WORLD GEOGR

myWorld INTERACTIVE

Active Journal

Boston, Massachusetts Chandler, Arizona
Glenview, Illinois New York, New York

Cover: Marco Bottigelli/AWL Images/Getty Images

Attributions of third party content appear on page 382, which constitutes an extension of this copyright page.

ISBN-13: 978-0-328-96028-6
ISBN-10: 0-328-96028-4
4 18

CONTENTS

Topic 1
Introduction to Geography

Topic 2
United States and Canada

Topic 3
Middle America

CONTENTS

Topic 4
South America

Topic 5
Europe Through Time

Topic 6
Europe Today

Topic 7
Northern Eurasia

Topic 8
Africa

Topic 9
Southwest Asia Through Time

Topic 10
Southwest Asia Today

CONTENTS

Topic 11
South Asia

Topic 12
East Asia

Topic 13
Southeast Asia

Topic 14
Australia and the Pacific

TOPIC 1

Introduction to Geography Preview

Essential Question How much does geography affect people's lives?

Before you begin this topic, think about the Essential Question by completing the following activities.

1. What do you think when you see or hear the word *geography*? What does *geography* mean to you? Record your thoughts in the space below.

Map Skills

Using the physical map in the Regional Atlas in your text, label the outline map with the continents and oceans listed. Then color in areas of land and water. Create a key to define what your colors signify.

Africa	Asia
Europe	Australia
North America	South America
Antarctica	Southern Ocean
Pacific Ocean	Atlantic Ocean
Indian Ocean	Arctic Ocean

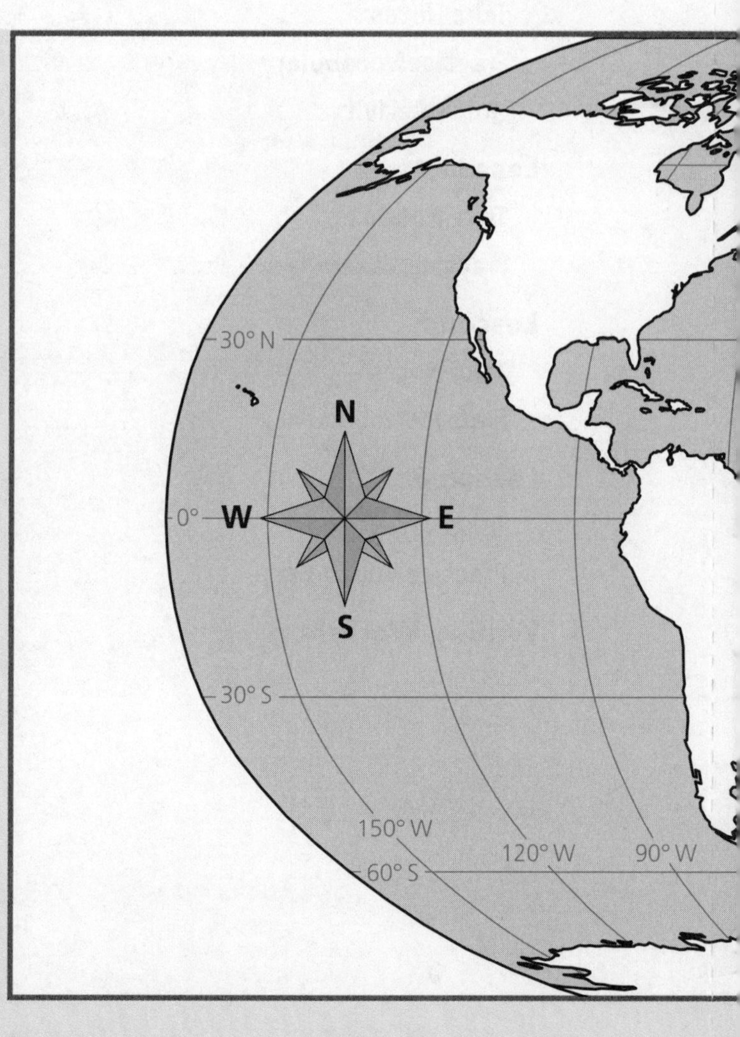

2. Preview the topic by skimming lesson titles, headings, and graphics. Then place a check mark next to the geographical features that you predict the text will show affecting people's lives. When you finish reading, circle the features that actually do affect people's lives, according to the text.

__citizenship	__climate	__command economy
__culture	__economics	__global positioning system
__government	__language	__maps
__monarchy	__plate tectonics	__religion
__time zones	__trade	__water cycle

0 2,000 mi
0 2,000 km
30° W 0° 30° E 60° E 90° E 120° E 150° E 180°

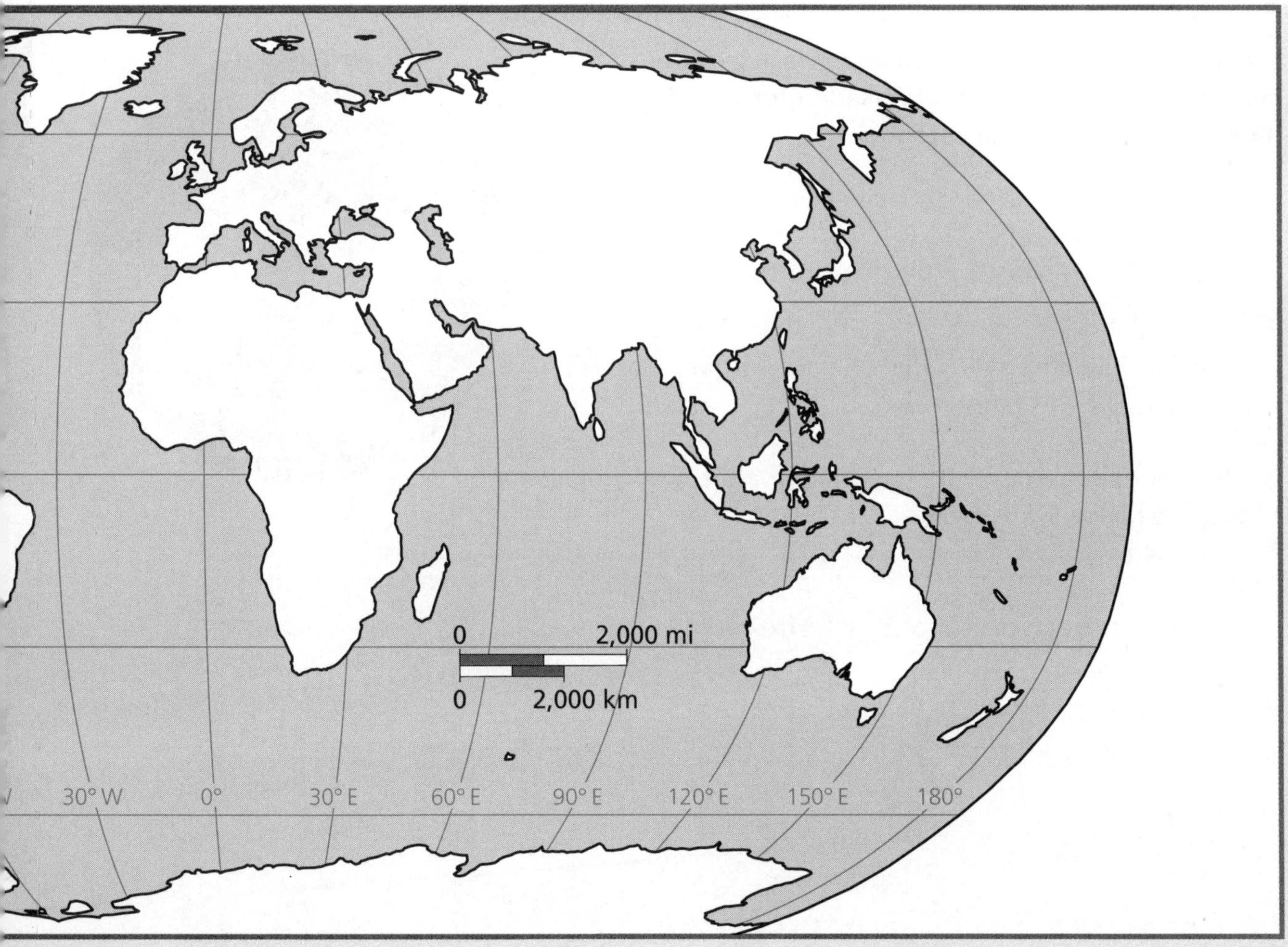

Balancing Development and the Environment

On this Quest, you will work with a team to identify an example of economic development in your area that has an impact on the environment locally or far away. You will ask and research questions about the economic and environmental costs and benefits of the development, and draw conclusions about whether the development is worth the cost. At the end of the Quest, your team will write a blog post in which you present your findings.

1 Ask Questions

As you begin your Quest, keep in mind the Guiding Question: **Can economic development justify its impact on the environment?** and the Essential Question: **How much does geography affect people's lives?**

What other questions do you need to ask in order to draw your conclusion? Two questions are filled in for you. Add at least two more questions for each category.

Theme Benefits of Development

Sample questions:

What positive effects does this development project have on the economy?

How can this development project improve the quality of life for people who live in the area?

Theme Impact on Quality of Life

Theme Harm to the Environment

Theme Financial Impact on the Community

Theme Role of Government

Theme My Additional Questions

INTERACTIVE

For extra help with Step 1, review the 21st Century Skills Tutorial: **Ask Questions**.

Quest CONNECTIONS

2 Investigate

As you read about concepts related to the economy and geography, collect five connections from your text to help you answer the Guiding Question. Three connections are already chosen for you.

Connect to People and the Environment

Lesson 4 Land Use

Here's a connection! Look at the World: Land Use map in your text. Which kinds of land use by people cover large areas, and which kinds of land use cover less area?

How do you think each type of use affects the environment?

Connect to Trade and Development

Lesson 7 Trade Barriers and Free Trade

Here is another connection! Read about economic development and look at the World: Levels of Human Development map. In which areas of the map would you expect to find the greatest human impact on the environment? Why?

What is the environmental impact of expanding trade?

Connect to Government

Lesson 8 Introduction to Government

Read about the powers and responsibilities of governments. What power does a government need to take steps to protect the environment, and what are the limits on those powers?

How can a government balance its responsibility to people's economic well-being with its responsibility to the environment?

It's Your Turn! **Find two more connections. Fill in the title of your connections, then answer the questions. Connections may be images, primary sources, maps, or text.**

Your Choice | Connect to

Location in text

What is the main idea of this connection?

What does it tell you about balancing development and the environment?

Your Choice | Connect to

Location in text

What is the main idea of this connection?

What does it tell you about balancing development and the environment?

3 Conduct Research

Form teams as directed by your teacher. Meet to decide who will research and write about each theme from Step 1 of the Quest as it relates to your local development project.

You will then research only the theme for which you are responsible. Use the ideas in the connections to explore your theme. Find at least five facts about your development project in relation to your theme. Record key points and reliable sources in the chart below.

Local Economic Development Project:

Theme:

Fact	Source

INTERACTIVE

For help with Step 3, review the 21st Century Skills Tutorials: **Search for Information on the Internet** and **Evaluate Web Sites**.

4 Write Your Blog Post

Now it's time to put together all of the information you have gathered and write your blog post.

1. **Prepare to Write** Your team has examined connections and conducted research about the environmental impact of a local economic development project. Together, review your notes and consider your team's position on the development project. Are the benefits worth the environmental costs? Note your thoughts in this space.

Thoughts

2. **Write a Draft** Write a draft of your blog post. Each team member will draft a paragraph about his or her theme in relation to the development project. Introductory and concluding sentences will express an opinion, and the body of the paragraph will contain supporting facts.

3. **Review and Revise** Compile the team's paragraphs. Read them and put them in order. Revise them together, correcting any grammatical or spelling errors and adding transition words as needed. As a team, develop introductory and concluding paragraphs that tie it all together relative to the Guiding Question and the Essential Question. Your blog post should present a unified opinion.

4. **Create a Visual** Now that you have the text for your blog post, find or create a visual to support your key points.

5. **Share** Finally, publish your blog post, following your teacher's instructions. Read the blog posts by other teams. On a separate sheet of paper, take notes on the information they shared.

6. **Reflect** Think about your experience completing this topic's Quest. What did you learn about the environmental impact of economic development? What questions do you still have about this subject? How will you answer them?

Reflections

INTERACTIVE

For extra help, review the 21st Century Skills Tutorials: **Work in Teams** and **Publish Your Work**.

Take Notes

Literacy Skills: Summarize Use what you have read to complete the table. Summarize the information for each lesson subheading. The first one has been completed for you.

Geography Basics	
Describing Locations	Geography is the study of human and nonhuman features of Earth. Geographers use the concepts of direction, absolute location, and relative location to describe where locations and objects are.
Geography's Five Themes	
How Do Geographers Show Earth's Surface?	
Understanding Maps	

INTERACTIVE

For extra help, review the 21st Century Skills Tutorial: **Summarize**.

Practice Vocabulary

Use a Word Bank **Choose one word from the word bank to fill in each blank. When you have finished, you will have a short summary of important ideas from the section.**

Word Bank

cardinal directions	distortion	geography
intermediate directions	latitude	longitude
projection	scale	

North, south, east, and west are the ______________.

Northwest, northeast, southwest, and southeast are examples of ______________. People use them to describe the location of places. They also use imaginary lines drawn across the surface of the Earth. Lines that run north to south are called lines of ______________, while those that run east to west are called lines of ______________.

People use maps and globes to represent the Earth's surface. Globes are round like the Earth. They show locations on Earth as they really are, but at a much smaller ______________.

To show Earth's round surface on a flat map, a mapmaker must use a ______________, such as the Robinson or Mercator. Therefore, even the best flat maps still show some ______________ of the size or position of objects.

The study of Earth and its human and nonhuman features is called ______________.

Take Notes

Literacy Skills: Interpret Visual Information Use the diagrams and your text to complete the concept web for Earth's seasons. A concept web for Earth's structure has already been completed. On a separate sheet of paper, make concept webs for forces within Earth that shape it, and forces on Earth's surface that shape it. Add spaces to the concept webs as needed.

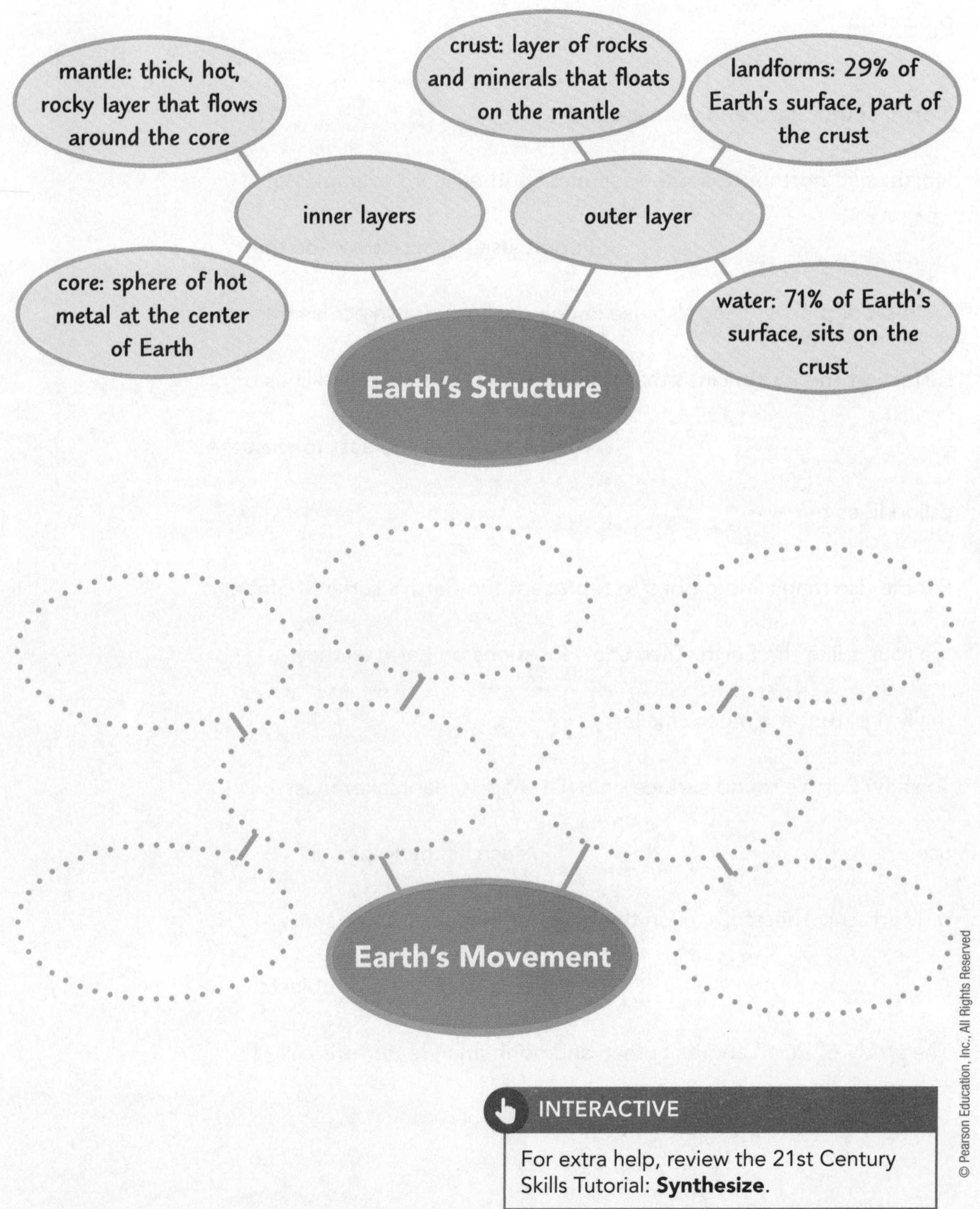

INTERACTIVE

For extra help, review the 21st Century Skills Tutorial: **Synthesize**.

Practice Vocabulary

Sentence Revision **Revise each sentence so that the underlined vocabulary term is used correctly. Be sure not to change the vocabulary term. The first one is done for you.**

1. Deposition is the process by which water, ice, and wind remove material.
   Deposition is the process by which water, ice, and wind deposit eroded material to create new landforms.

2. When volcanic lava erupts and flows, it is called magma.

3. Faults are huge blocks of Earth's crust.

4. At the equinox, all parts of Earth are an equal distance from the sun.

5. Erosion makes rocks break apart into tiny pieces.

6. Plate tectonics theory is that Earth's core is made of plates of rock that can move.

7. At a solstice, days are nearly equal in length everywhere on Earth.

8. Weathering is a force that carries away soil and bits of rock.

Take Notes

Literacy Skills: Determine Central Ideas Use what you have read to complete the chart. In the box in the second column, identify the central idea of the part of the lesson under the heading in the first column. The first section has been completed for you.

Climate and Weather	Weather is the condition of the air and sky at a certain time and place. Climate is the average weather of a place over many years. Climate graphs show climate for a place over a year's time.
Why Do Temperatures Differ?	
How Does Water Affect Climate?	
Air Circulation and Precipitation	
Types of Climate	
Biomes and Ecosystems	

INTERACTIVE

For extra help, review the 21st Century Skills Tutorial: **Identify Main Ideas and Details.**

Practice Vocabulary

Word Map Study the word map for the term *temperate zone*. Characteristics are words or phrases that relate to the term in the center of the word map. Non-characteristics are words and phrases not associated with the term. Use the blank word map to explore the meaning of the term *tropical cyclone*. Then make word maps of your own for these terms: *weather, climate, tropics, water cycle, prevailing winds, biome,* and *ecosystem.*

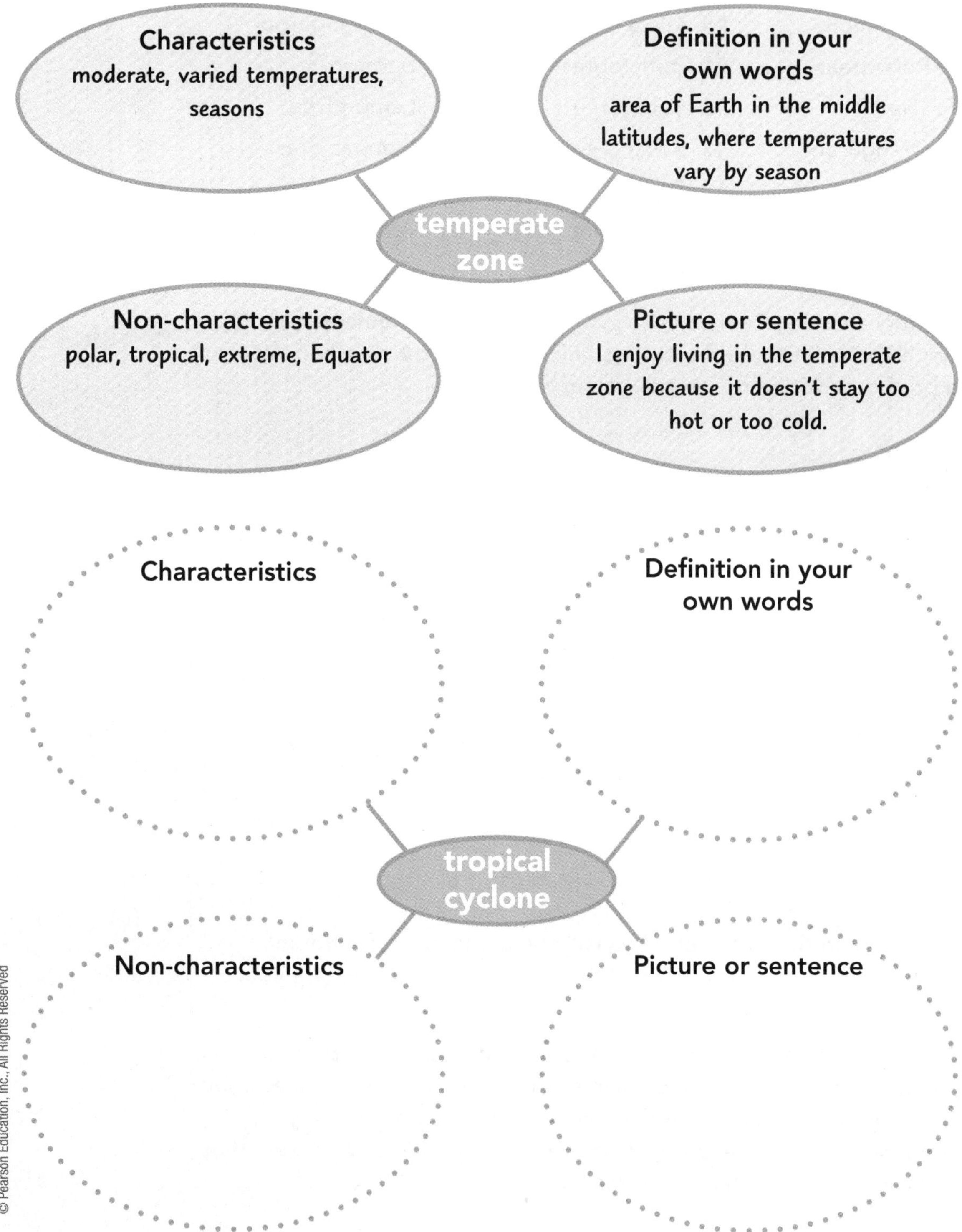

Quick Activity Exploring Ecosystems

As directed by your teacher, count off numbers around the classroom, then find the plant or animal below that corresponds to your number.

1. Parrot
2. Wildebeest
3. Bison
4. Chipmunk
5. Polar bear
6. Camel
7. Orangutan
8. Beaver
9. Caribou
10. Prairie dog
11. Redwood
12. Bearberry
13. Red maple
14. Olive
15. Buffalograss
16. Baobab
17. Swamp cypress
18. Saguaro cactus
19. Date palm
20. Banana
21. Emperor penguin
22. Jaguar
23. Yak
24. Red kangaroo
25. Baboon
26. Lemon tree
27. Pampas grass
28. Mahogany tree
29. African violet
30. Komodo dragon

Identify an ecosystem where your plant or animal can live. If you don't know, find reliable sources online, or ask your teacher. Write a brief description of the ecosystem here.

Look around the classroom. You will see the names of different ecosystems in different places. Move to an ecosystem where your plant or animal could live.

Team Challenge! Meet with classmates who also have a plant or animal in your ecosystem. Explain to them how you determined that your organism could live in that ecosystem. As a group, use your combined notes to prepare a brief description of the ecosystem that you can share with the rest of the class.

Take Notes

Literacy Skills: Draw Conclusions Use what you have read to complete the chart. In each column, write details about the topics listed. Then draw conclusions about people's interaction with the environment. The first one has been started for you.

People's Impact on the Environment	Population Growth and Movement
• Humans depend on resources from the environment for survival.	

Conclusions

INTERACTIVE

For extra help, review the 21st Century Skills Tutorial: **Draw Conclusions**.

Practice Vocabulary

Use a Word Bank **Choose one term from the word bank to fill in each blank. When you have finished, you will have a short summary of important ideas from the section.**

Word Bank

deforestation	urbanization	emigrate
pull factors	natural resources	push factors
biodiversity	industrialization	fossil fuels

____________ are useful materials found in the environment. Nonrenewable resources include minerals, metal ores, and ____________. ____________ is the development of machine-powered production and manufacturing. ____________ is the loss of forest cover in a region and can reduce ____________, the number of types of living things in a region or ecosystem. When people leave their home country, they ____________, which means to migrate out of a place. ____________ drive people to leave their home country. ____________ attract people to new countries. The movement of people from rural areas to urban areas is called ____________.

Take Notes

Literacy Skills: Use Evidence Use what you have read to complete the chart. In each column, write details about the elements of culture. Then use this evidence you have gathered from the text to draw a conclusion about what culture means and what makes a culture unique. The first section has been completed for you.

Families and Societies	Language and Religion	Arts, Science, and Technology
Families • Families are the basic units of societies. • Nuclear families are made up of parents and children. • Extended families include grandparents and other relatives.	Language	Arts
Societies	Religion	Science and Technology

Conclusion

INTERACTIVE

For extra help, review the 21st Century Skills Tutorial: **Support Ideas with Evidence**.

Practice Vocabulary

True or False? Decide whether each statement below is true or false. Circle T or F, and then explain your answer. Be sure to include the underlined vocabulary term in your explanation. The first one is done for you.

1. **T / F** A society is the beliefs, customs, practices, and behaviors of a group of people.
   False; a society is a group of humans with a shared culture who have organized themselves to meet their basic needs.

2. **T / F** Members of the same social class may have very different economic conditions.

3. **T / F** Advances in science and technology often raise the standard of living.

4. **T / F** Culture is the basic needs and wants shared by all people, such as food, clothing, and shelter.

5. **T / F** A person's social structure is made of the various social groups the person is part of.

6. **T / F** Cultural diffusion can include the spread of ideas, values, objects, foods, and art forms from one culture to another culture.

Take Notes

Literacy Skills: Compare and Contrast Use what you have read to complete the chart. In each column write the unique characteristics of the economic system listed. Also note any similarities with other economic systems. The first one has been completed for you.

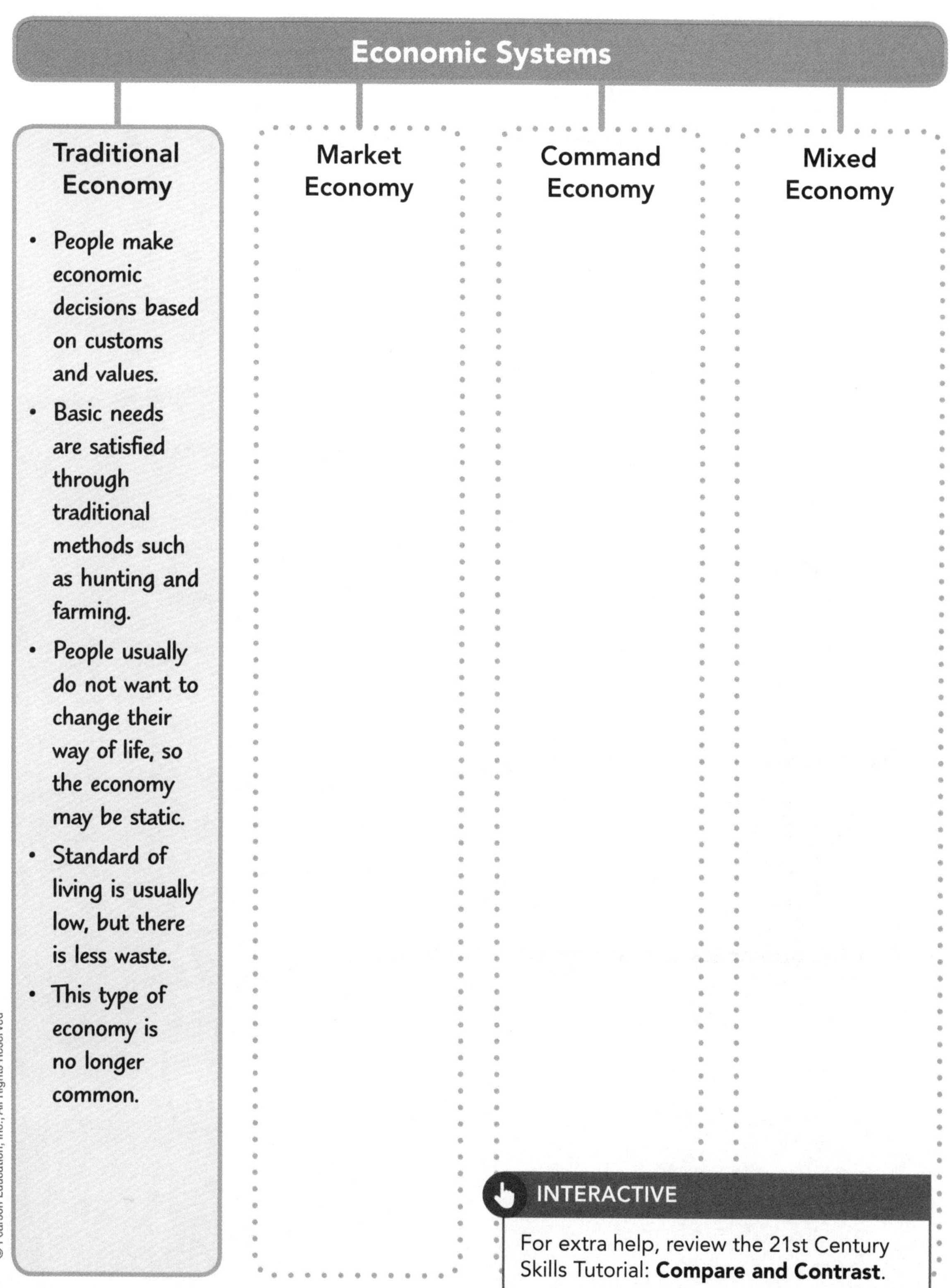

INTERACTIVE

For extra help, review the 21st Century Skills Tutorial: **Compare and Contrast**.

Practice Vocabulary

Words in Context For each question below, write an answer that shows your understanding of the boldfaced key term.

1. How does **demand** affect the price of a good or service?

2. How is the principle of **opportunity cost** related to economic decision making?

3. What is the role of **consumers** in a pure market economy?

4. What is **supply** in economics?

5. What is the role of **producers** in a country's economy?

6. Why does **economics** have an impact on everyday life?

Quick Activity Your Local Economy

As directed by your teacher, break into small groups to discuss the economy in your town, city, or county. Use the questions below to guide your group discussion.

1. Who are the producers in your local area, and who are the consumers?

2. What goods and services are in high demand in your area?

3. What goods and services are scarce? Describe the prices of these items.

4. Based on what you have read in this lesson, what kind of economy does your local area have? How can you tell?

Team Challenge! **As a group, imagine a scenario that would drastically change your local economy. Be creative! What if the entire economic system changed due to a shift in government? What if an essential good or service became scarce? What effects would the change have on the local economy? How might the change affect people's everyday lives or affect the environment? Write a short paragraph or draw a picture that describes your group's imagined economic scenario and the changes it would bring to your local community.**

Take Notes

Literacy Skills: Identify Cause and Effect Use what you have read to complete the charts. In each space, write details about the causes that contribute to the listed effect. The first chart has been started for you.

Decision What to Trade and Produce

Scarcity	Comparative Advantage	Physical Geography
Scarcity of resources due to limited supply and uneven distribution of resources can make it impossible for a country to produce everything it needs. Countries must trade the resources, goods, and services that they can produce to obtain resources, goods, and services that they want.		

Increase in Economic Development

Trade Barriers vs. Free Trade	Human Capital Improvements	Resources and Capital Goods

INTERACTIVE

For extra help, review the 21st Century Skills Tutorial: **Analyze Cause and Effect.**

Practice Vocabulary

Word Map Study the word map for the word *tariff*. Characteristics are words or phrases that relate to the word in the center of the word map. Non-characteristics are words and phrases not associated with the word. Use the blank word map to explore the meaning of the word *trade*. Then make word maps of your own for these terms: *comparative advantage, trade barrier, free trade, development, developed country, developing country, gross domestic product* (GDP), and *productivity*.

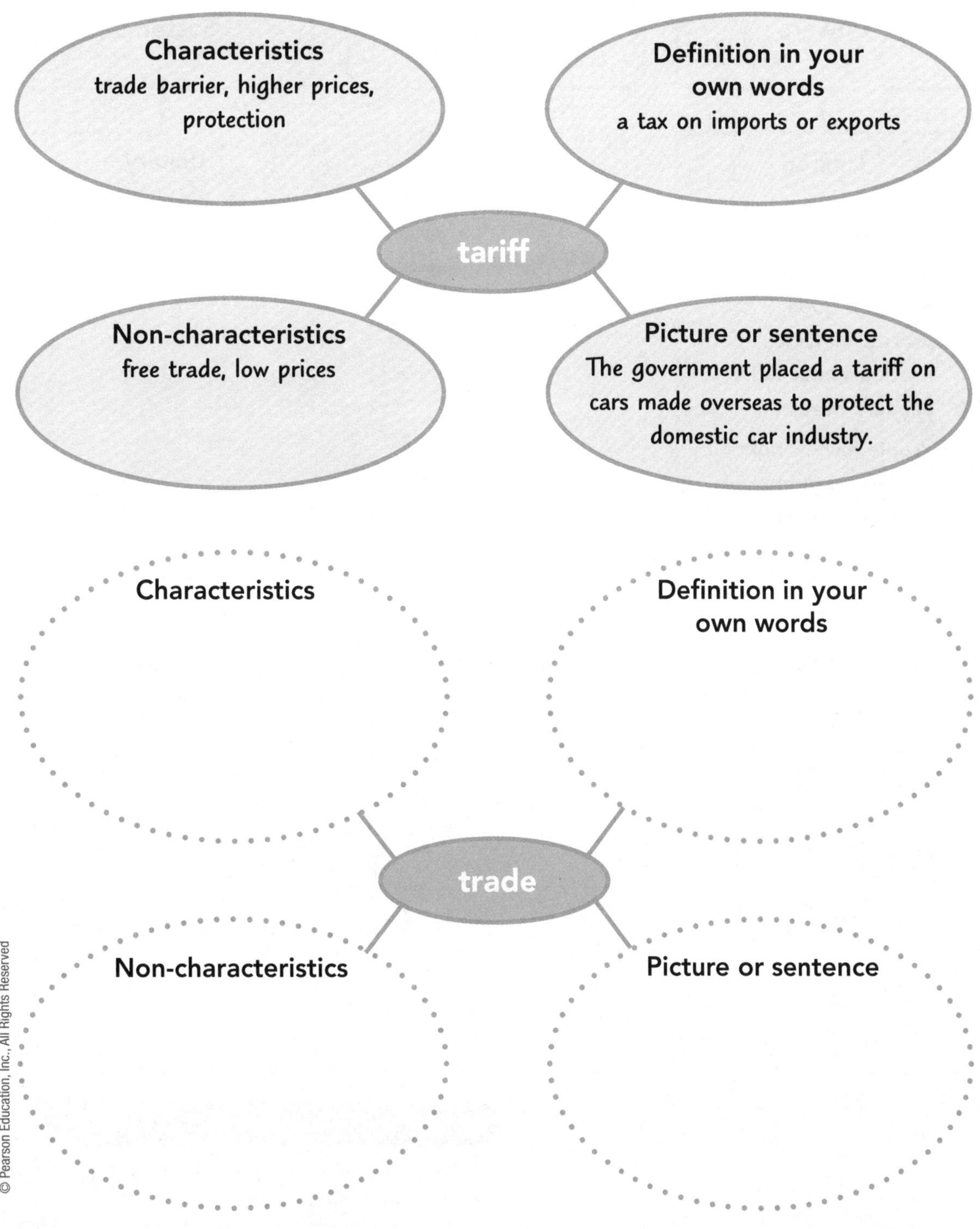

Take Notes

Literacy Skills: Classify and Categorize Use what you have read to complete the chart. In each space write key details that describe the type or characteristic of government listed. The first section has been completed for you.

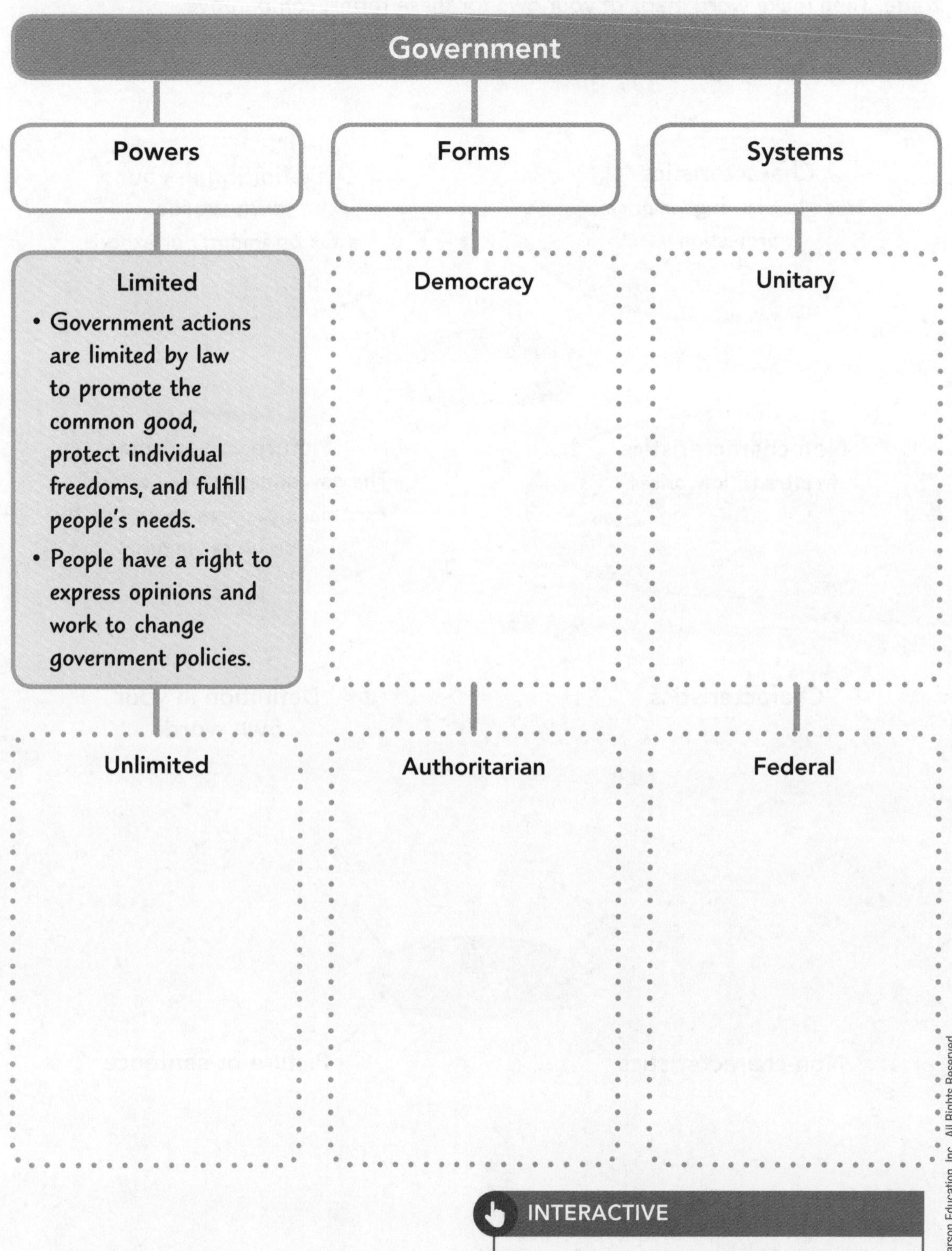

INTERACTIVE

For extra help, review the 21st Century Skills Tutorial: **Categorize**.

Practice Vocabulary

Sentence Revision **Revise each sentence so that the underlined vocabulary term is used logically. Be sure not to change the vocabulary term. The first one is done for you.**

1. Democracy is an international organization in which citizens hold political power.
   Democracy is a form of government in which citizens hold political power.

2. A constitution identifies the freedoms of individual citizens and outlines the rules and principles citizens must follow.

3. The United Kingdom is an example of authoritarian government, in which all power is held by one person.

4. In a federal system, all power is held by a central government.

5. A monarchy is headed by an elected king or queen.

6. A government is a group of people from the same area who obey the same laws.

7. The unitary system determines whether a government has limited or unlimited power over its citizens.

Take Notes

Literacy Skills: Identify Main Ideas Use what you have read to complete an outline that highlights the main ideas of the lesson. As you create your outline, pay attention to headings, subheadings, and key terms that you can use to organize the information. The first section of the outline has been completed for you.

I. Defining citizenship
   A. A citizen is a legal member of a country.
   B. Citizens of countries have both rights and responsibilities.

II.

INTERACTIVE

For extra help, review the 21st Century Skills Tutorial: **Identify Main Ideas and Details.**

Practice Vocabulary

Matching Logic **Using your knowledge of the underlined vocabulary terms, draw a line from each sentence in Column 1 to match it with the sentence in Column 2 to which it logically belongs.**

Column 1	Column 2
1. The democratization of societies has been happening gradually for more than 200 years.	Legal members of the United States have several rights and responsibilities.
2. Annika has the full rights and responsibilities of a United States citizen.	You have be at least 18 years old and live in the United States legally for at least ten years to be eligible.
3. Participating in civic life is both a right and a responsibility for citizens of the United States.	Eduardo votes in every election and stays informed about the issues affecting his community.
4. At the naturalization ceremony, 75 adults became U.S. citizens.	After the dictatorship ended, people voted for government representatives who would protect their freedoms.

Take Notes

Literacy Skills: Identify Main Ideas Use what you have read to complete the tables. In each space write one main idea and at least two details that support it. The first one has been completed for you.

Using a Timeline	Organizing Time
Main Idea: Timelines are one method historians use to measure time and determine chronology. **Details:** • Put events in a chronology. • Evaluate patterns and analyze continuity. • Portray a period characterized by specific events.	**Main Idea:** **Details:**

Historical Sources	Historical Maps	Other Sources
Main Idea: **Details:**	**Main Idea:** **Details:**	**Main Idea:** **Details:**

INTERACTIVE

For extra help, review the 21st Century Skills Tutorial: **Identify Main Ideas and Details**.

Practice Vocabulary

Use a Word Bank Choose one term from the word bank to fill in each blank. When you have finished, you will have a short summary of important ideas from the section.

Word Bank

secondary source	timelines	archaeology
prehistory	period	artifacts
chronology	anthropology	primary sources

__________ help historians identify and evaluate patterns of change. Historians use them to put events in a __________, a list of events in the order in which they occurred. A __________ can be defined by a set of developments that happened during that time. __________ is the time before humans invented writing and could begin to record events. __________ include letters, diaries, and photographs. __________, or objects made by human beings, are primary sources. A __________ has information about an event that does not come from a person who experienced that event. __________ is the scientific study of past cultures through the examination of artifacts and other evidence. __________ is the study of humankind in all aspects, especially development and culture.

Writing Workshop Narrative Essay

As you read, build a response to this question: How have geographic experiences affected your life? The prompts below will help walk you through the process.

Lessons 1 through 8 Writing Task: Gather Evidence Consider the experiences you have had with elements of geography throughout your life. In the table below, write a sentence or two about each area. You will use one or more of these ideas to write your narrative essay.

Ways geography has affected my life	
My experience(s) with the seasons, extreme weather, and/or natural disasters	
My experience(s) with the climate or ecosystem where I live	
My experience(s) interacting with my environment	
My experience(s) with my culture or the culture of the people around me	
My experience(s) with my local economy	
My experience(s) with items made in another country	
My experience(s) with a person who works in my local government or for a government agency	

Lesson 9 Writing Task: Use Descriptive Details Descriptive details and sensory language bring life to a story. The reader can "see" and "hear" the things or events the author is describing. Use descriptive details to write about the experience(s) you've had with an element of geography.

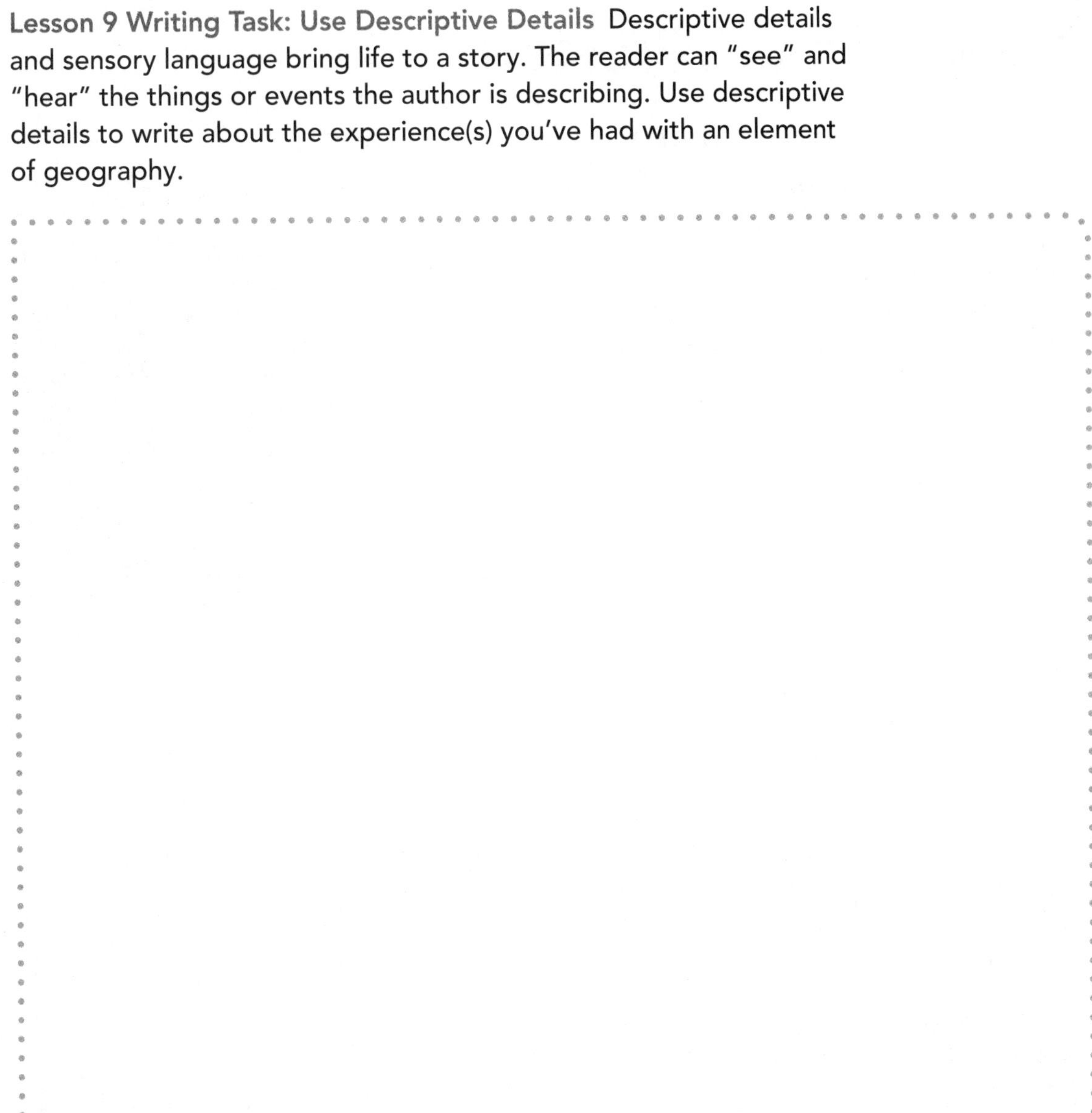

Lesson 10 Writing Task: Add Details Revisit your ideas on the previous page. Add descriptive details to them to make your ideas more complete and interesting.

Writing Task Using your notes from this workshop, write a narrative essay that answers the following question: How have geographic experiences affected your life? As you write, consider using one or more narrative techniques, and describe events using sensory language. The conclusion of your narrative should provide the reader with closure by filling in any missing details needed for the narrative to make sense. The conclusion also sums up the point made by the essay.

TOPIC 2

The United States and Canada Preview

Essential Question What should governments do?

Before you begin this topic, think about the Essential Question by completing the following activities.

1. List three ways government programs have affected your life. Then write whether you think government should do more or less in each of the areas in which government has affected your life.

2. Preview the topic by skimming lesson titles, headings, and graphics. Then, below or on a separate sheet of paper, make a drawing of something you expect to learn about.

Map Skills

Using the political and physical maps in the Regional Atlas in your text, label the outline map with the places listed. Then color in the bodies of water and major mountain ranges.

Ottawa	Great Plains	California	Canadian Shield
Rocky Mountains	Alberta	Hudson Bay	Appalachian Mountains
British Columbia	Gulf of Mexico	Bering Strait	Mississippi River
Georgia	Lake Michigan	St. Lawrence River	

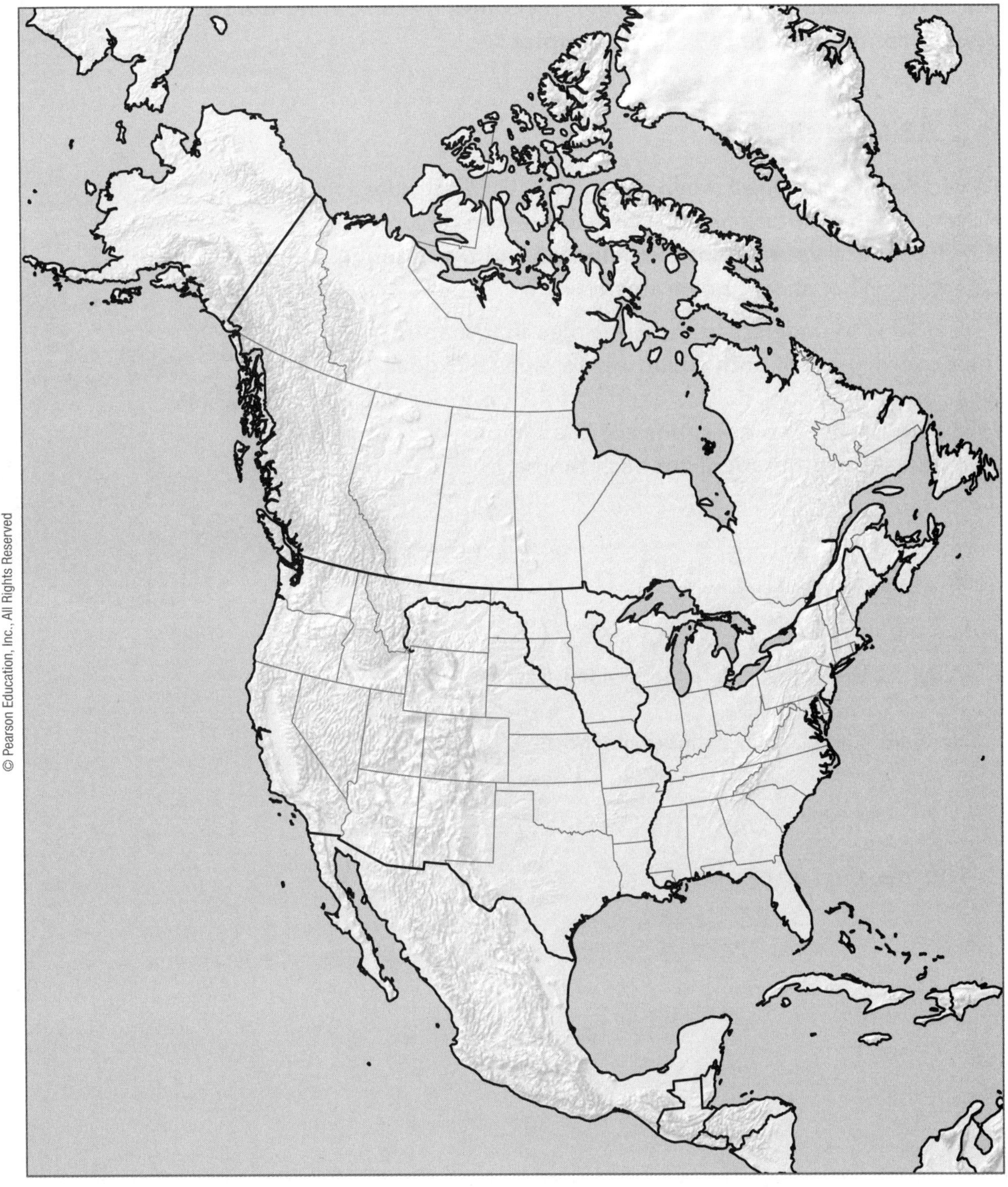

Studying Founding Documents

On this Quest, you will compare the founding documents of the United States and Canada. You will examine as sources documents that established both countries' governments. At the end of the Quest you will write an essay for publication in both countries comparing the two governments and their founding principles.

1 Ask Questions

As you begin your Quest, keep in mind the Guiding Question: **How do the constitutions and other important documents of the United States and Canada compare?** and the Essential Question: **What should governments do?**

Your goal is to understand the principles that shaped the governments of both countries. To meet this goal, what other questions do you need to ask? Consider the following issues. Two questions are filled in for you. Add at least two questions for each theme.

Theme Independence

Sample questions:

Why did the United States seek independence?

How did Canada gain its independence?

Theme Government

Theme Democracy

Theme Rights

Theme My Additional Questions

INTERACTIVE

For extra help with Step 1, review the 21st Century Skills Tutorial: **Ask Questions**.

Quest CONNECTIONS

2 Investigate

As you read about Canadian and American documents that established new governments, collect five connections from your text to help you answer the Guiding Question. Three connections are already chosen for you.

Connect to Rights

Lesson 4 Canada Unifies

Here's a connection! How did the different ways in which the United States and Canada developed their national identities affect the founding documents of each nation?

The United States Bill of Rights was ratified in 1791 and certain individual rights were included in Canada's 1982 constitution. What impact do you think the 191-year difference had on the rights Canada listed?

Connect to Government

Lesson 6 Comparing Systems of Government

Here's another connection! What impact did the founding documents of Canada and the United States have on the structures of the countries' governments?

What's the difference between the way the President is chosen in the United States and the way the prime minister is selected in Canada?

Connect to Social Issues

Lesson 7 Social Challenges

How have the founding documents of the United States and Canada affected each country's ability to deal with its social challenges?

Do the protections provided by the Constitution of the United States apply to people who come to the country illegally?

It's Your Turn! Find two more connections. Fill in the title of your connections, then answer the questions. Connections may be images, primary sources, maps, or text.

Your Choice | Connect to

Location in text

What is the main idea of this connection?

What does it tell you about the founding principles of the United States and Canada?

Your Choice | Connect to

Location in text

What is the main idea of this connection?

What does it tell you about the founding principles of the United States and Canada?

3 Examine Primary Sources

Examine the primary and secondary sources provided online or by your teacher. Fill in the chart to show how these sources reflect the origins and founding principles behind the governments of the United States and Canada. The first one is completed for you.

Source	This reflects a founding principle by . . .
The United States Declaration of Independence	saying that everybody is created equal and is endowed with certain unalienable rights, or rights that cannot be taken away
A Timeline of the U.S. Constitutional Convention	
The United States Constitution and Bill of Rights	
The Canadian Constitution Act of 1867	
The Canadian Constitution Act of 1982	

INTERACTIVE

For extra help with Step 3, review the 21st Century Skills Tutorial: **Analyze Primary and Secondary Sources**.

4 Write Your Essay

Now it's time to put together all of the information you have gathered and use it to write your essay comparing the founding principles of the United States and Canada.

1. **Prepare to Write** You have collected connections and explored primary and secondary sources about important documents of the United States and Canada and the process by which these documents were developed. Look through your notes and decide which facts you want to highlight in your essay. Record them here.

Facts

2. **Write a Draft** Using evidence from the information in your text and the primary and secondary sources you explored, write a draft of your essay. Be sure to include details about both countries' documents. Include details from the evidence in the material you've studied in this Quest.

3. **Share with a Partner** Exchange your draft with a partner. Tell your partner what you like about his or her draft and suggest any improvements.

4. **Finalize Your Report** Revise your essay based on your partner's comments. Also correct any grammatical or spelling errors.

5. **Reflect on the Quest** Think about your experience completing this topic's Quest. What did you learn about the founding documents of Canada and the United States? What questions do you still have about the two countries and their founding principles? How will you answer them?

Reflections

INTERACTIVE

For extra help with Step 4, review the 21st Century Skills Tutorial: **Write an Essay**.

Take Notes

Literacy Skills: Classify and Categorize Use what you have read to complete the table. The first one has been completed for you.

Key Features of Culture Regions	
Region	Key Features
Arctic	kayaks, hunted sea animals, underground homes, igloos
Subarctic	
Northwest Coast	
California	
Plateau and Great Basin	
Southwest	
Great Plains	
Northeastern	
Southeastern	

INTERACTIVE

For extra help, review the 21st Century Skills Tutorial: **Categorize**.

Practice Vocabulary

Vocabulary Quiz Show **Some quiz shows ask a question and expect the contestant to give the answer. In other shows, the contestant is given an answer and must supply the question. If the blank is in the Question column, write the question that would result in the answer in the Answer column. If the question is supplied, write the answer.**

Question	Answer
1. What are domed houses made from blocks of snow?	1.
2.	2. potlatch
3.	3. tepees
4. What is a home formed by bending the trunks of young trees and tying them together to make a round frame?	4.
5. What type of home is similar to a wigwam but is larger and rectangular?	5.

Take Notes

Literacy Skills: Synthesize Visual Information Use what you have read and the images you have studied to complete the charts. The first one has been started for you. To complete the first chart analyze the text and the photo on the first page of this lesson. For the second chart, analyze the text and photo on the second page of the lesson.

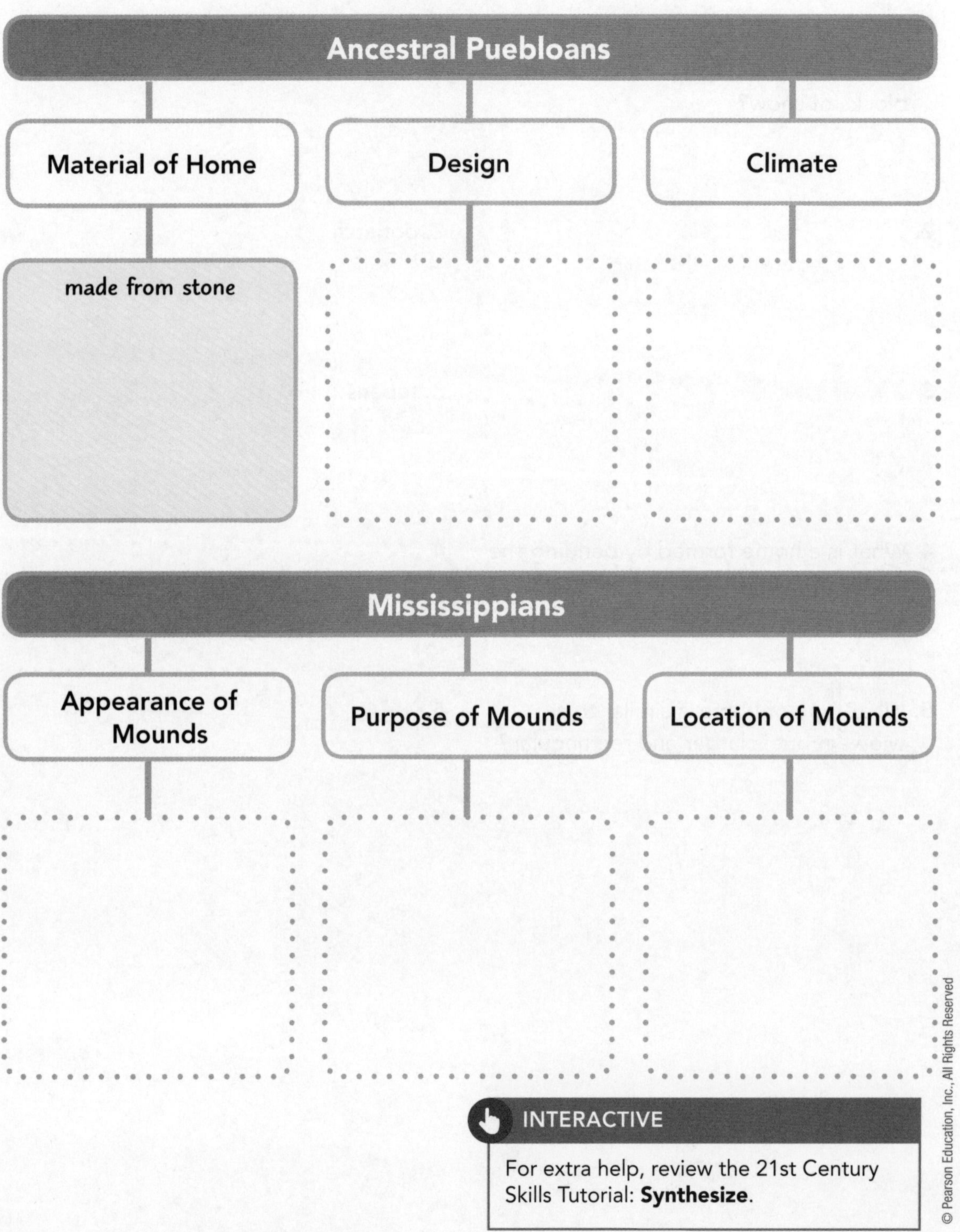

INTERACTIVE

For extra help, review the 21st Century Skills Tutorial: **Synthesize**.

Practice Vocabulary

Matching Logic **Using your knowledge of the underlined vocabulary words, draw a line from each sentence in Column 1 to match it with the sentence in Column 2 to which it logically belongs.**

Column 1	Column 2
1. Women chose hoyaneh in the Iroquois League.	Women could remove a leader from his position if he did a poor job.
2. Long droughts around the year 1300 made farming difficult for the Ancestral Puebloan people.	They have learned about groups' crops, clothing, tools, and homes.
3. Scientists have learned about North American Indians by studying their artifacts.	This joint council decided important matters.
4. The five Iroquois nations formed the Iroquois League in the 1500s.	Groups left their villages and moved closer to water sources.

Take Notes

Literacy Skills: Synthesize Visual Information Use what you have read and the images you have observed to complete the charts. The first one has been started for you. To complete the first chart analyze the map titled "European Settlement in North America, About 1640" along with the text on that page. For the second chart, analyze the maps of North America in 1753 and 1763 along with the text on that page.

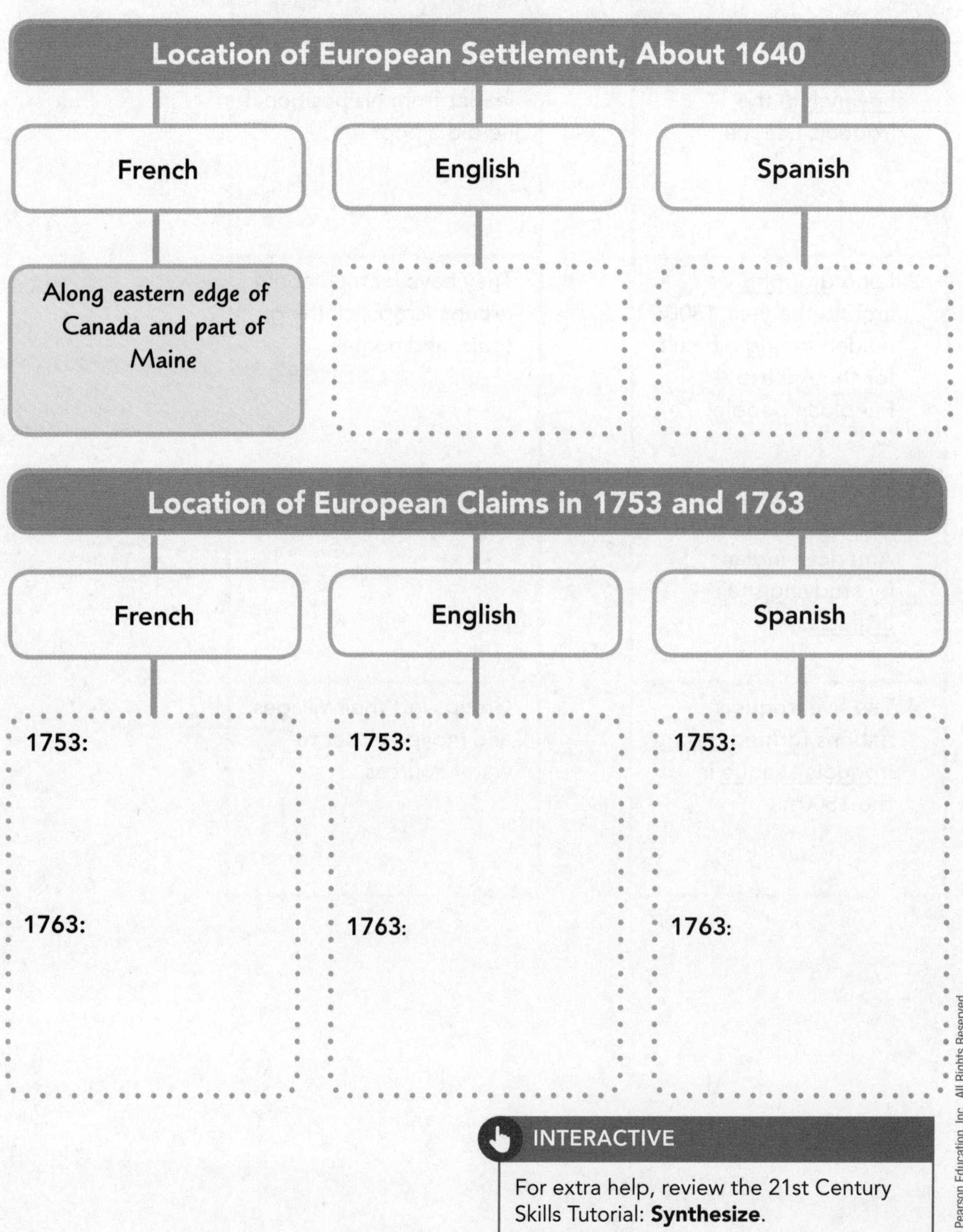

INTERACTIVE

For extra help, review the 21st Century Skills Tutorial: **Synthesize**.

Practice Vocabulary

True or False? Decide whether each statement below is true or false. Circle T or F, and then explain your answer. Be sure to include the underlined vocabulary term in your explanation. The first one is done for you.

1. **T / F** Eventually, a Northwest Passage was discovered in North America.
   False; The French, the Dutch, and the English looked for a Northwest Passage, but eventually it became clear that it did not exist.

2. **T / F** Enslaved Africans were chained together to prevent escapes and mutinies.

3. **T / F** About 500,000 enslaved Africans were transported to the Americas across the Middle Passage between 1500 and 1870.

4. **T / F** Pilgrims settled in Virginia in 1620 and were also called Puritans.

5. **T / F** The triangular trade linked Africa, the Caribbean, and the English colonies.

Quick Activity European Settlement

When European colonists settled in North America, they became residents of a continent that had previously been the home of only American Indians. There were costs and benefits to Europeans settling in North America as well as to American Indians. In the chart below, list both the costs and benefits of European settlement of North America.

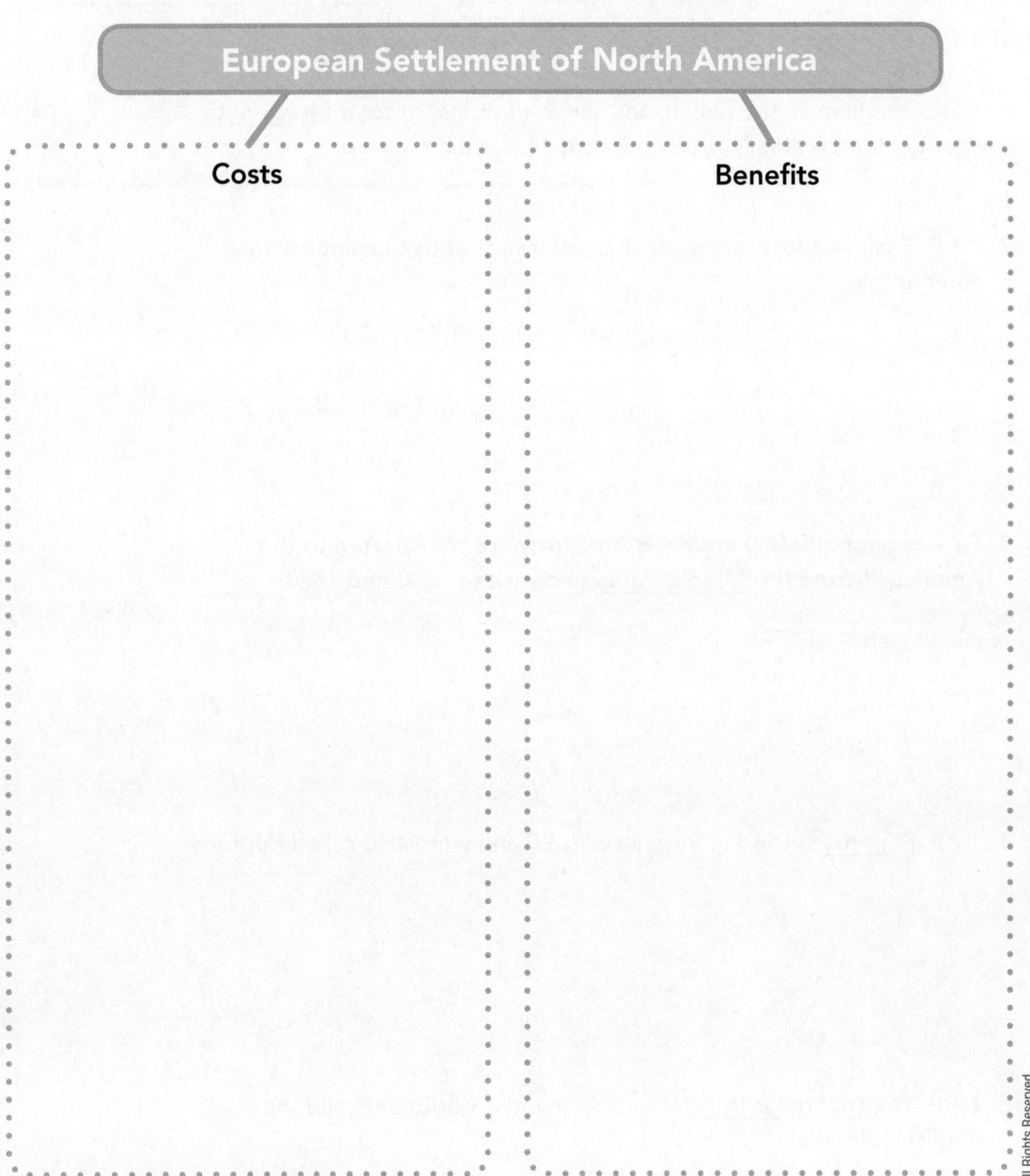

Team Challenge! **With a partner, discuss the costs and benefits of European settlement. Be sure to include perspectives from all sides.**

Take Notes

Literacy Skills: Sequence Use what you have read to complete the charts. Enter events in the sequence they occurred. The first one has been started for you.

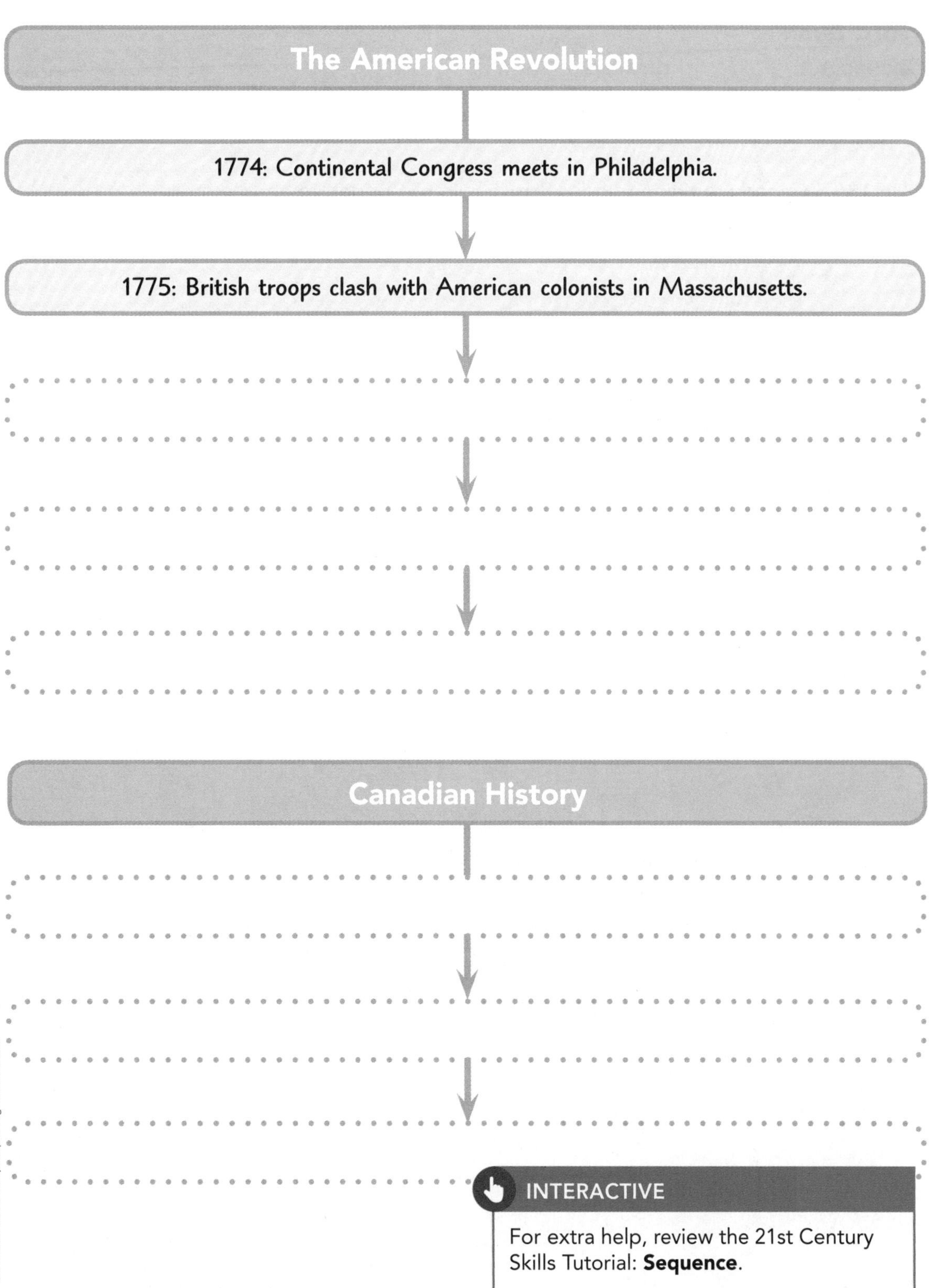

INTERACTIVE

For extra help, review the 21st Century Skills Tutorial: **Sequence**.

Practice Vocabulary

Sentence Builder **Finish the sentences below with a key term from this lesson. You may have to change the form of the terms to complete the sentences.**

Word Bank

Quebec Act	dominion
Great Depression	civil rights movement

1. In 1867, Canada remained under British rule but began to handle more of its affairs when it became a

   .

2. The efforts of African Americans in the 1950s through the 1960s to win equal rights was called the

   .

3. French Canadians had their religious freedom and laws protected with the passage of the

   .

4. In 1929, a financial collapse in the United States led to the

   .

Take Notes

Literacy Skills: Draw Conclusions Use what you have read to complete the charts. Draw conclusions from the actions in the top boxes. The first one has been started for you.

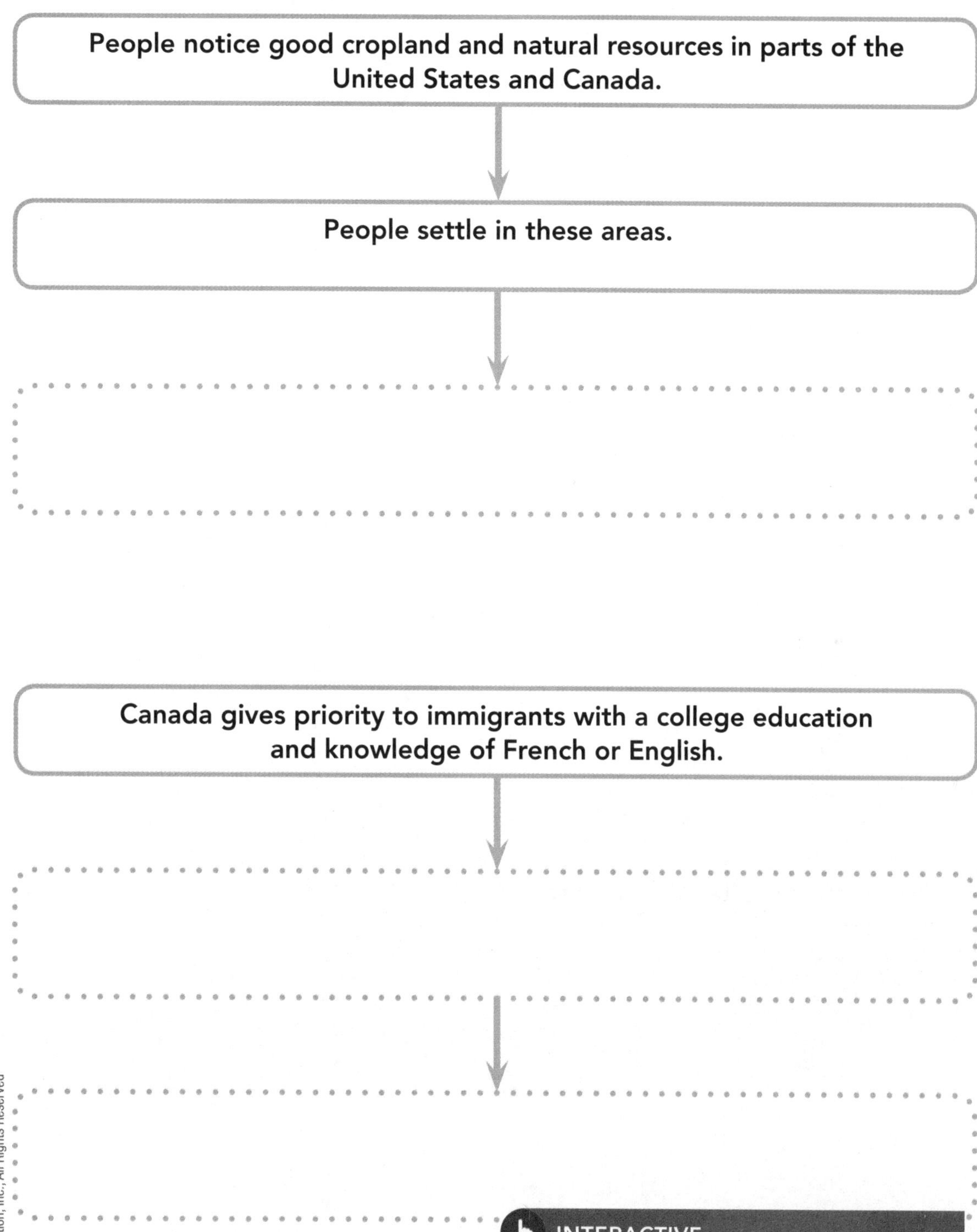

INTERACTIVE

For extra help, review the 21st Century Skills Tutorial: **Draw Conclusions**.

Practice Vocabulary

Words in Context **For each question below, write an answer that shows your understanding of the boldfaced key term.**

1. What impact has economic change had on **migration**?

2. Under U.S. **immigration** laws, who is prioritized?

3. What are the characteristics of a **taiga** biome?

Take Notes

Literacy Skills: Compare and Contrast Use what you have read to complete the Venn diagrams with similarities and differences. The first entry has been completed for you.

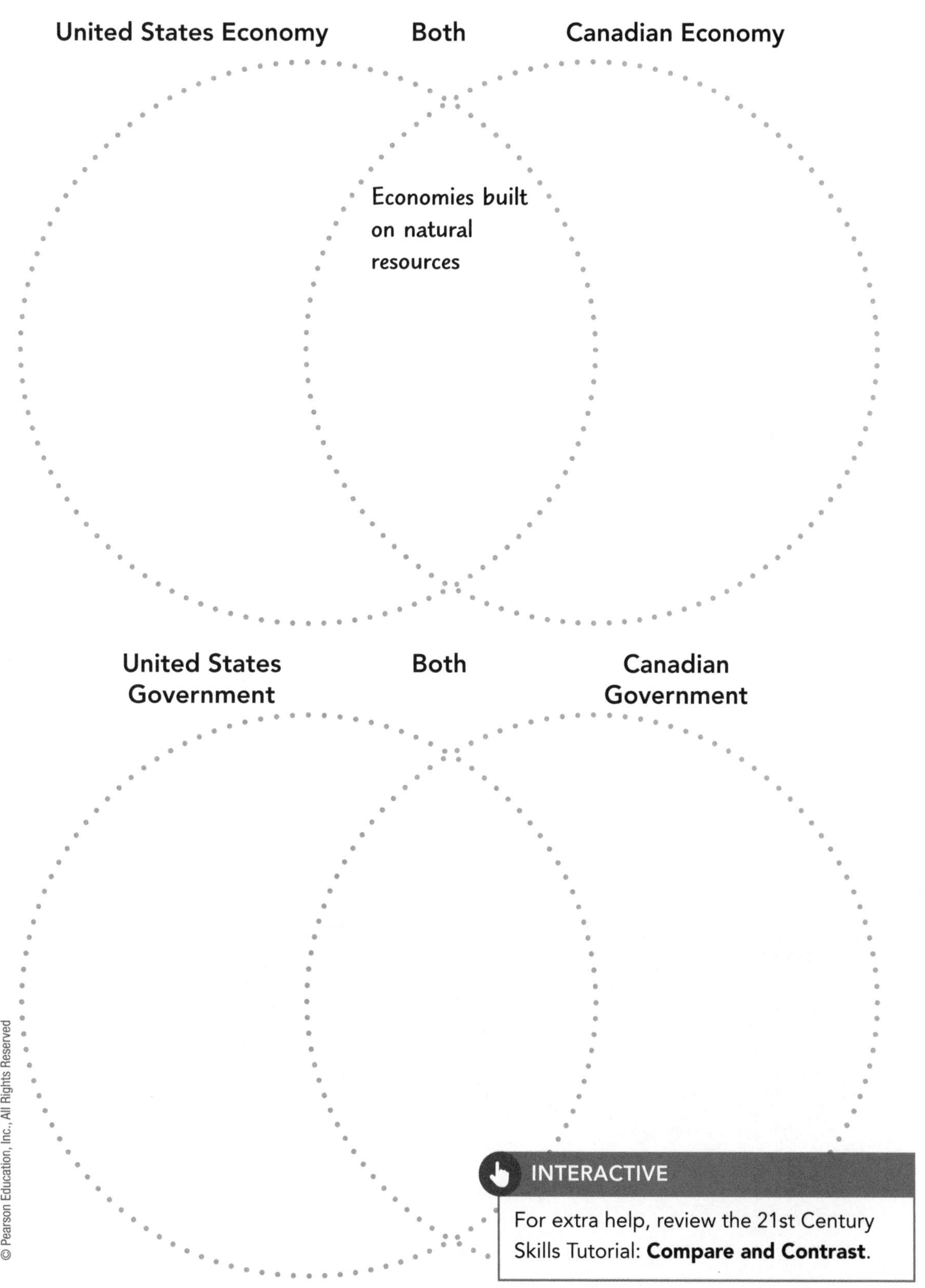

INTERACTIVE

For extra help, review the 21st Century Skills Tutorial: **Compare and Contrast**.

Practice Vocabulary

Words in Context For each question below, write an answer that shows your understanding of the boldfaced key term.

1. Where is an **import** shipped?

2. What are the most valuable **exports** of the United States and Canada?

Quick Activity Technology in the Workplace

Over the past 30 years, new technologies have changed the workplace. They've led to the creation of some jobs, but other jobs have been lost. Write a list of some technologies that have developed over the past 30 years.

Team Challenge! Discuss with your classmates the lists everybody came up with. Then, have a conversation about the costs and benefits of these new technologies. Consider the jobs gained in new technological sectors and the jobs lost to automation or software.

Take Notes

Literacy Skills: Use Evidence Use what you have read to complete the charts. Fill in the spaces with evidence that supports the conclusion. The first one has been started for you.

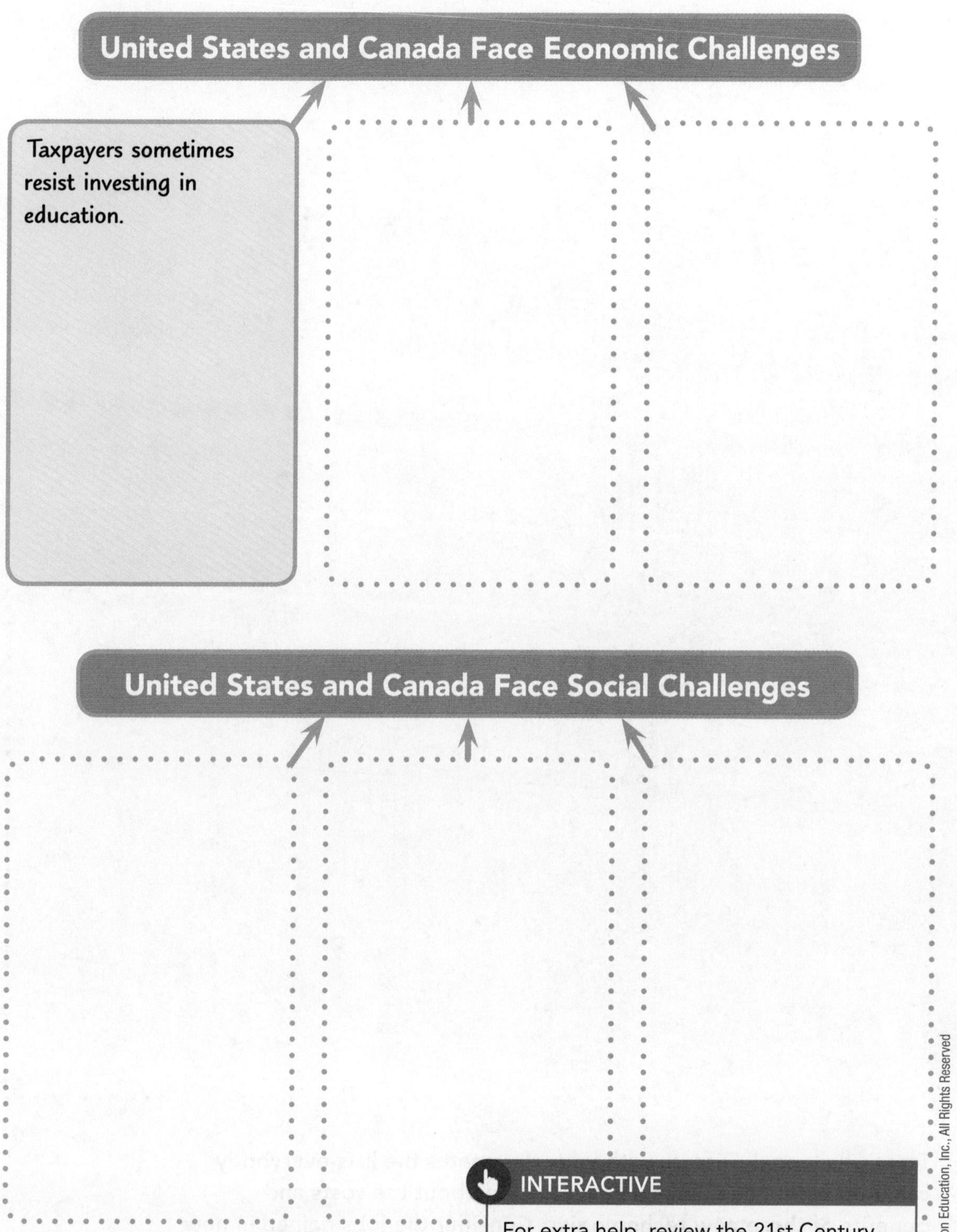

INTERACTIVE

For extra help, review the 21st Century Skills Tutorial: **Identify Evidence**.

Practice Vocabulary

Vocabulary Quiz Show **Some quiz shows ask a question and expect the contestant to give the answer. In other shows, the contestant is given an answer and must supply the question. If the blank is in the Question column, write the question that would result in the answer in the Answer column. If the question is supplied, write the answer.**

Question	**Answer**
1. What is the practice of moving a company outside North America, where wages and other costs are lower?	1.
2. What is the money people make through work or investments?	2.
3.	3. globalization

Writing Workshop Argument

As you read, build a response to this question: What impact has technology had on the environment in the United States and Canada? The prompts below will help walk you through the process.

Lessons 1, 2, and 3 Writing Task: Introduce and Support Claims

Write three claims about the impact of technology on the environment in the early history of the United States and Canada, and record supporting evidence. Be sure to use logical reasoning and relevant evidence. You will use these ideas for the argument you will write at the end of the topic.

Claim	Supporting Evidence

Lessons 4 and 5 Writing Task: Distinguish Claims from Opposing Claims and Choose an Organizing Strategy Write a sentence opposing one of your claims. Then write a sentence defending your claim against this opposing claim. On a separate sheet of paper, determine how you will structure your essay to incorporate opposing claims and your responses to them.

Lesson 6 Writing Task: Use Transition Words Write transition words that you could use in your argument to compare and contrast ideas and information or to transition from one argument to another.

Lesson 7 Writing Task: Write a Conclusion Write a paragraph drawing a conclusion about the impact of technology on the environment in the United States and Canada.

Writing Task Building on the work you have done, write an argument of at least four paragraphs on the impact of technology on the environment in the United States and Canada. Cite credible sources to support your arguments.

Middle America Preview

Essential Question Who should benefit from a country's resources?

Before you begin this topic, think about the Essential Question by completing the following activities.

1. Think about your own community or the country as a whole. Make a list of some of the natural resources that are important. Note who you think benefits most from some of those resources.

Map Skills

Using the political and physical maps in the Regional Atlas in your text, label the outline map with the places listed. Then color in water, desert, and areas of fertile land.

Guatemala	Atlantic Ocean
Greater Antilles	Costa Rica
Gulf of Mexico	Jamaica
Isthmus of Panama	Cuba
Dominican Republic	Caribbean Sea
Panama	Pacific Ocean
Yucatán Peninsula	Mexico
Lesser Antilles	Haiti

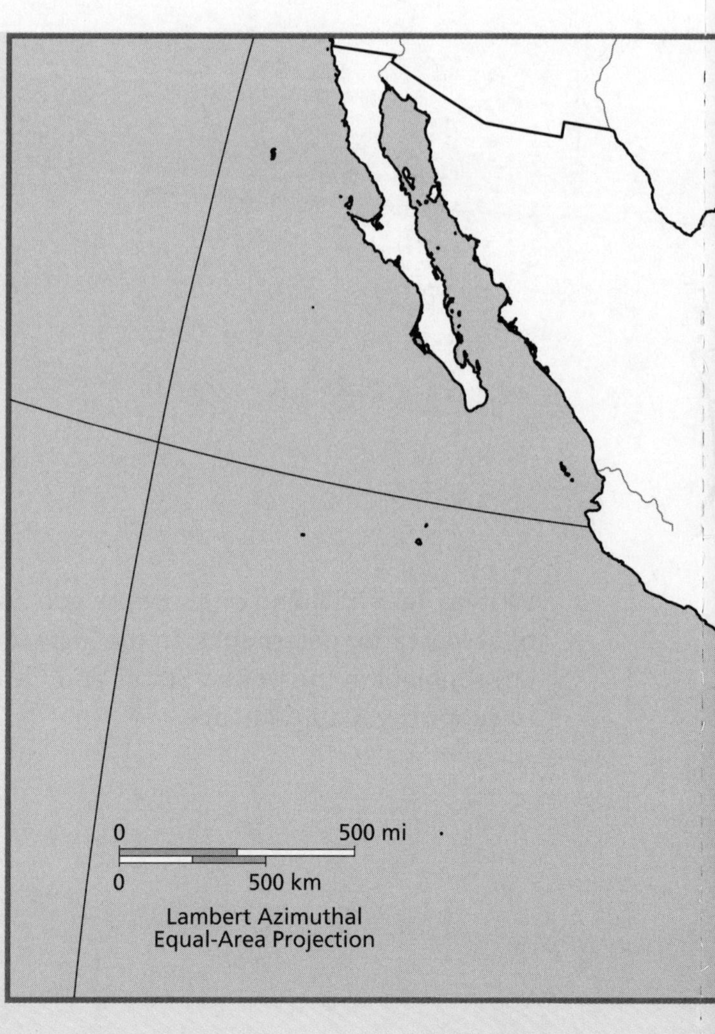

2. Preview the topic by skimming lesson titles, headings, and graphics. Then place a check mark next to the major natural resources you predict the text will cover. After you finish reading the topic, circle the predictions that were correct.

__hydroelectric power	__coal	__oil
__timber	__gas	__soil
__skilled labor	__minerals	__spring water

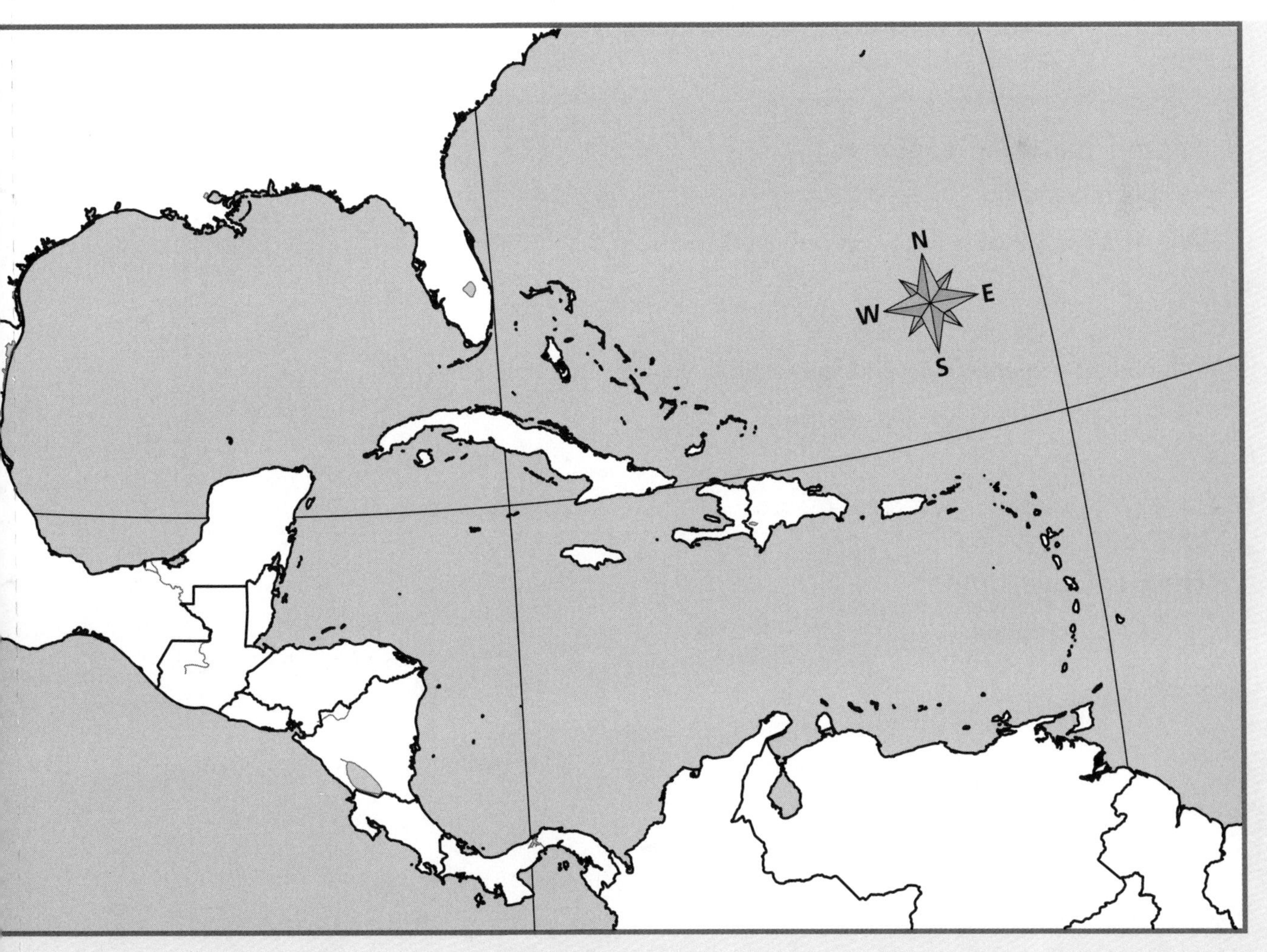

Debate Ownership of a Key Resource

On this Quest, you will explore sources and gather information about one of Mexico's key resources. You will take the role of an economist advising the government whether or not to privatize the government-owned oil industry. Then, you will participate in a discussion about the Guiding Question.

1 Ask Questions

As you begin your Quest, keep in mind the Guiding Question: **Should oil production in Mexico be privatized?** and the Essential Question: **Who should benefit from a country's resources?** What other questions do you need to ask in order to take a position on this issue? Two questions are filled in for you. Add at least two questions for each category.

Theme Natural Resources

Sample questions:

Why is oil so valuable in the modern world economy?

Why might a country's government want to control its supply of oil?

Theme Government

Theme Economic Systems

Theme Social Conditions

Theme Wealth

Theme My Additional Questions

INTERACTIVE

For extra help with Step 1, review the 21st Century Skills Tutorial: **Ask Questions**.

2 Investigate

As you read about Middle America, collect five connections from your text to help you answer the Guiding Question. Three connections are already chosen for you.

Connect to the Mexican Revolution

Lesson 4 A Troubled History

Here's a connection! Why do you think the Mexican government took steps to nationalize the oil industry in the years after the revolution?

Who might have favored this decision? Who might have opposed it?

Connect to Cuba's Economy

Lesson 5 The Cuban Revolution

Here's another connection! Why would Castro have opposed outside control of Cuba's industries?

What impact did Castro's decision to nationalize industries have on the Cuban economy?

Connect to Mexico's Economy

Lesson 7 Making a Living in Mexico and Central America

What does this connection tell you about the kind of economy Mexico has? What is the role of oil in Mexico's economy?

What are the benefits and drawbacks of recent changes in Mexico's oil industry?

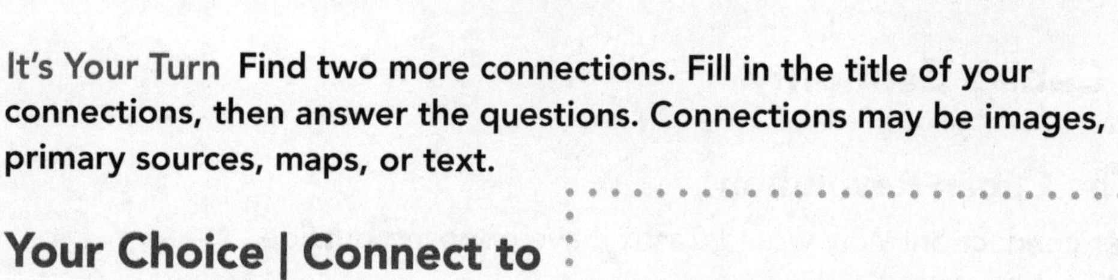

It's Your Turn **Find two more connections. Fill in the title of your connections, then answer the questions. Connections may be images, primary sources, maps, or text.**

Your Choice | Connect to

Location in text

What is the main idea of this connection?

What does it tell about what Mexico should consider when debating whether to privatize its oil industry?

Your Choice | Connect to

Location in text

What is the main idea of this connection?

What does it tell about what Mexico should consider when debating whether to privatize its oil industry?

3 Examine Primary Sources

Examine the primary and secondary sources provided online or from your teacher. Fill in the chart to show how these sources provide further information about the costs and benefits of privatizing Mexico's oil industry. The first one has been started for you.

Source	Yes or No? Why?
How Mexico plans to revitalize its energy industry through privatization	YES. Introducing market forces will promote Mexico's gas industry and help the economy grow.
Good News in Mexico	
Mexico's Oil Belongs to Its Citizens, Not the Global 1%	
Privatizing Mexico's Oil Industry Spells Disaster	

INTERACTIVE

For extra help with Step 3, review the 21st Century Skills Tutorial: **Compare Viewpoints**.

4 Discuss!

Now that you have explored sources about the costs and benefits of privatizing Mexico's oil industry, you are ready to discuss with your fellow economists the Guiding Question: Should oil production in Mexico be privatized? Follow the steps below, using the spaces provided to prepare for your discussion.

You will work with a partner in a small group of economists. Try to reach consensus, a situation in which everyone is in agreement, on the question. Can you do it?

1. **Prepare Your Arguments** You will be assigned a position on the question, either YES or NO.

   My position:

   Work with your partner to review your Quest notes from the Quest Connections and Quest Sources.

   - If you were assigned YES, agree with your partner on what you think were the strongest arguments from Harrison and *The Washington Times* editors.
   - If you were assigned NO, agree on what you think were the strongest arguments from Okón and Buscaglia.

2. **Present Your Position** Those assigned YES will present their arguments and evidence first. As you listen, ask clarifying questions to gain information and understanding.

What is a Clarifying Question?	
These types of questions do not judge the person talking. They are only for the listener to be clear on what he or she is hearing.	
Example: **Can you tell me more about that?**	**Example:** **You said [x]. Am I getting that right?**

INTERACTIVE

For extra help with Step 4, review the 21st Century Skills Tutorial: **Participate in a Discussion or Debate.**

While the opposite side speaks, take notes on what you hear in the space below.

3. **Switch!** Now NO and YES will switch sides. If you argued YES before, now you will argue NO. Work with your same partner and use your notes. Add any arguments and evidence from the clues and sources. Those *now* arguing YES go first.

When both sides have finished, answer the following:

Before I started this discussion with my fellow economists, my opinion was that oil production in Mexico	*After* I finished this discussion with my fellow economists, my opinion was that oil production in Mexico
____should be privatized.	____should be privatized.
____should not be privatized.	____should not be privatized.

4. **Point of View** Do you all agree on the answer to the Guiding Question?

- ____Yes
- ____No

If not, on what points do you all agree?

Take Notes

Literacy Skills: Identify Cause and Effect Use what you have read to complete the charts. For each statement, identify three effects that the cause had on the development of civilizations in Middle America. The first effect has been completed for you.

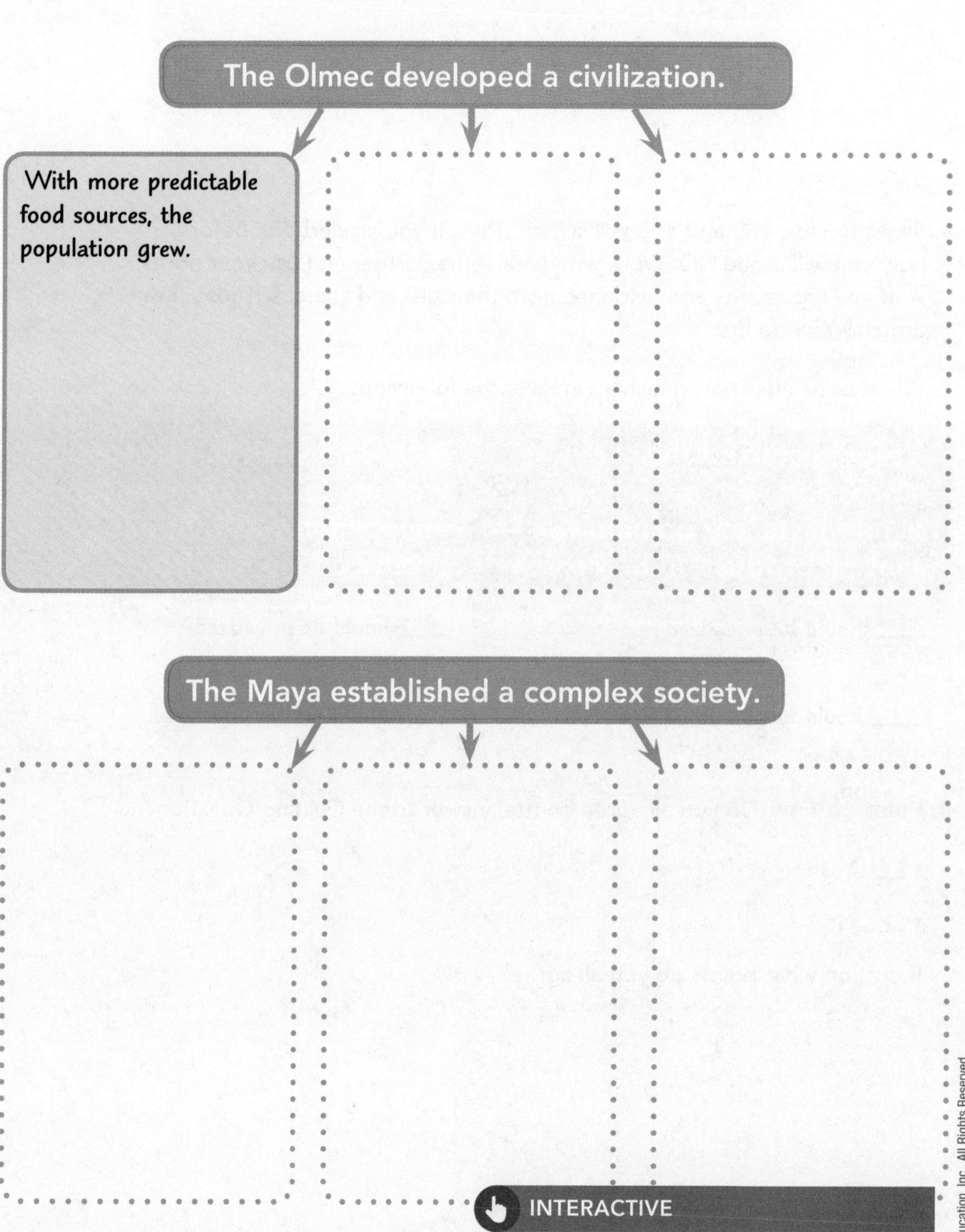

INTERACTIVE

For extra help, review the 21st Century Skills Tutorial: **Analyze Cause and Effect**.

Practice Vocabulary

Matching Logic Using your knowledge of the underlined vocabulary words, draw a line from each sentence in Column 1 to the sentence in Column 2 to which it logically belongs.

Column 1	Column 2
1. The Maya traded across the region for quetzal feathers.	They cleared and set fire to land to enrich the soil for farming.
2. The Maya built temples and observatories in all their cities.	This writing system uses picture representations of words and ideas.
3. The Olmecs used a technique called slash-and-burn agriculture.	They tracked the sun, moon, and stars to know when to plant and harvest.
4. The Maya developed a complex system of hieroglyphics.	These items were important for religious rituals.

Take Notes

Literacy Skills: Summarize Use what you have read to complete the table. List two or three important facts about Aztec civilization for each theme. The first one has been started for you. Then use these notes to write a short summary of the lesson.

Geography	Government and Society	Achievements
• The Aztecs built their capital city in the middle of a lake so they could easily defend it.		

Summary Statement

INTERACTIVE

For extra help, review the 21st Century Skills Tutorial: **Summarize**.

Practice Vocabulary

Sentence Revision **Revise each sentence so that the underlined vocabulary word is used correctly. Be sure not to change the vocabulary word. The first one is done for you.**

1. Aqueducts allowed merchants to carry trade over water.

   Aqueducts allowed fresh water to be carried across the salty lake.

2. The Aztecs built their civilization in a basin so that it was easier to do laundry.

3. The Aztecs constructed dikes to keep invaders out of their city.

4. The Aztecs built chinampas to paddle around the lake where they built their city.

Take Notes

Literacy Skills: Sequence Use what you have read to complete the chart. Sequence important events concerning Spanish colonization of Middle America. The first one has been completed for you.

INTERACTIVE

For extra help, review the 21st Century Skills Tutorial: **Sequence**.

Practice Vocabulary

Use a Word Bank **Choose one word from the word bank to fill in each blank. When you have finished, you will have a short summary of important ideas from the section.**

Word Bank

creoles	Columbian Exchange	conquistadors	mestizos
mulattoes	encomienda	peninsulares	

In search of gold, riches, and converts to Christianity, Spanish ______ colonized many territories in Middle America. They established the ______ system, which required American Indians to pay tribute in goods or labor. Many American Indians died from disease and harsh treatment. New Spain had a very rigid social structure. ______, or people born in Spain, were at the top of the social ladder. Next came ______, or people born in the Americas to Spanish settlers. The lower social classes included people of mixed American Indian and European descent who were called ______ and people who were of mixed African and European descent, who were called ______. Colonization also linked America to the rest of the world, leading to the ______, in which goods and ideas were exchanged between the Eastern and Western Hemispheres.

Take Notes

Literacy Skills: Determine Central Ideas Use what you have read to complete the table. Use the supporting details provided to determine the central idea. The first one has been completed for you.

Central Idea	Supporting Details
The Enlightenment inspired revolt and a push toward independence in Mexico and Central America.	• Many people in the Spanish colonies had few rights. • Creoles were tired of being dominated by peninsulares. • People were starting to question the divine right of rulers.
	• Common people in Mexico worked long hours and had very few rights and not enough food. • Juárez wanted to create reforms that would help the poor, but wealthy people were afraid of losing power. • Díaz ignored election results to make someone he favored president.
	• Many newly independent countries looked to the United States to help build their economies. • The United States supported Panama's independence in return for control of a planned canal. • Guatemalan reform and nationalization ended with U.S.-backed overthrow of its elected government.
	• Reforms made in Mexico led to democratic elections in 2000. • There is now free trade in most Central American countries. • Many foreign countries are now investing in Central American countries.

INTERACTIVE

For extra help, review the 21st Century Skills Tutorial: **Identify Main Ideas and Details.**

Practice Vocabulary

Vocabulary Quiz Show Some quiz shows ask a question and expect the contestant to give the answer. In other shows, the contestant is given an answer and must supply the question. If the blank is in the Question column, write the question that would result in the answer in the Answer column. If the question is supplied, write the answer.

Question	Answer
1.	1. nationalizing
2.	2. Mexican Cession
3. In 1910, what happened when Díaz tried to install someone he favored as the Mexican president?	3.

Quick Activity Living Timeline

Based on instructions from your teacher, form a group of three or four students. Use the workspace below to name and briefly explain a few people or events that are important to Mexican history. Each student should choose one to use for this activity. As a group, arrange the events and people in chronological order, or the order in which they happened.

Team Challenge! **Construct a living timeline of important people and events in Mexican history. Each team member will be responsible for presenting one person or event. Stand in chronological order and describe to the class your person or event and that person's or event's importance to Mexican history.**

Take Notes

Literacy Skills: Text Structure Use what you have read to complete the table. For each heading, write one sentence that describes the importance of that segment. The first one has been completed for you.

How Colonization Changed the Course of Caribbean History	
Segment Heading	**Importance of Events**
Who Were the First Caribbean Peoples?	The first Caribbean peoples were Arawaks and Caribs, who were mostly hunters and gatherers but also planted some staple crops.
European Colonization	
What Was the Transatlantic Slave Trade?	
Larger Countries Win Independence First	
The Cuban Revolution	
Late Moves Toward Independence	

INTERACTIVE

For extra help, review the 21st Century Skills Tutorial: **Take Effective Notes**.

Practice Vocabulary

Word Map Study the word map for the word *dictatorship*. Characteristics are words or phrases that relate to the word in the center of the word map. Non-characteristics are words and phrases that are not associated with the word. Use the blank word map to explore the meaning of the word *embargo*.

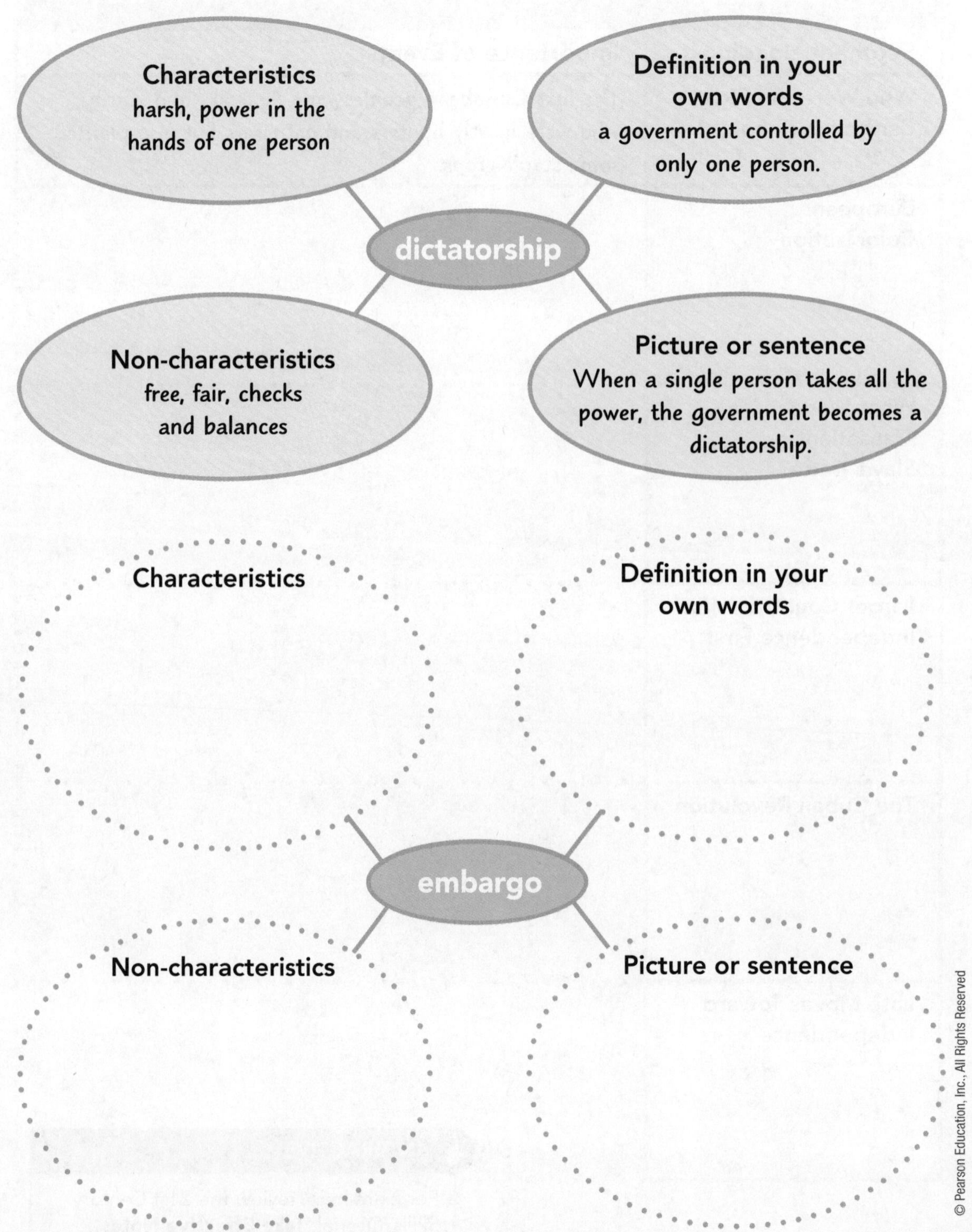

Take Notes

Literacy Skills: Synthesize Visual Information Use what you have read to complete the chart. The chart provides space to take notes on what you learn from each image as you read the text that accompanies it. Notes on the first photo have been started for you. Add any other notes on this photo and notes on the other photo, map, and graph.

Living in Mexico and Central America

Photos	Map and graphs
• The photo shows a densely developed town with narrow streets, so at least some people in this region live in cities.	

INTERACTIVE

For extra help, review the 21st Century Skills Tutorial: **Synthesize**.

Practice Vocabulary

Words in Context For each question below, write an answer that shows your understanding of the boldfaced key term.

1. What is a **diaspora**?

2. What is the effect of **cultural diffusion**?

3. What is a **mural**, and what purpose can it serve?

Quick Activity Quiz Show!

Based on instructions from your teacher, form a group of three or four students. Together you will come up with three questions about the regions of Mexico and Central America to ask the other teams in your class. Make sure you know the answer to your questions.

Did you know?

Hint! Consider the themes of population, culture, language, history, and geography.

Team Challenge! Test your classmates' knowledge. Each team presents their three questions to the rest of the teams, and the other teams try to answer them correctly. After all of the teams have had a chance to present, the team with the most correct answers wins.

Take Notes

Literacy Skills: Classify and Categorize Use what you have read to complete the charts. For each topic, categorize information about each country listed. The first one has been started for you.

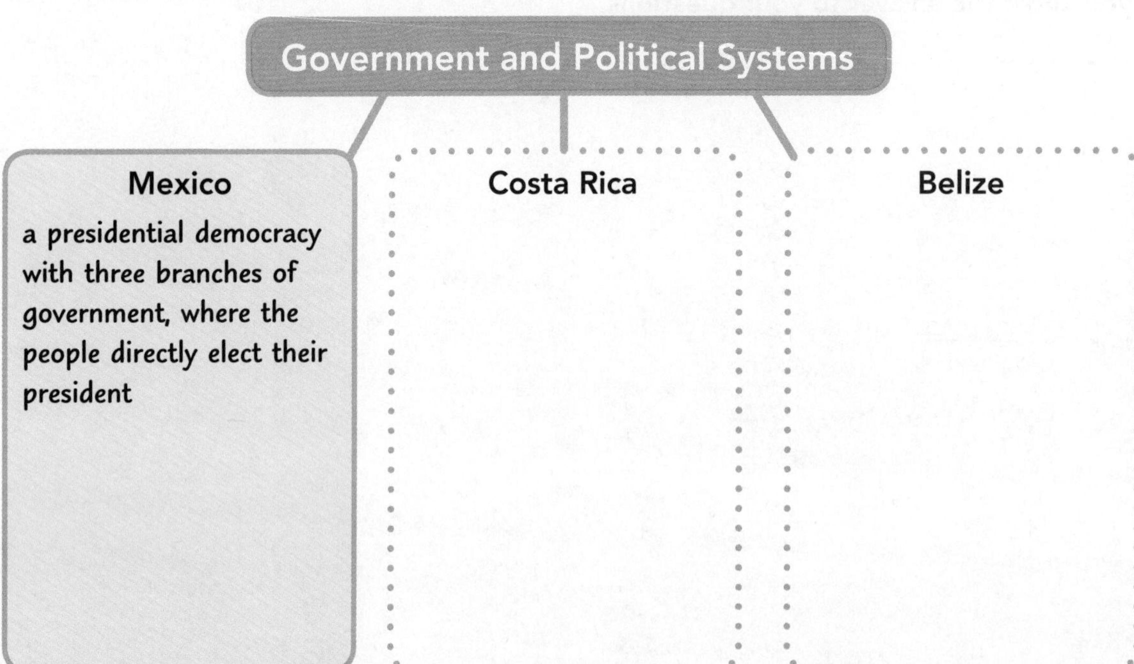

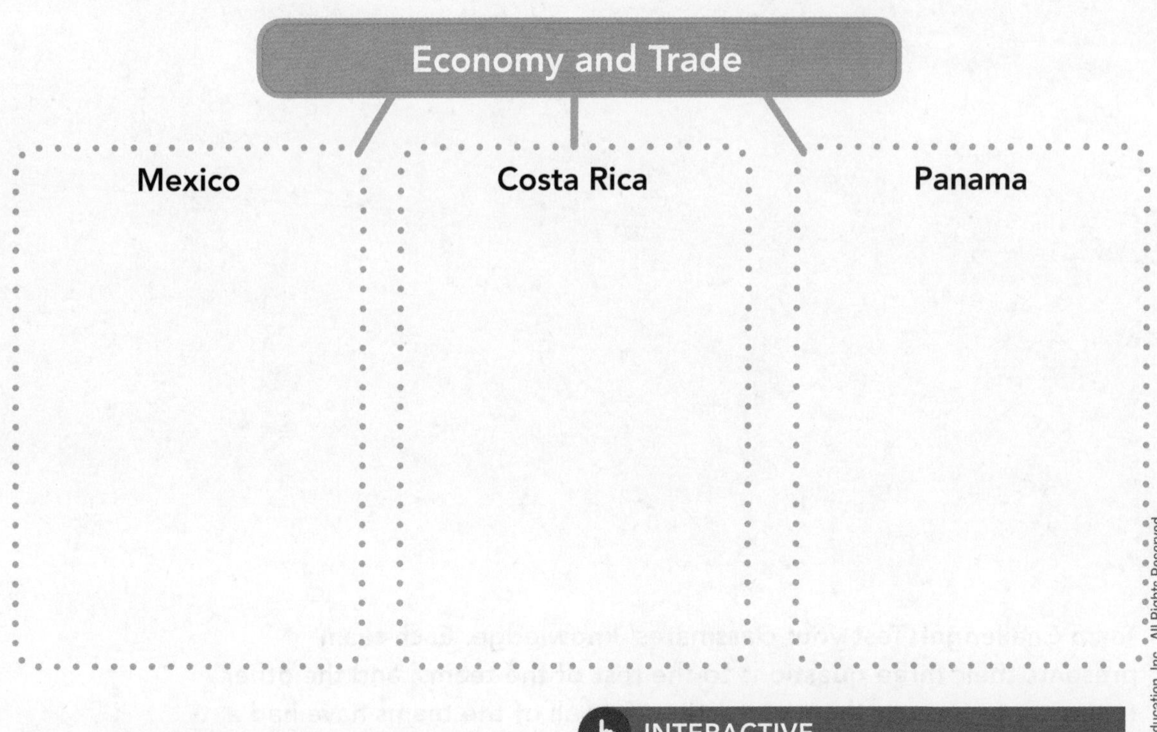

INTERACTIVE

For extra help, review the 21st Century Skills Tutorial: **Categorize**.

Practice Vocabulary

True or False? **Decide whether each statement below is true or false. Circle T or F and then explain your answer. Be sure to include the underlined vocabulary word in your explanation. The first one is done for you.**

1. **T / F** When someone goes abroad to find work, their family may send them money called remittances.
   False; when someone goes abroad to find work, they may send their family money called remittances.

2. **T / F** Specialization helps with trade because countries focus on producing items they can do well.

3. **T / F** Interdependence for Central American countries means each country produces everything it needs on its own.

4. **T / F** Costa Rica's ecotourism industry is important because it limits the environmental impact of tourism.

Take Notes

Literacy Skills: Use Evidence **Use what you have read to complete the table. Supply at least two pieces of evidence from the text to support each claim. The first one has been started for you.**

Claim	Evidence
The environment affects economic growth in the Caribbean.	• The area is prone to natural disasters, like hurricanes, that can hurt the economy.
Tourism is a critical part of the economy in Caribbean nations.	
Cuba suffers from a communist government and command economy.	

INTERACTIVE

For extra help, review the 21st Century Skills Tutorial: **Support Ideas with Evidence.**

Practice Vocabulary

Sentence Builder **Finish the sentences below with a key term from this section. You may have to change the form of the words to complete the sentences.**

Word Bank

Santeria hurricane creole

1. A language that mixes elements from other languages is called a

.

2. One religion that combines Roman Catholic and West African practices is

.

3. Another word for a tropical cyclone is

.

Take Notes

Literacy Skills: Draw Conclusions Use what you have read to complete the chart. Identify some of the environmental, economic, and social challenges that the governments and people of Middle America face. Then draw conclusions about the impact of these factors on these countries and the people that live there.

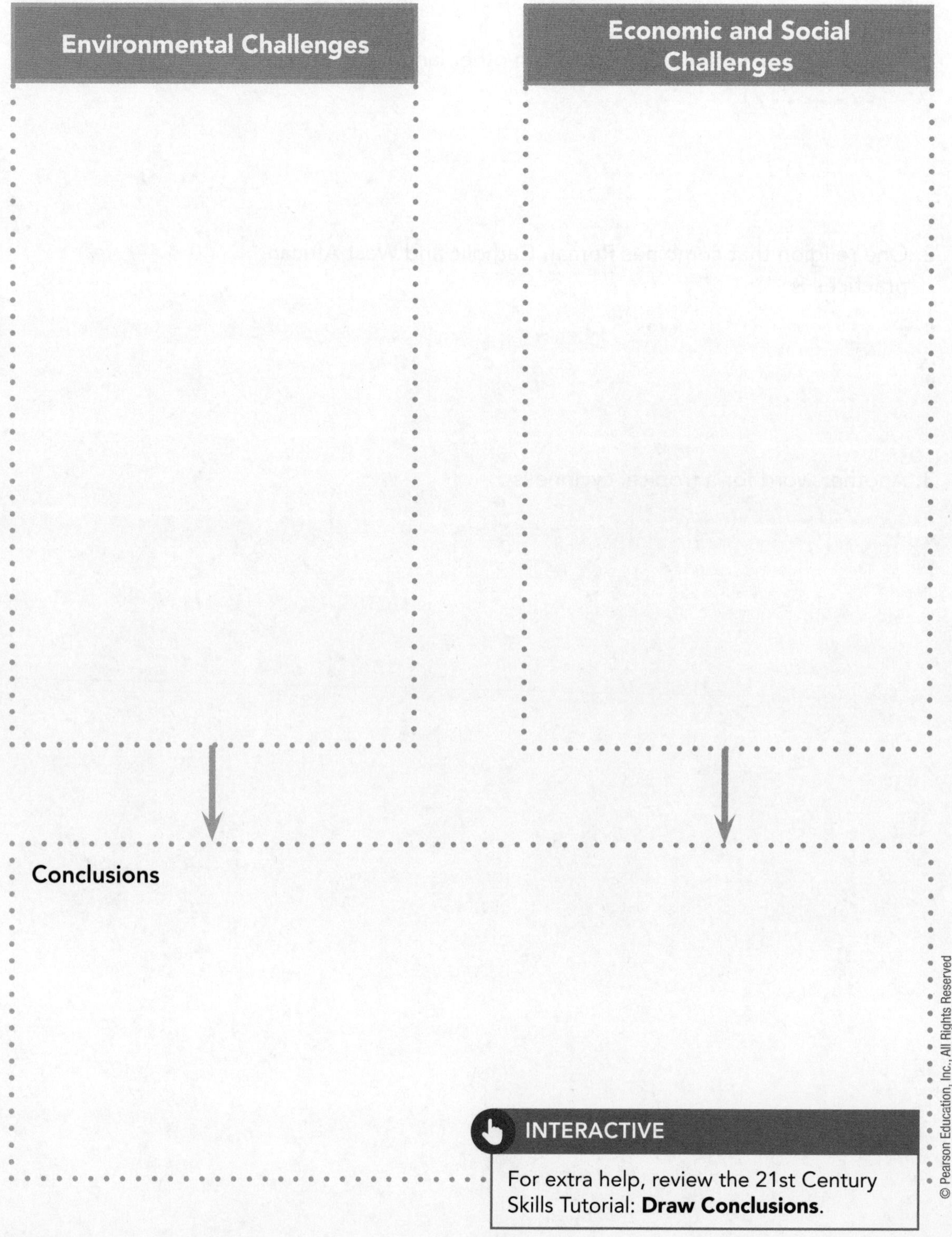

INTERACTIVE

For extra help, review the 21st Century Skills Tutorial: **Draw Conclusions**.

Practice Vocabulary

Matching Logic **Using your knowledge of the underlined vocabulary words, draw a line from each sentence in Column 1 to match it with the sentence in Column 2 to which it logically belongs.**

Column 1	Column 2
1. One of the causes of educational gaps in the region is the <u>digital divide</u>.	Poverty and the illegal drug trade lead to a high rate of crime, which hurts the economy.
2. One effect of earthquakes is that they sometimes cause <u>mudslides</u>.	In some places, fewer than 17 percent of people have access to the Internet at home.
3. <u>Cartels</u> have been responsible for thousands of murders in recent years.	With no tree roots to hold it down, the soil is easily washed away.
4. A consequence of deforestation is <u>erosion</u>.	When lots of dirt slides down the slope of a hill or mountain, homes and whole towns can be buried.
5. A lack of good <u>infrastructure</u> holds the region's economy back.	Reliable transportation, clean water, and electricity attract businesses to a region.

Writing Workshop Explanatory Essay

As you read, build a response to this question: How does Middle America use its resources? The prompts below will help walk you through the process.

Lesson 1 Writing Task: Consider Your Purpose Write your thoughts about how people use natural resources. How might you write an explanation of those uses?

Lesson 2 Writing Task: Develop a Clear Thesis Write a clear sentence explaining how people in Middle America have used natural resources. This sentence will be the main point of an essay you will write on this subject at the end of the topic.

Lesson 3 Writing Task: Support Your Thesis with Details Add details about how the Spanish colonists used resources. Review your thesis statement. Revise it if you think that's necessary based on what you've read in this lesson.

Lessons 4 through 7 Writing Task: Pick an Organizing Strategy and Support Your Thesis with Details Use the table to develop an organizing strategy for the body of your essay and to group key details. In the left column, identify three main points to write paragraphs about. Make sure these main points support your thesis. In the right column, note details that support each of these main points. As you work, review your thesis statement and revise it if you think that is necessary.

Lessons 8 and 9 Writing Task: Write an Introduction and a Conclusion Draft your introductory paragraph, which should include your thesis statement and three main points that support it. Draft a conclusion, explaining that resource use is important to Middle America. Use transition words to clarify relationships between ideas.

Writing Task Using the material you've already written, write your explanatory essay on the following topic: How does Middle America use its resources? After you write, read through your essay. Revise it, correcting all spelling and grammar errors.

South America Preview

Essential Question What should governments do?

Before you begin this topic, think about the Essential Question by completing the following activities.

1. Think about your own community and state, as well as the federal government. Make a list of ten things that you know the government does. Choose and rank what you consider to be the five most important things.

2. Preview the topic by skimming lesson titles, headings, and graphics. Then place a check mark next to the government activities that you predict the text will discuss. After reading the topic, circle the predictions that were correct.

__establish military	__pay for art	__abolish slavery
__collect taxes	__establish order	__build monuments
__organize economy	__create colonies	__take control of businesses

Map Skills

Using the political and physical maps in the Regional Atlas in your text, label the outline map with the places listed. Then draw in any major mountain ranges or rivers.

Brazil	Atlantic Ocean	Peru	Buenos Aires
Santiago	Pacific Ocean	Venezuela	Argentina
Caribbean Sea	Colombia	Brasília	The Guianas

Setting Priorities

On this Quest, you are part of a team that will be advising a government committee that is deciding whether or not to host a future Olympics in a South American country. You will gather information about the costs and benefits of hosting the Olympics by examining sources and conducting research. At the end of this Quest, your team will make a recommendation about whether hosting the Olympics is a good economic decision for your country.

1 Ask Questions

As you begin your Quest, keep in mind the Guiding Question: **What economic priorities should a government set?** and the Essential Question: **What should governments do?**

What other questions do you need to ask in order to make your recommendation? Two questions are filled in for you. Add at least two questions in each category.

Theme Economic Development

Sample questions:

What factors lead to economic growth in a country?

How can governments best encourage growth?

Theme Culture

Theme Government

Theme Transportation and Urban Development

Theme My Additional Questions

INTERACTIVE

For extra help with Step 1, review 21st Century Skills Tutorial: **Ask Questions.**

Quest CONNECTIONS

2 Investigate

As you read about South American countries and the relationships between governments and their economies, collect five connections from your text to help you answer the Guiding Question. Three connections are already chosen for you.

Connect to the Incas

Lesson 2 How Did the Incas Live Together?

Here's a connection! How did the Incan government use the Incas' resources?

Connect to Industrialization

Lesson 4 Dictatorship and Development

Here's another connection! Examine the efforts of dictators to industrialize their countries. How successful were they?

Connect to Venezuela

Lesson 6 South America's Economies

Examine the role Venezuela's government played in the country's economy under Hugo Chávez. What role did the government play in the country's economy under Chávez?

How did supporters and opponents view that role?

It's Your Turn! Find two more connections. Fill in the title of your connections, then answer the questions. Connections may be images, primary sources, maps, or text.

Your Choice | Connect to

Location in text

What is the main idea of this connection?

What does it tell you about whether using resources to host the Olympics is a good decision for your country?

Your Choice | Connect to

Location in text

What is the main idea of this connection?

What does it tell you about whether using resources to host the Olympics is a good decision for your country?

3 Conduct Research

Form teams based on your teacher's instructions. Use the table below to develop your research plan. Meet to decide who will research each segment, and list team members' names under their segments. The goal of your research is to help you decide on and support a recommendation on whether or not to host the Olympics.

You will research only the segment that you are responsible for. Be sure to find valid sources and take good notes so you can properly cite your sources. Record key information to help your team make a decision and to include in your written recommendation. Brainstorm ways to enhance your points with visuals.

Segment	Ideas	Sources
Economic Development		
Culture		
Government		
Transportation and Urban Development		

INTERACTIVE

For extra help with Step 3, review the 21st Century Skills Tutorials: **Search for Information on the Internet** and **Make Decisions**.

4 Write Your Recommendations

Now it's time to put together all of the information you have gathered and write your segment.

1. **Prepare to Write** Review the research you've collected, then meet as a team and decide whether your research supports the government using resources to host the Olympics. Then write notes below on how research on your segment supports the team's decision.

Segment's main point:

Supporting details:

Sources:

Supporting visuals:

2. **Write a Draft** Your segment of the report should fit on one page. That means you will need to get straight to the point. Use transition words and formal grammar.

3. **Share with a Partner** Exchange your segment with a partner. Tell your partner what you like about his or her segment and suggest any improvements. Check for clarity, for evidence-based claims, and for formal language. Revise your segment based on your partner's comments. Correct any grammar or spelling errors and revise your text based on the feedback.

4. **Create a Visual** Now that you have the text of your segment, find or create a visual to support your key points. Aim to make your points more memorable. With your team, decide on a style for the visuals in your committee's report.

5. **Put Together Your Written Recommendation** Once all committee members have written and revised their segments, it's time to put them together. Write an introduction and conclusion paragraph. Ensure smooth transitions from one segment to the next. Review your visuals together.

6. **Reflect on the Quest** After delivering the committee's recommendation, discuss your thoughts. Reflect on the project and list what you might do differently next time so that the project goes more smoothly.

Reflections

INTERACTIVE

For extra help, review the 21st Century Skills Tutorial: **Work in Teams**.

Take Notes

Literacy Skills: Cite Evidence Use what you have read to complete the table. Cite at least three pieces of evidence for each claim about the development of early South American cultures. The first one has been started for you.

Early South American Cultures	
Claim	**Evidence**
Groups of people living in different regions developed different cultures.	• The way people interacted with their environment affected how people lived.
Farming developed in some, but not all, regions of South America.	
Some groups that farmed developed civilizations.	

INTERACTIVE

For extra help, review the 21st Century Skills Tutorial: **Support Ideas with Evidence.**

Practice Vocabulary

Matching Logic **Using your knowledge of the underlined vocabulary words, draw a line from each sentence in Column 1 to match it with the sentence in Column 2 to which it logically belongs.**

Column 1	Column 2
1. The Andes are a difficult place to live.	They had no permanent homes and moved around to look for food.
2. Early people began to domesticate wild plants.	The mountains are so high that the elevation makes the air thin and cold.
3. To farm on the mountainsides, people developed terraces.	These flat strips of land allowed people to farm without losing soil and water.
4. Some groups of people continued to be nomads.	Instead of gathering food, they planted seeds and tended gardens.

Take Notes

Literacy Skills: Compare and Contrast **Use what you have read to complete the chart. Write notes about the Incan civilization and civilizations of the Maya and Aztecs that you read about earlier. Then, use your notes to write one to three sentences comparing the civilizations. One note has been completed for you.**

Incan Civilization	Maya and Aztec Civilizations
The Incas used a mix of peaceful and military means to build a huge empire.	

Compare and Contrast

INTERACTIVE

For extra help, review the 21st Century Skills Tutorial: **Compare and Contrast**.

Practice Vocabulary

True or False? **Decide whether each statement below is true or false. Circle T or F, and then explain your answer. Be sure to include the underlined vocabulary word in your explanation. The first one is done for you.**

1. T / F A quipu was how the Incas kept records.
True; a quipu was a record-keeping device, made of knotted strings, used to track goods and people.

2. T / F A hierarchy is a way to carry water up the mountainside.

3. T / F An ayllu is the name of an animal similar to a llama or alpaca.

4. T / F The Inca paid taxes through the mita system.

Take Notes

Literacy Skills: Identify Cause and Effect Use what you have read to complete the chart. List five specific results of European colonization of South America and the effects they had on South American Indians. The first one has been completed for you.

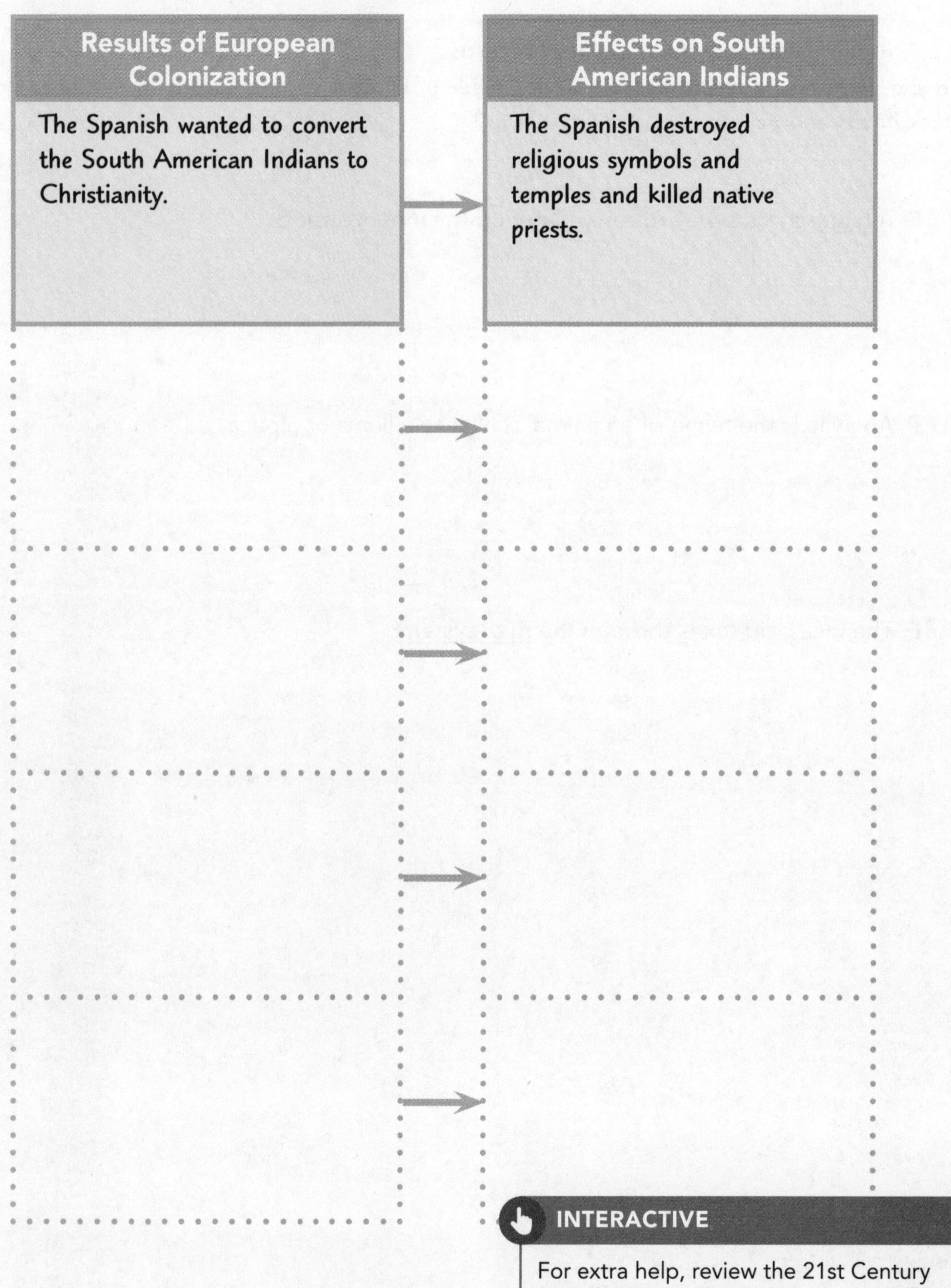

Results of European Colonization		Effects on South American Indians
The Spanish wanted to convert the South American Indians to Christianity.	→	The Spanish destroyed religious symbols and temples and killed native priests.
	→	
	→	
	→	
	→	

INTERACTIVE

For extra help, review the 21st Century Skills Tutorial: **Analyze Cause and Effect**.

Practice Vocabulary

Sentence Revision **Revise each sentence so that the underlined vocabulary word is used correctly. Be sure not to change the vocabulary word. The first one is done for you.**

1. Millions of South American Indians survived smallpox because they had immunity.
   Millions of South American Indians died from smallpox because they lacked immunity.

2. The Treaty of Tordesillas was a treaty the Spanish signed with the Incas.

3. Bandeiras were Portuguese explorers who were aided by native peoples.

4. The Line of Demarcation divided Africa in half.

5. Early settlers built houses out of brazilwood.

Quick Activity Sort It Out!

With your classmates, sort out which South American countries that you read about in this lesson were colonized by which European country, based on information provided in this lesson and the South America: Political map in the Regional Atlas.

Your teacher will assign students to represent French Guiana, Suriname, Guyana, Venezuela, Colombia, Ecuador, Peru, Bolivia, Chile, Argentina, Paraguay, Brazil, and Uruguay; and one student each to the colonial empires: Spain, Portugal, the Netherlands, France, and Britain. Make a sign with your country's name in big, bold letters so it can be read from across the room. Students representing the colonial empires should stand in five different parts of the room. Students representing the present or former colonies should move to the correct empire.

Team Challenge! **Divide evenly into two teams. Which side can remember the greatest number of impacts of colonization on South America? Your teacher or a student will record the list and keep score.**

Take Notes

Literacy Skills: Sequence Use what you have read to complete the chart. Sequence the important events leading up to the independence of the South American colonies. The first one has been completed for you.

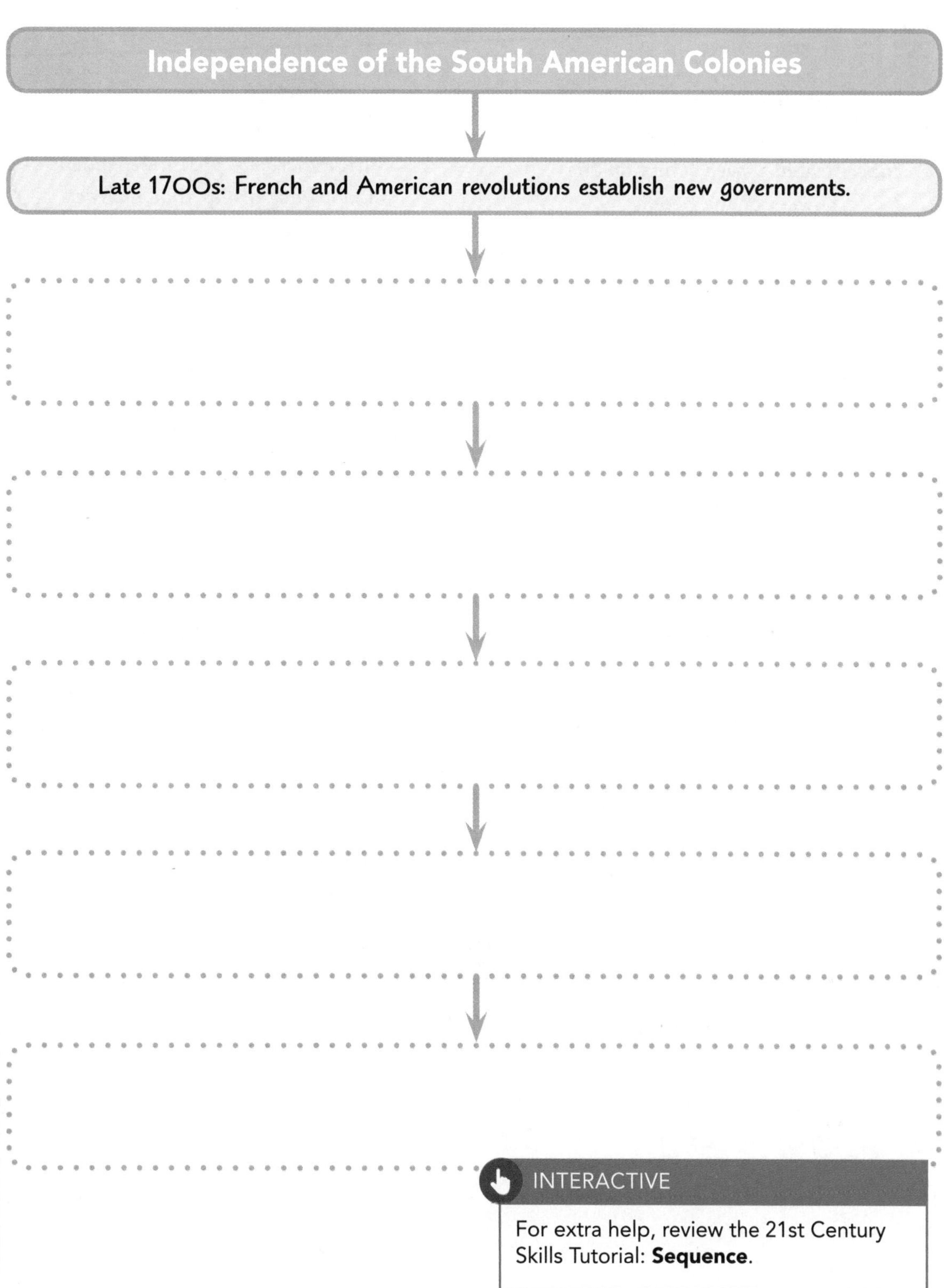

INTERACTIVE

For extra help, review the 21st Century Skills Tutorial: **Sequence**.

Practice Vocabulary

Word Map Study the word map for the word *oligarchy*. Characteristics are words or phrases that relate to the word in the center of the word map. Non-characteristics are words and phrases not associated with the word. Use the blank word map to explore the meaning of the word *abolitionist*. Then make word maps of your own for these words: *coup* and *nationalize*.

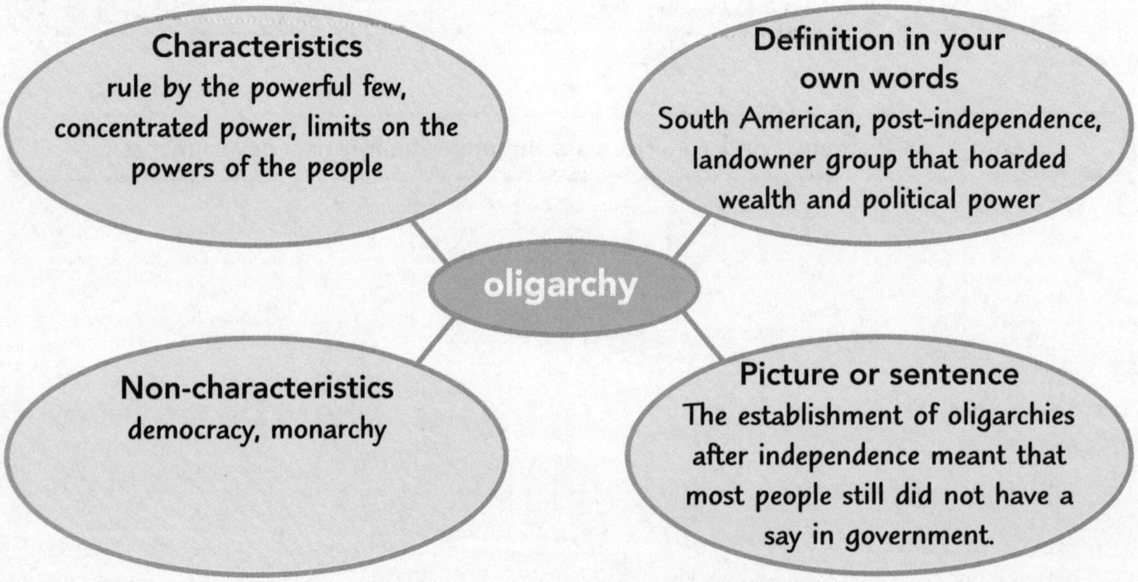

oligarchy

Characteristics
rule by the powerful few, concentrated power, limits on the powers of the people

Definition in your own words
South American, post-independence, landowner group that hoarded wealth and political power

Non-characteristics
democracy, monarchy

Picture or sentence
The establishment of oligarchies after independence meant that most people still did not have a say in government.

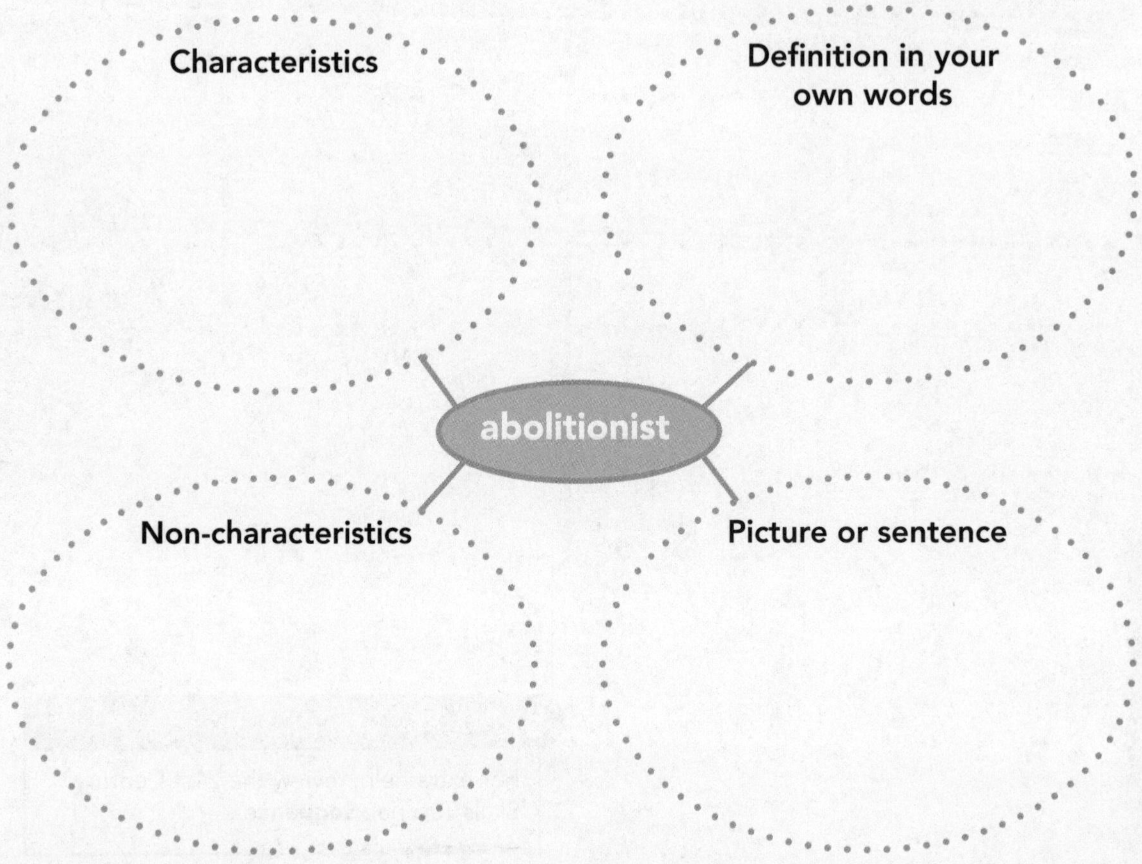

abolitionist

Characteristics

Definition in your own words

Non-characteristics

Picture or sentence

Take Notes

Literacy Skills: Classify and Categorize Use what you have read to complete the chart. List at least three facts about each region that distinguish it from other areas of South America. Be sure to include information about languages spoken and population distribution. The first one has been started for you.

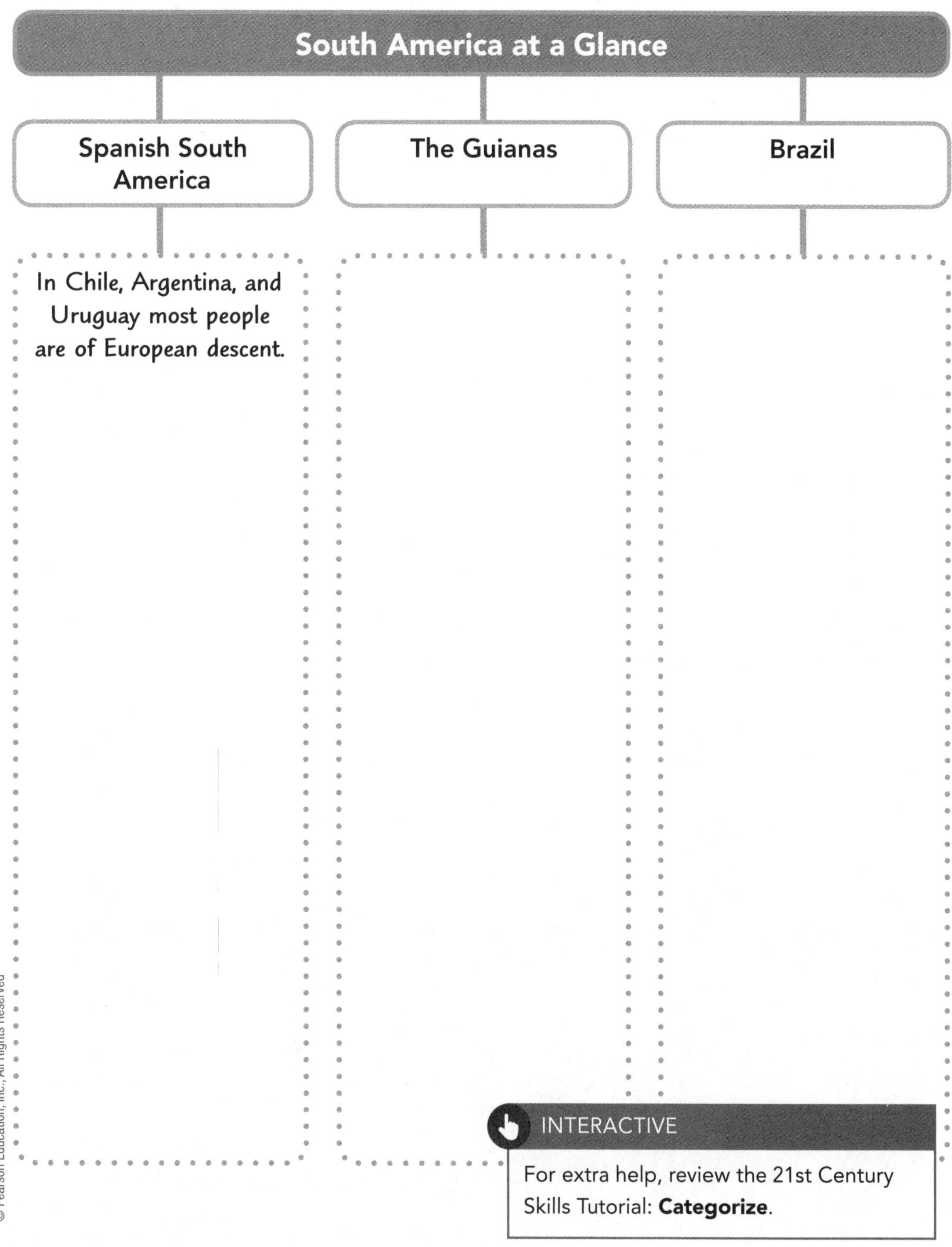

INTERACTIVE

For extra help, review the 21st Century Skills Tutorial: **Categorize**.

Practice Vocabulary

Vocabulary Quiz Show Some quiz shows ask a question and expect the contestant to give the answer. In other shows, the contestant is given an answer and must supply the question. If the blank is in the Question column, write the question that would result in the answer in the Answer column. If the question is supplied, write the answer.

Question	Answer
1.	1. Carnival
2. What is it called when machines do the work that humans used to do?	2.
3. Brazil is a major producer of what kind of soap opera?	3.
4. What is the name of a Brazilian style of dance performed in parades?	4.
5.	5. ethnic group

Take Notes

Literacy Skills: Determine Central Ideas Use what you have read to complete the charts. Using complete sentences, identify three central ideas from the text that support each headline. The first one has been started for you.

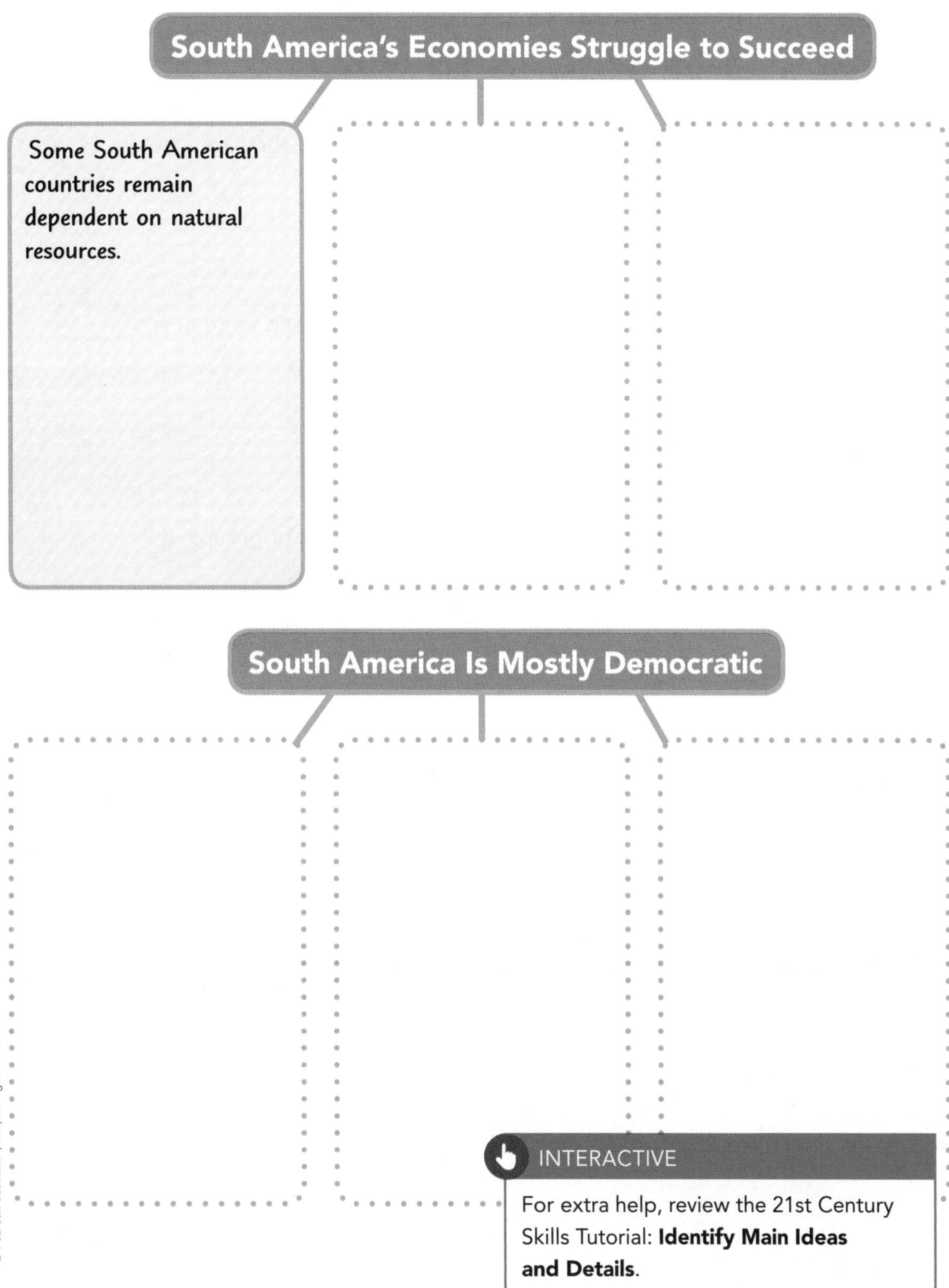

INTERACTIVE

For extra help, review the 21st Century Skills Tutorial: **Identify Main Ideas and Details**.

Practice Vocabulary

Sentence Builder **Finish the sentences below with a key term from this section. You may have to change the form of the words to complete the sentences.**

Word Bank

infrastructure	hydroelectric power	literacy rate
privatizing	interdependent	diversified

1. Countries can't make everything they need themselves, so they are

   .

2. If a high percentage of people in a certain place can read and write, it is said to have a high

   .

3. When a government sells businesses it owns to individuals or groups, it is called

   .

4. When countries produce lots of different products, their economy is said to be

   .

5. Roads and power lines are important examples of a country's

   .

6. Fast-running rivers can produce electricity called

   .

Quick Activity Workers Needed!

Examine the map showing the land use and major resources of South America.

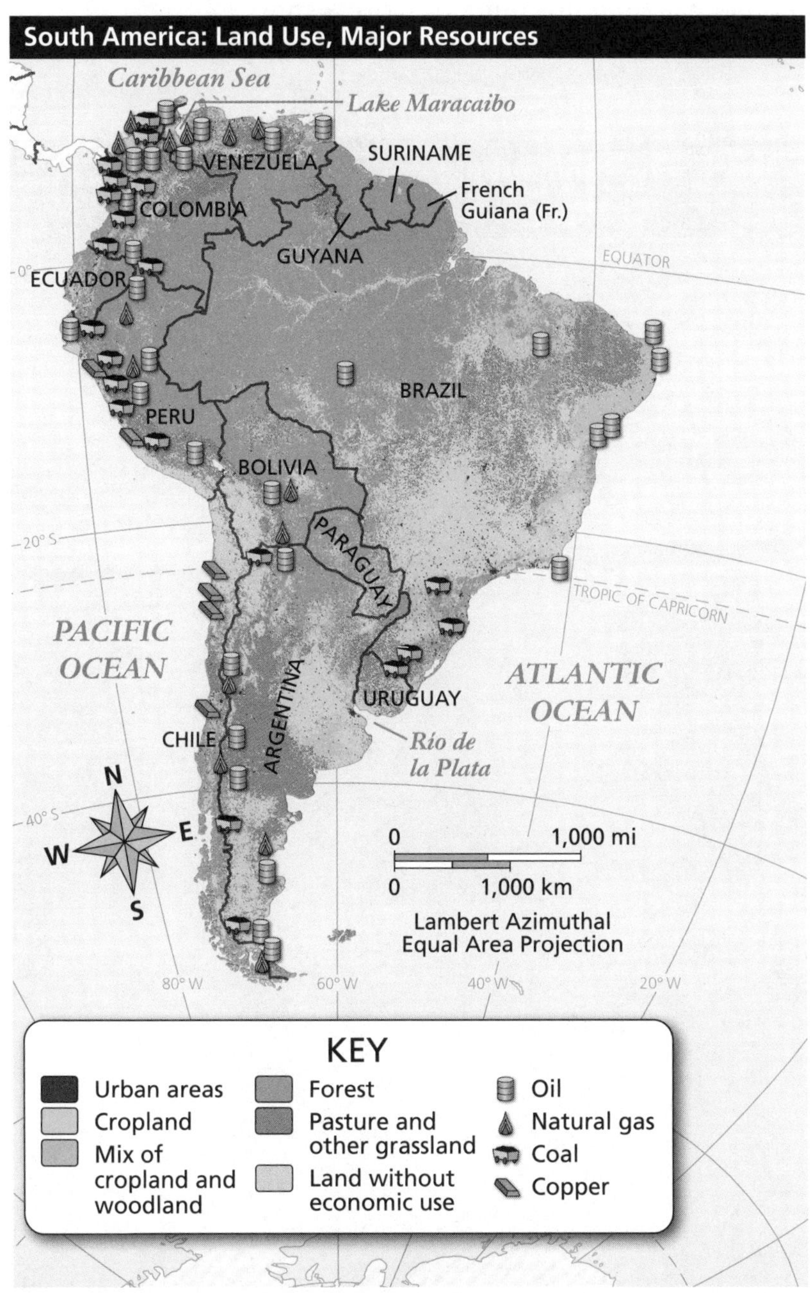

Team Challenge! With a partner, look at this map and think of a business you could start by taking advantage of one of South America's resources. Write a short ad to post on a business website to attract investors to invest money in your business. Mention where your business will be located and the resource it will use.

Take Notes

Literacy Skills: Summarize Use what you have read to complete the chart. Write two or three sentences that summarize each category of challenges facing South America. Then use them to write a short summary of the lesson. The first sentence has been completed for you.

Political Challenges	Environmental Challenges	Economic Challenges
Corruption is a widespread problem in many South American countries.		

Summary

INTERACTIVE

For extra help, review the 21st Century Skills Tutorial: **Summarize**.

Practice Vocabulary

Words in Context **For each question below, write an answer that shows your understanding of the boldfaced key term.**

1. How has **corruption** affected countries in South America?

2. Why are **nongovernmental organizations** important?

3. What are the causes of **deforestation**?

4. Why are **free trade zones** important?

Writing Workshop Argument

As you read, build a response to this question: Should a government have a strong or weak role in its country's economy? The prompts below will help walk you through the process.

Lessons 1 and 2 Writing Task: Introduce Claims Think about how governments affect the economy. How strong a role do you think they should play in the economy? List your ideas below.

Lesson 3 Writing Task: Develop a Clear Thesis Consider what you have learned about government involvement in South America's economies. Write a thesis statement—a clear sentence stating your main argument—on the role you think a government should play in an economy.

Lesson 4 Writing Task: Distinguish Claims From Opposing Claims Consider the strong and weak government roles described in this lesson. On a separate sheet of paper, write at least one benefit and one drawback of each kind of system.

Lessons 5 through 7 Writing Task: Support Claims List details from your reading, including from earlier lessons, that support the claim you made in your thesis statement.

Writing Task Think about what you have learned about the economic roles of different South American governments. Using your thesis and the supports for your claim, answer the following question in a five-paragraph argument on a separate sheet of paper: Should a government have a strong or weak role in its country's economy?

TOPIC 5

Europe Through Time Preview

Essential Question How should we handle conflict?

Before you begin this topic, think about the Essential Question by completing the following activities.

1. Consider the times you've experienced a conflict or a disagreement with someone in your life. Think about three of those times and write two or three sentences about each of them. Circle the example in which you were most satisfied with the way you handled the situation.

2. Preview the topic by skimming lesson titles, headings, and graphics. Then, place a check mark next to the examples that you predict will show ways that conflicts have been handled. After you finish reading the topic, circle the predictions that were correct.

__The Greek city-states of Sparta and Athens had different governments and values.

__The Romans built aqueducts to bring water to their cities.

__In Europe, the western and eastern Christian churches split apart.

__The king of England signed the English Bill of Rights.

__The Peace of Augsburg divided Germany into Catholic and Protestant states.

__People in Eastern Europe protested against communist rule.

__Countries formed the European Union.

Map Skills

Using the political and physical maps in the Regional Atlas in your text, label the outline map with the places listed. Then, color in water and areas of fertile land.

Alps	Iberian Peninsula	Ireland
Black Sea	Balkan Peninsula	Danube River
English Channel	Germany	Baltic Sea
Great Britain	North European Plain	Italian Peninsula
France	Scandinavian Peninsula	Poland
Rome	Mediterranean Sea	Greece
Paris		

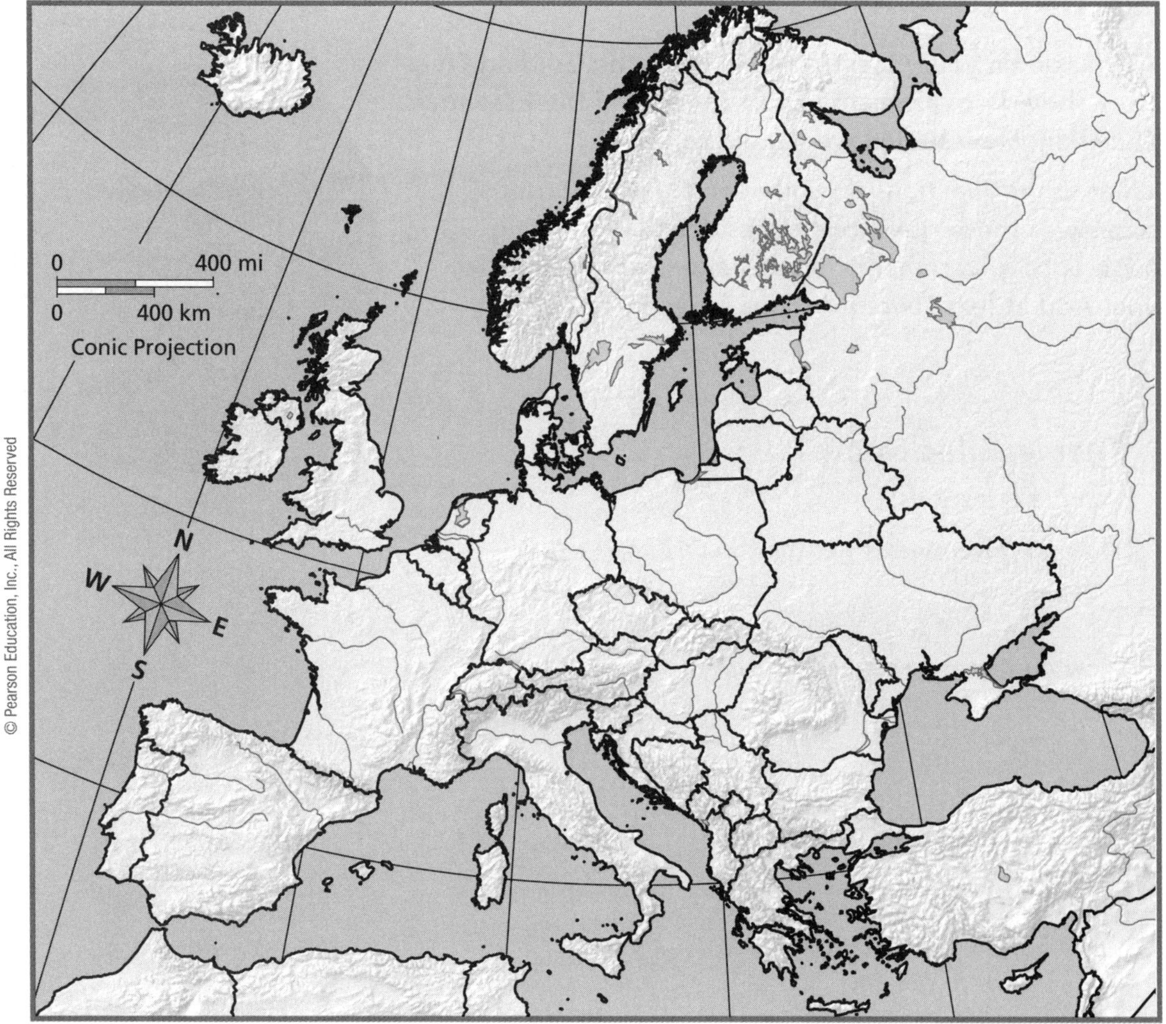

Planning a New Government

On this Quest, you will explore different forms of government. You will examine sources about different forms of government. By the end of the Quest, you will determine which form of government you believe works best and write an official recommendation on the form of government you think a newly independent country should adopt.

1 Ask Questions

As you begin your Quest, keep in mind the Guiding Question: **How should governments be formed?** and the Essential Question: **How should we handle conflict?**

What other questions do you need to ask in order to answer these questions? Consider the following aspects of government. Two questions are filled in for you. Add at least two questions for each category.

Theme Effectiveness

Sample questions:

How do governments get their work done?

How do governments keep order?

Theme Citizens' Rights

Theme Security

Theme Economic Well-Being

Theme The Common Good

Theme My Additional Questions

INTERACTIVE

For extra help with Step 1, review the 21st Century Skills Tutorial: **Ask Questions**.

2 Investigate

As you read about forms of government, collect five connections from your text to help you answer the Guiding Question. Three connections are already chosen for you.

Connect to Plato's Opinion on Leadership

Lesson 2 Greek Culture and Achievements

Here's a connection! What qualities did Plato believe a good leader should have?

Why do you think these qualities are important in government?

Connect to English Bill of Rights

Lesson 6 Powerful Kingdoms

Here's another connection! How did the government of England in the late 1600s differ from governments in the rest of Europe at the time?

What would be the advantages and disadvantages of a constitutional monarchy?

Connect to the Enlightenment

Lesson 7 Science and the Enlightenment

What did Enlightenment thinkers say about government?

What effect did Enlightenment thinkers have on the establishment of governments in North America and elsewhere?

It's Your Turn! **Find two more connections. Fill in the title of your connections, then answer the questions. Connections may be images, primary sources, maps, or text.**

Your Choice | Connect to

Location in text

What is the main idea of this connection?

What does it tell you about forms of government?

Your Choice | Connect to

Location in text

What is the main idea of this connection?

What does it tell you about forms of government?

3 Examine Primary Sources

Examine the primary and secondary sources provided online or from your teacher. Fill in the chart to show how these sources provide further information about forms of government. The first one has been started for you.

Source	The form of government supported and the reasons for that support:
Funeral Oration	democracy because it provides justice to all and opens government office to anyone with abilities
The Republic	
Leviathan	
Two Treatises of Government	
Origins of Totalitarianism	

INTERACTIVE

For extra help with Step 3, review the 21st Century Skills Tutorial: **Analyze Primary and Secondary Sources**.

4 Write Your Essay

Now it's time to put together all of the information you have gathered and use it to write your report.

1. **Prepare to Write** You have collected connections and explored primary and secondary sources about different forms of government. Look through your notes and decide which ideas you want to highlight in your report and what kind of government you are going to recommend. Record them here.

Ideas:

Recommendation:

2. **Write a Draft** Using evidence from the textbook and the primary and secondary sources you explored, write a draft of your report. Be sure to discuss various forms of government, not just your recommendation. Include details from the evidence in the material you've studied in this Quest.

3. **Share with a Partner** Exchange your draft with a partner. Tell your partner what you like about his or her draft and suggest any improvements.

4. **Finalize Your Report** Revise your essay based on the comments you receive from your partner. Correct any grammatical or spelling errors.

5. **Reflect on the Quest** Think about your experience completing this topic's Quest. What did you learn about the different forms of government? What questions do you still have about forms of government? How will you answer them?

Reflections

INTERACTIVE

For extra help with Step 4, review the 21st Century Skills Tutorial: **Write an Essay**.

Take Notes

Literacy Skills: Main Ideas and Details Use what you have read to complete the table. In each row write details that support the main idea provided. The first one has been completed for you.

Main Idea	Details
The first people arrived in Europe about 1 million years ago, and over time, societies developed.	• The first humans to arrive in Europe came from Africa by way of Asia. • Over time, these early humans developed into Neanderthals. • Eventually, *Homo sapiens* came out of Africa and displaced Neanderthals. • *Homo sapiens*, who had larger brains, learned how to use fire, made cave paintings, and held religious beliefs.
Farming changed Europe.	
Europeans produced better and stronger tools.	

INTERACTIVE

For extra help, review the 21st Century Skills Tutorial: **Identify Main Ideas and Details**.

Practice Vocabulary

Words in Context **For each question below, write an answer that shows your understanding of the boldfaced key term.**

1. Who were the **Neanderthals**?

2. Where in Europe did ***Homo sapiens*** live?

3. What happened in Europe during the **Bronze Age**?

Take Notes

Literacy Skills: Determine Central Ideas Use what you have read to complete the charts. In the top box, write the central idea. Then, complete the lower boxes with missing details. Both charts have been started for you.

Solon ended the practice of selling into slavery poor people who could not pay their debts.

Cleisthenes increased the number of citizens who could vote.

The Greeks created a mythology to explain the world.

Philosophers such as Socrates, Plato, and Aristotle used reason, or logic, to understand reality.

INTERACTIVE

For extra help, review the 21st Century Skills Tutorial: **Determine Central Ideas**.

Practice Vocabulary

Vocabulary Quiz Show Some quiz shows ask a question and expect the contestant to give the answer. In other shows, the contestant is given an answer and must supply the question. If the blank is in the Question column, write the question that would result in the answer in the Answer column. If the question is supplied, write the answer.

Question	Answer
1. What is the term for an independent state consisting of a city and its surrounding territory?	1.
2. What is the worship of many gods?	2.
3.	3. aristocracy
4.	4. mythology
5. What is membership in a community that gives a person civil and political rights and obligations?	5.
6. What is a system of rule by the people?	6.
7.	7. Socratic method

Take Notes

Literacy Skills: Summarize Use what you have read to complete the tables. Note the most important details from the section provided. The first row has been completed for you.

How Was the Republic Governed?	Important Details
Rome's Constitution	• Government included strong leaders, aristocrats, and average people. • Government was organized by basic rules and principles. • Constitution was based on tradition and custom, not written.
Principles of Republican Government	
Citizens and Officials	

The Empire and the Roman Peace	Important Details
Augustus and the Pax Romana	
Other Emperors	

INTERACTIVE

For extra help, review the 21st Century Skills Tutorial: **Summarize**.

Practice Vocabulary

True or False? **Decide whether each statement below is true or false. Circle T or F, and then explain your answer. Be sure to include the underlined vocabulary word in your explanation. The first one is done for you.**

1. **T / F** A <u>republic</u> is a government in which a monarch, such as a king, makes every decision.
   False; a republic is a government in which citizens have a right to vote and elect officials.

2. **T / F** An <u>empire</u> is a state that contains only one country.

3. **T / F** A <u>constitution</u> is a system of basic rules and principles by which a government is organized.

Take Notes

Literacy Skills: Draw Conclusions Use what you have read to complete the charts. The top box lists a conclusion you might draw from the text. In the bottom box, list evidence from the text that supports each conclusion. The first one has been started for you.

Two separate Christian churches developed—one in Western Europe and the other in the Byzantine empire.

- The western church used Latin, while the eastern church used Greek.

The Byzantine empire slowly shrank and fell 800 years later.

INTERACTIVE

For extra help, review the 21st Century Skills Tutorial: **Draw Conclusions**.

Practice Vocabulary

Sentence Builder **Finish the sentences below with a key term from this section. You may have to change the form of the words to complete the sentences.**

Word Bank

Great Schism	Justinian's Code
missionary	icon

1. The western church and the eastern church became permanently split as a result of the

   ______________________.

2. The western and eastern churches decorated church buildings with

   ______________________.

3. People who try to convert others to a particular religion are called

   ______________________.

4. In 529, Roman law was collected and organized into a few texts known as

   ______________________.

Quick Activity Prepare a Statement

Every major event throughout history has had many causes and many effects. Select one of the four pictures below and write a brief statement that explains what it illustrates and its causes and effects.

▲ Humans use bronze to make tools and weapons.

▲ The Greeks develop city-states.

▲ The church in the Byzantine empire is closely connected to the government.

▲ Caesar Augustus becomes first Roman emperor.

Team Challenge! After everybody in your class posts their statements around the classroom, read them. Discuss with your classmates why they chose to write what they did. Do you have different ideas about the causes and effects your classmates chose? Discuss them.

Take Notes

Literacy Skills: Identify Cause and Effect Use what you have read to complete the charts. In the bottom boxes, enter three causes of each listed effect. The first one has been started for you.

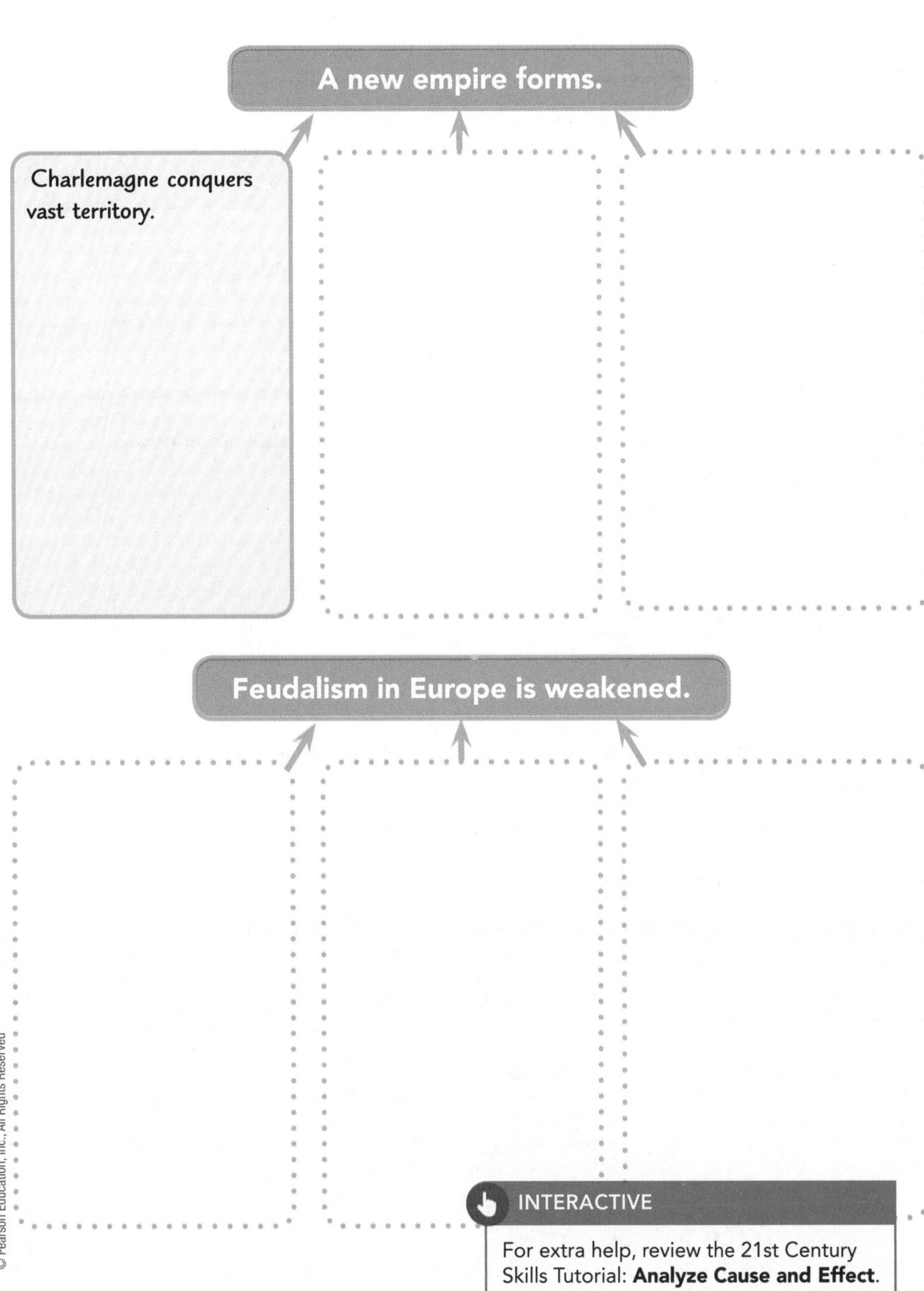

INTERACTIVE

For extra help, review the 21st Century Skills Tutorial: **Analyze Cause and Effect**.

Practice Vocabulary

Sentence Revision **Revise each sentence so that the underlined vocabulary word is used logically. Be sure not to change the vocabulary word. The first one is done for you.**

1. After the collapse of the western Roman empire, a system of marketplace reform called feudalism was established.
   After the collapse of the western Roman empire, a system of government called feudalism was established.

2. Most lords in medieval Europe were serfs who were required to live and work at a specific manor.

3. The disease called the Black Death contributed to a population increase in medieval Europe.

4. Under feudalism, lords kept land to themselves.

5. The heart of the medieval economy was the manor, which was a town center.

6. The Crusades began after Charlemagne's defeat of feudal lords.

7. Vassals were the most powerful lords.

Take Notes

Literacy Skills: Use Evidence Use what you have read to complete the table. In each column write details about the topic provided. The first one has been completed for you. Then, use the information you have gathered to draw a conclusion about the question provided.

Renaissance	Age of Discovery	Reformation
• Italians discovered teachings of ancient Greeks and Romans and learned new ideas. • Thinkers began to rely more on reason than on religious authority to understand the world. • Art became more realistic and scientists made great discoveries. • William Shakespeare wrote brilliant plays and poems.		

Conclusion: How did changes in Europe from the 1300s to the 1500s affect the way people understood the world and practiced religion?

INTERACTIVE

For extra help, review the 21st Century Skills Tutorial: **Identify Evidence**.

Practice Vocabulary

Matching Logic **Using your knowledge of the underlined vocabulary terms, draw a line from each sentence in Column 1 to match it with the sentence in Column 2 to which it logically belongs.**

Column 1	Column 2
1. The Protestant Reformation started as a movement to reform the Catholic Church.	This cultural flowering included new artistic methods as well as new ways of looking at the world.
2. French King Louis XIV embraced the idea of absolute monarchy.	Luther challenged the church's authority and stressed spirituality.
3. Italians rediscovered the learning of the ancient Greeks and Romans, spurring the Renaissance.	Missionary orders, such as the Jesuits, were formed.
4. People who believed in humanism sought a better life on earth.	Under this belief, the king had an unlimited right to rule.
5. During the Counter-Reformation, reformers founded religious groups with their own particular structure and purpose.	Thinkers began to focus on improving life on earth instead of just achieving salvation after death.

Take Notes

Literacy Skills: Classify and Categorize Use what you have read about the Enlightenment and revolutions in Europe to complete the tables. Categorize events based on the subject matter. The first one has been started for you.

Scientific Revolution	The Enlightenment
• Scientists started to use the scientific method to determine the truth. • Newton used the scientific method to prove the existence of gravity.	

Nationalism	Imperialism

INTERACTIVE

For extra help, review the 21st Century Skills Tutorial: **Categorize**.

Practice Vocabulary

Words in Context **For each question below, write an answer that shows your understanding of the boldfaced key term.**

1. What does a supporter of **nationalism** want?

2. What was the **Industrial Revolution**?

3. What happened during the **Enlightenment**?

4. What is **imperialism**?

5. How did the **French Revolution** begin?

Take Notes

Literacy Skills: Analyze Text Structure Use what you have read to complete the outlines. Fill in each outline to summarize the main ideas of the lesson. The outline has been started for you.

I. Why Were There Two World Wars?

A. World War I

1. Allied powers of France, Britain, Russia, and the United States fought and defeated Germany, Austria-Hungary, Bulgaria, and the Ottoman Empire; the defeated countries lost land and had to pay heavy reparations.

B. Inflation and Depression

1. Reparations led to hyperinflation in defeated countries, and the U.S. stock market crashed in 1929.

2.

C. Totalitarian Governments

1.

2.

3.

D. World War II

1.

2.

E. Effects of World War II

1.

2.

3.

INTERACTIVE

For extra help, review the 21st Century Skills Tutorial: **Summarize**.

Practice Vocabulary

Vocabulary Quiz Show **Some quiz shows ask a question and expect the contestant to give the answer. In other shows, the contestant is given an answer and must supply the question. If the blank is in the Question column, write the question that would result in the answer in the Answer column. If the question is supplied, write the answer.**

Question	Answer
1. What is the economic and political partnership among member nations in Europe?	1.
2. What name was given to the mass murder of Jews and others by Nazis during World War II?	2.
3.	3. Cold War
4.	4. hyperinflation

Quick Activity Nazism and World War II Timeline

Write a timeline of events during the rise of Nazism and of the outbreak of World War II. Then, write one or two sentences about the effect on the people of Europe during the 1930s and 1940s.

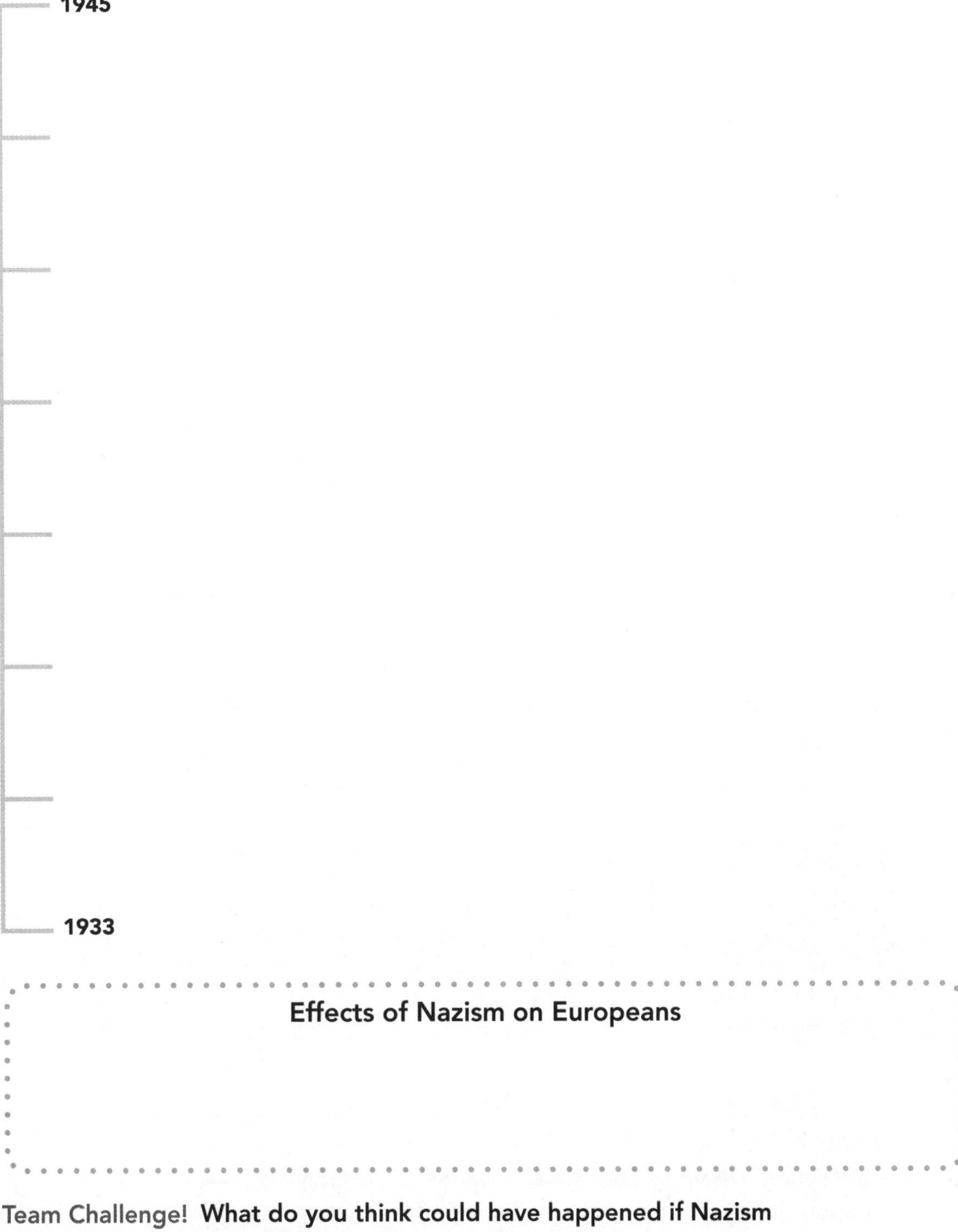

Team Challenge! What do you think could have happened if Nazism had not arisen in Germany? List some ideas on a piece of paper, and when your list is finished, take part in a classroom discussion about the alternative history in which Germany never started World War II.

Writing Workshop Explanatory Essay

As you read, build a response to this question: What causes war and conflict? The prompts below will help walk you through the process.

Lesson 1 Writing Task: Generate Questions In the box below, write two to four questions about the causes of war and conflict through time to help focus your research.

Lesson 2 Writing Task: Draft a Thesis Statement In the box below, write a thesis statement summarizing your position on the main causes of war and conflict.

Lessons 3 through 6 Writing Task: Cite Evidence On a separate piece of paper, cite evidence from your reading of the text and source documents that supports your thesis statement. If necessary, revise your thesis statement to align your position to the evidence that supports your position.

Lesson 7 Writing Task: Compare and Contrast List three wars or conflicts described in the lesson. In a few sentences, compare and contrast the causes of these wars or conflicts.

Lesson 7 Writing Task: Write an Introduction Write a paragraph that introduces your explanatory essay and includes your thesis statement.

Writing Task Using your thesis statement, the evidence you gathered, and your introduction, answer the following question in a five-paragraph explanatory essay: What causes war and conflict?

As you write, consider using the following cause-and-effect signal words to transition between points: *because, consequently, therefore, for this reason,* and *as a result.*

TOPIC 6

Europe Today Preview

Essential Question What makes a culture unique?

Before you begin this topic, think about the Essential Question by completing the following activities.

1. Briefly describe what culture means to you. How would you describe your culture, and what makes it different from other cultures?

2. Preview the topic by skimming lesson titles, headings, and graphics. Then place a check mark next to the factors that you predict the text says contribute to the existence of many unique cultures in Europe.

__language	__environment	__government
__religion	__ecotourism	__economy
__jazz	__migration	__geographic barriers

Map Skills

Using the Regional Atlas maps in your text, label the outline map with the places listed. Use a symbol to indicate urban areas with populations of more than 5 million, and create a key that explains your symbol. Then color in the land areas of Europe and the bodies of water.

Athens	Brussels	Bucharest	Budapest
Kiev	Lisbon	London	Madrid
Milan	Paris	Rhine-Ruhr	Warsaw

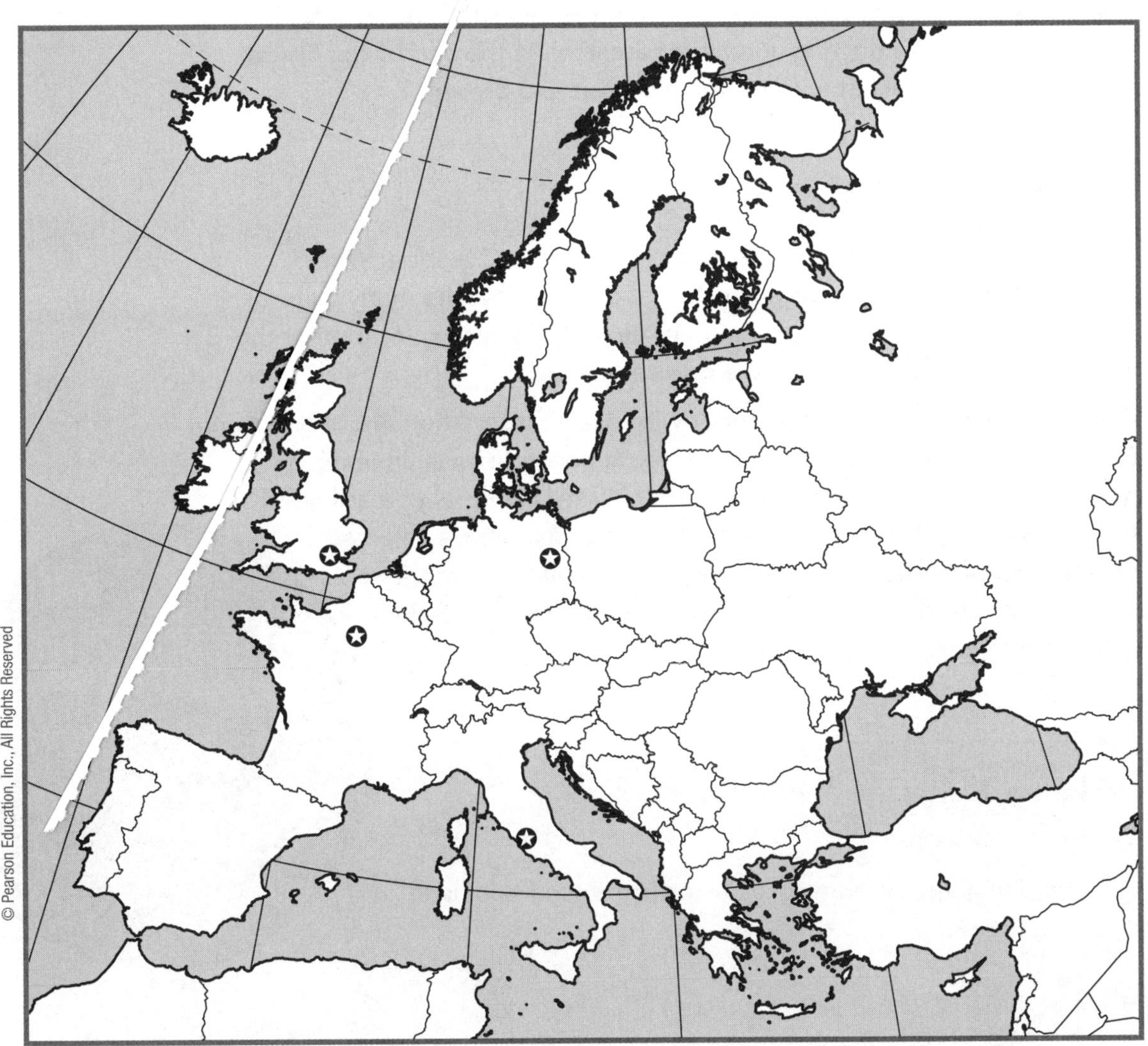

Create a Museum Exhibit

On this Quest, you have been asked by a museum curator to work with a team to create an exhibit about cultural diversity in modern Europe. You will gather information about Europe's cultures by examining sources in your text and by conducting your own research. At the end of the Quest, you will build a model of your museum exhibit and present it.

1 Ask Questions

As you begin your Quest, keep in mind the Guiding Question: **What distinguishes one culture from another?** Consider how the many cultures of Europe are distinct from one another as part of your exploration of the Essential Question: **What makes a culture unique?**

For your project, each team member will collect information about a different European culture that will be used to create part of a museum exhibit. To get a better understanding of how each culture is unique, you will need to consider the following themes for the culture you have selected. Create a list of questions that will help guide your research. Two questions are filled in for you. Add at least two more questions for each category.

Theme Language and Religion

Sample questions:

What language or languages are spoken by individuals in this culture?

What religious beliefs, if any, are most common among people from this culture?

Theme History and Settlement Patterns

Theme Family and Social Structure

Theme Arts, Beliefs, and Values

Theme My Additional Questions

INTERACTIVE

For extra help with Step 1, review the 21st Century Skills Tutorial: **Ask Questions**.

Quest CONNECTIONS

2 Investigate

As you read about modern Europe, collect five connections from your text to help you answer the Guiding Question. Three connections are already chosen for you.

Connect to Language

Lesson 1 Why Does Europe Have So Many Languages?

Here's a connection! Read the section on Europe's languages. How did history contribute to the development of diverse languages in the past? What role did geographic barriers play?

How do you think modern transportation and communication methods have overcome geographic barriers and affected Europe's linguistic and cultural diversity?

Connect to Migration

Lesson 3 How Is the European Union Run?

Here is another connection! Read about the government of the European Union in the infographic. How do European Union policies affect the movement of people among member countries?

What effects does this movement have on cultural diversity?

Connect to Ethnic Identity

Lesson 4 Challenges Facing the European Union

Read about criticisms of the European Union. How has ethnic identity contributed to those criticisms?

How have economic conditions contributed to those criticisms?

It's Your Turn! Find two more connections. Fill in the title of your connections, then answer the questions. Connections may be images, primary sources, maps, or text.

Your Choice | Connect to

Location in text

What is the main idea of this connection?

What does it tell you about cultural diversity?

Your Choice | Connect to

Location in text

What is the main idea of this connection?

What does it tell you about cultural diversity?

3 Conduct Research

Form teams based on your teacher's instructions. As a team, decide which cultures to showcase and who will research each culture. The cultures your group chooses to research should include cultures of historically European ethnic groups and at least one example of a more recent immigrant culture.

You will do further research on the culture that you are responsible for. Use the Quest themes and connections to explore the culture that you selected. Find reliable primary and secondary sources about the culture. Record sources and key information in the table below. You may want to investigate additional themes to get a fuller understanding of the culture.

Theme	Source(s)	Notes
Language and Religion		
History and Settlement Patterns		
Family and Social Structure		
Beliefs and Values		
Arts		

INTERACTIVE

For extra help, review the 21st Century Skills Tutorials: **Evaluate Web Sites** and **Search for Information on the Internet**.

4 Create Your Exhibit

Now it's time to put together all of the information you have gathered and then plan and create your exhibit.

1. **Prepare to Create** Before you start to build your exhibit, organize your information and make a plan to help ensure that your exhibit is fact-based, logically organized, and eye-catching.

Culture:

Key information about the culture:

Sources to cite:

Possible visual or audio material to use:

2. **Create a Diagram** To plan your exhibit as a team, each member will make a diagram. The diagrams will be sketches or layouts that show how your exhibit will look. Begin by agreeing on a plan for the overall exhibit, and then independently develop a diagram for your own part. Your diagram should include a title, text, and at least one visual element. Visuals should have captions. Remember to plan your part with the complete exhibit in mind.

3. **Share** Share your diagram with the team. Discuss how all the diagrams work together and whether any changes are needed. Revise your diagram based on the team discussion.

4. **Build a Model** Once all team members have finalized plans, work together to create an exhibit model to present to the class.

5. **Present Your Exhibit** Present your exhibit model to the class. View the other teams' exhibits, and take notes on the information they shared.

Notes on other exhibits:

6. **Reflect** After viewing all the exhibit models, share your thoughts. What did you learn about cultural diversity in Europe from your team's research and the exhibit models presented by other teams? Which culture or cultures would you like to learn more about?

Reflections:

INTERACTIVE

For extra help, review the 21st Century Skills Tutorials: **Give an Effective Presentation** and **Work in Teams**.

Take Notes

Literacy Skills: Identify Cause and Effect Use what you have read to complete the charts. In each space write details about the causes that have led to the identified effect. The first chart has been started for you.

Europe's Language Diversity

Indo-European Languages

Invaders brought Proto-Indo-European language to Central Europe about 5,000 years ago. Dialects spread across Europe and grew into distinct languages.

Influence of the Roman Empire

Impact of Geography

Europe's Religious Diversity

Judaism and Christianity

Islam and Protestantism

Recent Changes

INTERACTIVE

For extra help, review the 21st Century Skills Tutorial: **Analyze Cause and Effect.**

Practice Vocabulary

Words in Context For each question below, write an answer that shows your understanding of the boldfaced key term.

1. Explain how Proto-Indo-European **dialects** led to Europe's language diversity.

2. Why are most Basques **bilingual**?

Take Notes

Literacy Skills: Analyze Text Structure Use what you have read to create an outline of the main ideas of the lesson. As you create your outline, pay attention to headings, subheadings, and key terms that you can use to organize the information. The first section of the outline has been completed for you.

I. How Geographic Features Affect Where People Live
   A. Settlement Patterns
      1. Many early Europeans were farmers, and areas with rich farmland are still home to large populations.
      2. In western and northern Europe, people live near the coast where trade routes are easier to access and the climate is milder.
   B.

INTERACTIVE

For extra help, review the 21st Century Skills Tutorial: **Identify Main Ideas and Details.**

Practice Vocabulary

Matching Logic **Using your knowledge of the underlined vocabulary terms, draw a line from each sentence in Column 1 to match it to the sentence in Column 2 to which it logically belongs.**

Column 1	Column 2
1. Entrepreneurship is strong in the German and British economies.	Free university education in her country helped Anja complete a degree in computer science.
2. Many Europeans are employed in service sector jobs.	María works for the public transportation system as a bus driver.
3. One way for a country to invest in human capital is by providing its people with quality education.	After Malik moved to England, he started his own international importing business.

Quick Activity Create a Living Population Density Map

The table below shows how the population of Europe would be distributed if the total population of Europe were 20. For example, 3 of the 20 would live in France.

Population of Europe in Terms of 20 People Total		
France: 3/20	Germany: 3/20	Italy: 3/20
Netherlands: 1/20	Poland: 2/20	Romania: 1/20
Spain: 2/20	Ukraine: 2/20	United Kingdom: 3/20

Calculate how many students in your class would live in each country based on these proportions. To do so, multiply the proportion for each country by the number of students in your class and round to the nearest whole number.

For example, if there are 27 students in your class, you would multiply 3/20 by 27 students. That gives a result of 4.05. After rounding, you know that 4 students would represent the population of France.

Record the proportions for your class in the table below.

Number of Students to Represent Countries' Populations		
France:	Germany:	Italy:
Netherlands:	Poland:	Romania:
Spain:	Ukraine:	United Kingdom:

Team Challenge! Create a living population density map using the proportions that you calculated. Work together to assign each student a country. Look at a map of Europe. Arrange yourselves around the classroom by country to form a giant map, with students assigned to each country standing together. Look around and discuss as a class: Where is population most concentrated? Which countries are missing? Why might those countries have lower populations? In which parts of Europe are people most concentrated?

Take Notes

Literacy Skills: Classify and Categorize Use what you have read to complete the chart. In each space write details about a type of government in Europe. The first one has been started for you. Provide examples of countries with each form of government.

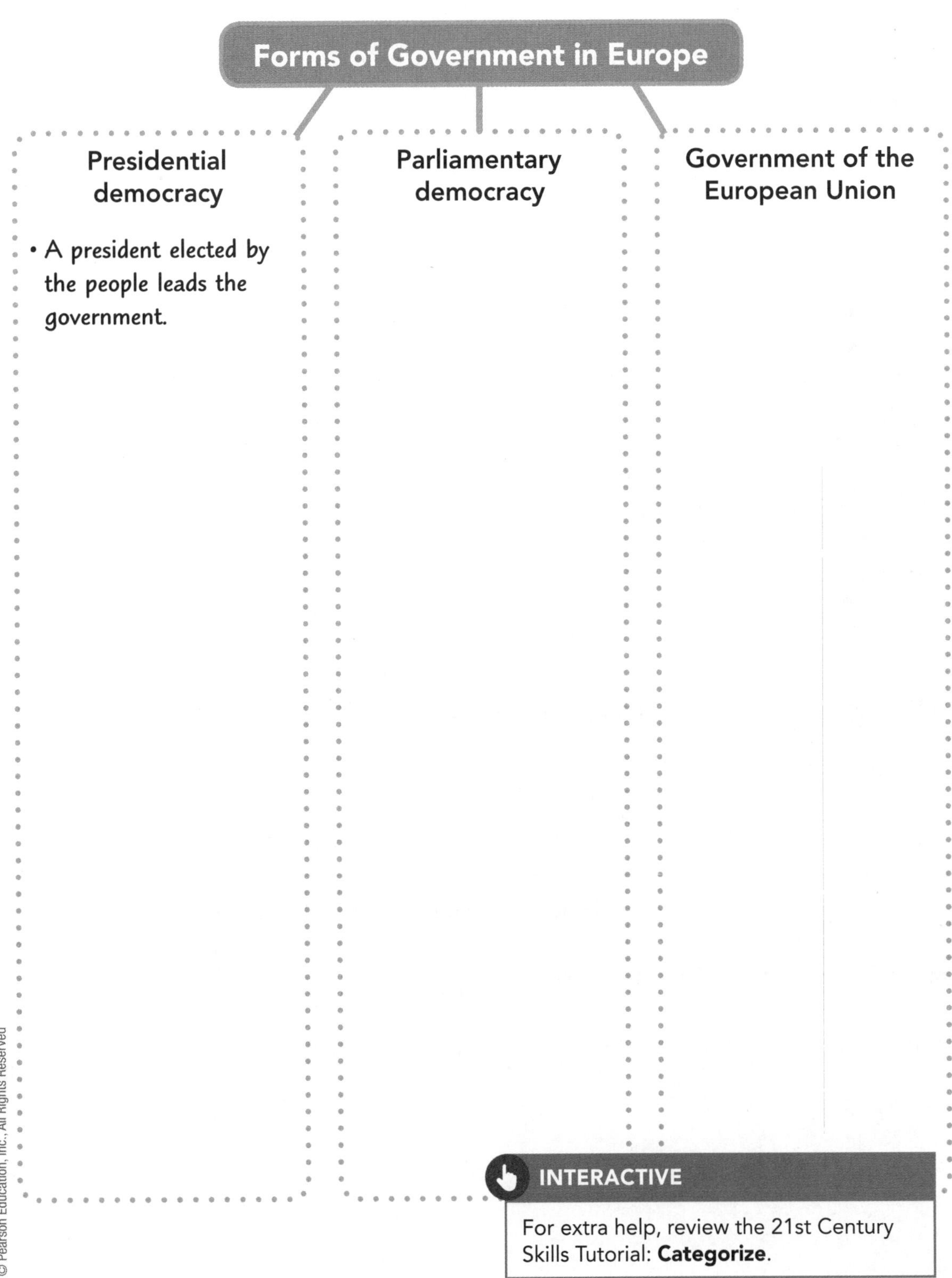

INTERACTIVE

For extra help, review the 21st Century Skills Tutorial: **Categorize**.

Practice Vocabulary

Use a Word Bank **Choose one word from the word bank to fill in each blank. When you have finished, you will have a short summary of important ideas from the section.**

Word Bank

dictatorship
constitutional monarchy
presidential democracy
parliamentary democracy
theocracy

Most European countries are democracies, but several types of democracy exist in Europe. In a ______________, the leader of the government is elected by the people, and the leader's power is balanced by the legislature. In a ______________, the head of government is a prime minister chosen by a majority of the legislature. These countries also usually have a president or monarch who is the symbolic head of state. The head of state in Britain is a monarch who inherits the position. Because the monarch's powers are limited by a system of laws and court decisions, the British government is considered a ______________. A few European countries are not democracies. The Vatican State, for example, is a ______________ headed by the Pope, the religious leader of the Roman Catholic Church. Belarus is a ______________, or autocracy, in which the people have little input in the government.

Take Notes

Literacy Skills: Draw Conclusions Use what you have read to complete the table. In each column write details about the challenges European countries are facing. The first details have been completed for you. Then use the notes you have taken to draw a conclusion related to the challenges facing Europe today.

Environmental challenges	Demographic challenges	Challenges facing the European Union
Air pollution • harms crops, forests, and human health • causes acid rain that damages buildings, forests, and water supplies	Aging population	Criticism of the EU
Nuclear fears	Economic effects	The euro crisis
Climate change		

Conclusion

INTERACTIVE

For extra help, review the 21st Century Skills Tutorial: **Draw Conclusions**.

Practice Vocabulary

Sentence Builder **Finish the sentences below with a key term from this section. You may have to change the form of the words to complete the sentence.**

Word Bank

climate change	demographic
greenhouse gases	Kyoto Protocol

1. Products of burning fossil fuels that scientists believe trap heat in Earth's atmosphere and make the planet warmer are called ______.

2. The international agreement the European Union signed in 1997 pledging to reduce the emission of greenhouse gases is the ______.

3. If data have to do with population change and the groups that make up the population of a place, those data are ______.

4. A long-term increase in Earth's temperature is one example of global ______.

Quick Activity Discussing Government Spending

An issue that every country faces is the question of government spending: How much should the government spend, and what should it spend its money on? How much spending is too much, and when is more spending justified? For countries in the European Union, there is another question: How will spending by the government of one member nation affect the other member nations?

Using what you have learned in this lesson, briefly write arguments for each of the positions provided in the table.

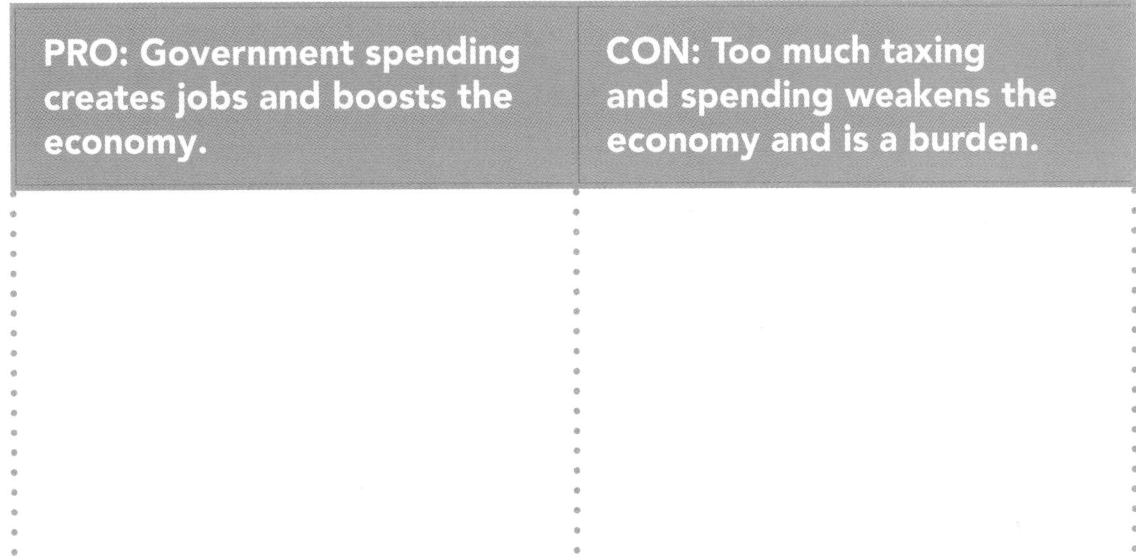

PRO: Government spending creates jobs and boosts the economy.	CON: Too much taxing and spending weakens the economy and is a burden.

Team Challenge! Form pairs and discuss the role of government spending and its effects on individual countries and on the European Union as a whole. Your teacher may assign you a side to take in this discussion. After discussing the issue with your partner, use the space below to record your opinion on the European Union's spending.

Writing Workshop Explanatory Essay

As you read, build a response to this question: **What is the impact of cultural diversity on Europe?** The prompts below will help walk you through the process.

Lesson 1 Writing Task: Develop a Clear Thesis Write a statement about the impact of cultural diversity in Europe. This sentence will be the thesis statement, or main idea, for the explanatory essay you will write at the end of the topic. Think about what you have read so far about Europe's diverse cultures and the effects of that diversity.

Lesson 2 Writing Task: Support Thesis with Details Record details from this lesson and the previous lesson that support your thesis. Continue recording details that support your thesis in the remaining lessons of the topic.

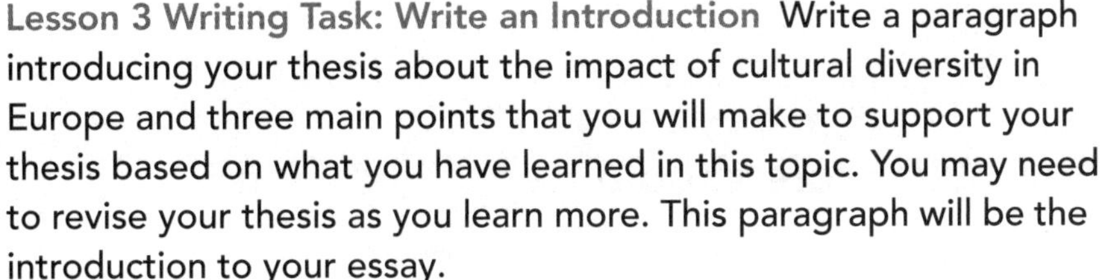

Lesson 3 Writing Task: Write an Introduction Write a paragraph introducing your thesis about the impact of cultural diversity in Europe and three main points that you will make to support your thesis based on what you have learned in this topic. You may need to revise your thesis as you learn more. This paragraph will be the introduction to your essay.

Lesson 4 Writing Task: Clarify Relationships with Transition Words Using transition words like *additionally* and *furthermore* strengthens writing by helping the reader see how ideas presented in a piece are connected. On a separate sheet of paper, create a rough outline for your essay, and write sentences that might connect parts of your outline using transition words.

Writing Task Using your thesis, introduction, and rough outline, answer the following question in a five-paragraph explanatory essay: What is the impact of cultural diversity on Europe? Incorporate some of the transition words you noted. For the conclusion, revisit your thesis and explain why the information in your essay is important. Re-read your essay carefully and edit it for proper spelling, grammar, and punctuation.

Northern Eurasia Preview

Essential Question What role should people have in their government?

Before you begin this topic, think about the Essential Question by completing the following activities.

1. Think about your community, state, or nation as a whole. List at least three ways that people participate in government. Then write a sentence about how you think people should participate in their government and explain why you think so.

Map Skills

Using the political and physical maps in the Regional Atlas in your text, label the outline map with the places listed.

Turkmenistan	Caspian Sea
Armenia	Georgia
Uzbekistan	Russia
Black Sea	Azerbaijan
Tajikistan	St. Petersburg
Kyrgyzstan	Kazakhstan
Moscow	Ural Mountains
Siberia	Arctic Ocean

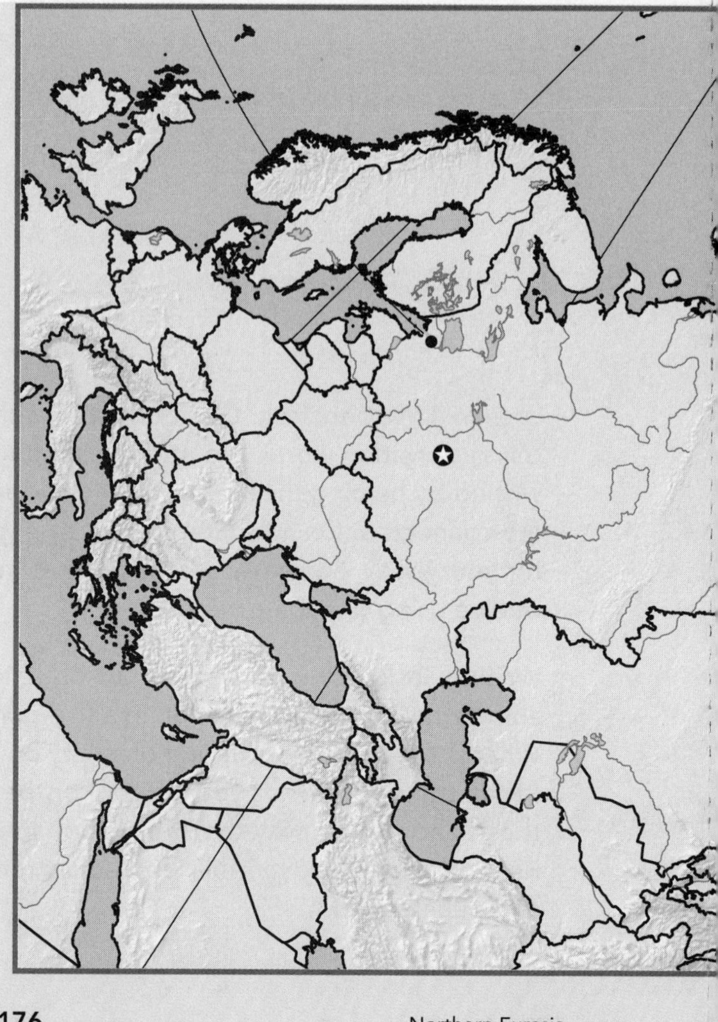

2. Preview the topic by skimming lesson titles, headings, and graphics. Then place a check mark next to the types of governments in Northern Eurasia that you predict will be discussed in the text. After you finish reading the topic, circle the predictions that were correct.

__parliamentary democracy

__dictatorship

__feudalism (serfdom)

__economic oligarchy

__communist regime

__theocracy

__direct democracy

__monarchy

__presidential democracy

__authoritarian regime

N
W
E
S

0 800 mi
0 800 km
Conic Projection

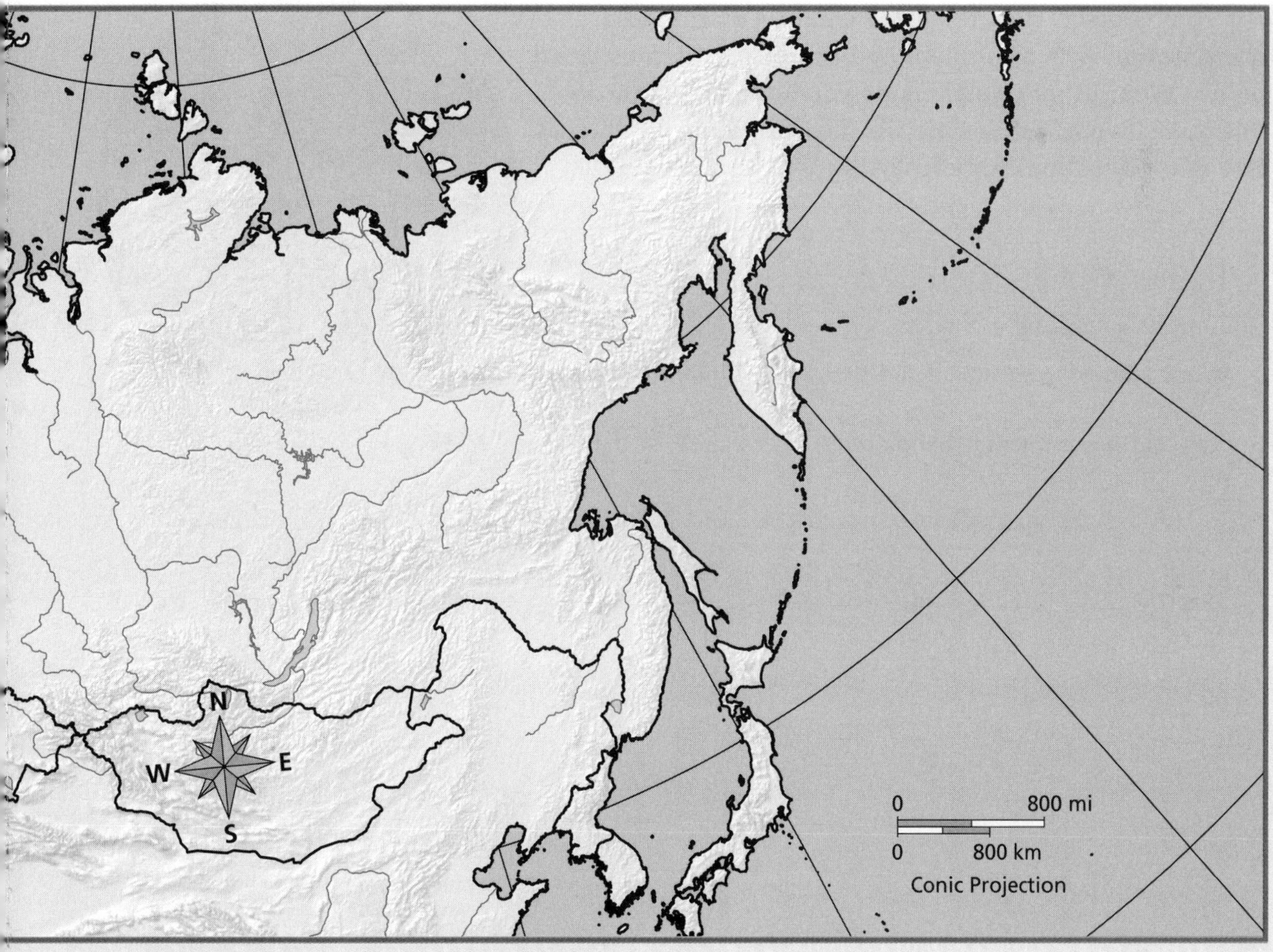

Project-Based Learning Inquiry

Evaluating the Soviet Legacy

On this Quest, you will work with a team to put together a multimedia presentation explaining how Soviet economic decisions affected the region's natural environments and what challenges the Soviet system created for the region's economies. You will gather information about contemporary regional issues by examining sources in your text and by conducting your own research. At the end of the Quest, you will create a multimedia presentation to educate others.

1 Ask Questions

As you begin your Quest, keep in mind the Guiding Question: **How has the Soviet Union left a mark on the economies and environments of Northern Eurasia?** and the Essential Question: **What role should people have in their government?**

For your project, each team will create a multimedia presentation with a segment on each of the themes listed below. What other questions do you need to ask to do this task? Two questions are filled in for you. Add at least two more questions for each category.

Theme Government Systems

Sample questions:

What kind of government did the Soviet Union have?

How did governments change after the collapse of the Soviet Union?

Theme Agriculture and Industry

Theme Trade

Theme Environment and Health

Theme My Additional Questions

INTERACTIVE

For extra help with Step 1, review the 21st Century Skills Tutorial: **Ask Questions**.

2 Investigate

As you read about Northern Eurasia, collect five connections from your text to help you answer the Guiding Question. Three connections are already chosen for you.

Connect to Command Economy

Lesson 2 Transition from Communism

Here's a connection! Examine the structure of the Soviet economy. What were the characteristics of the Soviet command economy?

How did those characteristics affect attempts to transition to a market economy after the breakup of the Soviet Union?

Connect to Market Economy

Lesson 4 Russia's Economy

Here's another connection! Take a closer look at the Russian economy today. What are some strengths?

How do you think it shows lingering effects of the Soviet system?

Connect to Challenges in the Region

Lesson 5 Political Challenges

What does this connection tell you about the challenges the Soviet Union left behind in Northern Eurasia?

How do these challenges affect the economies and the environment of the countries in the region?

It's Your Turn! **Find two more connections. Fill in the title of your connections, then answer the questions. Connections may be images, primary sources, maps, or text.**

Your Choice | Connect to

Location in text

What is the main idea of this connection?

What does it tell you about how the Soviet Union affected the environments and economies of the region?

Your Choice | Connect to

Location in text

What is the main idea of this connection?

What does it tell you about how the Soviet Union affected the environments and economies of the region?

3 Conduct Research

Form teams based on your teacher's instructions. Meet to decide who will create each segment of your presentation. Use the ideas in the connections to further explore the subject you have been assigned. Pick what you will report about, and find more sources about that subject.

Turn to the Country Databank at the end of your student text for data on the countries in the region. Look to sources like the CIA World Factbook or the World Bank's Databank for more current information and statistics. Take good notes so you can properly cite your sources. Brainstorm ways to express your findings by using various kinds of media.

Segment	Source	Notes
Government Systems		
Agriculture and Industry		
Trade		
Environment and Health		

INTERACTIVE

For extra help, review the 21st Century Skills Tutorials: **Analyze Media Content** and **Create Charts and Maps**.

4 Create Your Multimedia Presentation

Now it's time to put together all of the information you have gathered and create your multimedia presentation.

1. **Prepare to Write** Draw conclusions from the research you've collected and determine the main idea of your segment. Select one or two multimedia pieces that you will use to present your main idea. Below, write down your main idea and then record what two pieces you will use to support it, with a sentence explaining how each supports your main idea.

2. **Write a Draft** Write a short paragraph explaining your idea, then captions for each piece of media, summarizing the story that it tells. Clarify how it illustrates your theme in relation to the Guiding Question and the Essential Question. Include key facts, and cite sources.

3. **Plan and Revise with Your Team** Share your draft with your team. Discuss how you will combine your segments and the story they tell as a whole. Consider if anything needs to change to make the group presentation cohesive and concise. Plan how you will organize everyone's work. Remember, comparing and contrasting can help present opposing views in a cohesive way. Break down into pairs to examine each other's work in detail and to make changes discussed by the team.

4. **Share with Your Class** Follow teacher instructions for sharing your multimedia presentation. Include material from each team member. Present your project according to your team's organizational plan. Experience other presentations and note at least one impact each one had on you.

Notes on other presentations:

5. **Reflect** Think about your experience completing this topic's Quest. What did you learn about the effect of the Soviet Union on the environments and economies of the region? What questions do you still have? How will you answer them?

Reflections

INTERACTIVE

For extra help, review the 21st Century Skills Tutorials: **Give an Effective Presentation** and **Work in Teams**.

Take Notes

Literacy Skills: Summarize Use what you have read to complete the table. List important events or facts that describe how Russia formed, grew, and declined. The first detail has been completed for you. Then write a few sentences summarizing Russia's cultural history before World War I.

How Did Russia Form?	How Did Russia Grow?	How Did Russia Decline?
• Drawn by trade, Vikings settled in what would later become Ukraine, adopted Slavic practices, and eventually ruled the region as the Kievan Rus.		

Summary

INTERACTIVE

For extra help, review the 21st Century Skills Tutorial: **Summarize**.

Practice Vocabulary

Use a Word Bank **Choose one term from the word bank to fill in each blank. When you have finished, you will have a short summary of important ideas from the section.**

Word Bank

serfs	clans	inflation
tsar	Silk Road	westernize

Early in Russia's history, the settlers formed ______________, or family groups that lived and traded along the Black Sea. As people moved around and traded more, the ______________, a trade network linking China to the Mediterranean Sea, emerged.

Russian nobles gained great wealth through the labor of ______________, who worked the land but had no rights. Peter the Great became the first great ______________, or ruler, from the Romanov dynasty. He tried to ______________ Russia and bring new technology and culture in from western Europe. By the 1800s, Russia still depended on agriculture. The tsar emancipated, or freed, the serfs, hoping that would help Russia become more modern. A lot of people remained very poor, however. Russia's entry into World War I led to food shortages and ______________, and people could not afford what little food was available.

Take Notes

Literacy Skills: Sequence Use what you have read to complete the timeline. Using specific dates, list the important events of the rise and fall of communism in Russia. Then attach the boxes to the correct place on the timeline.

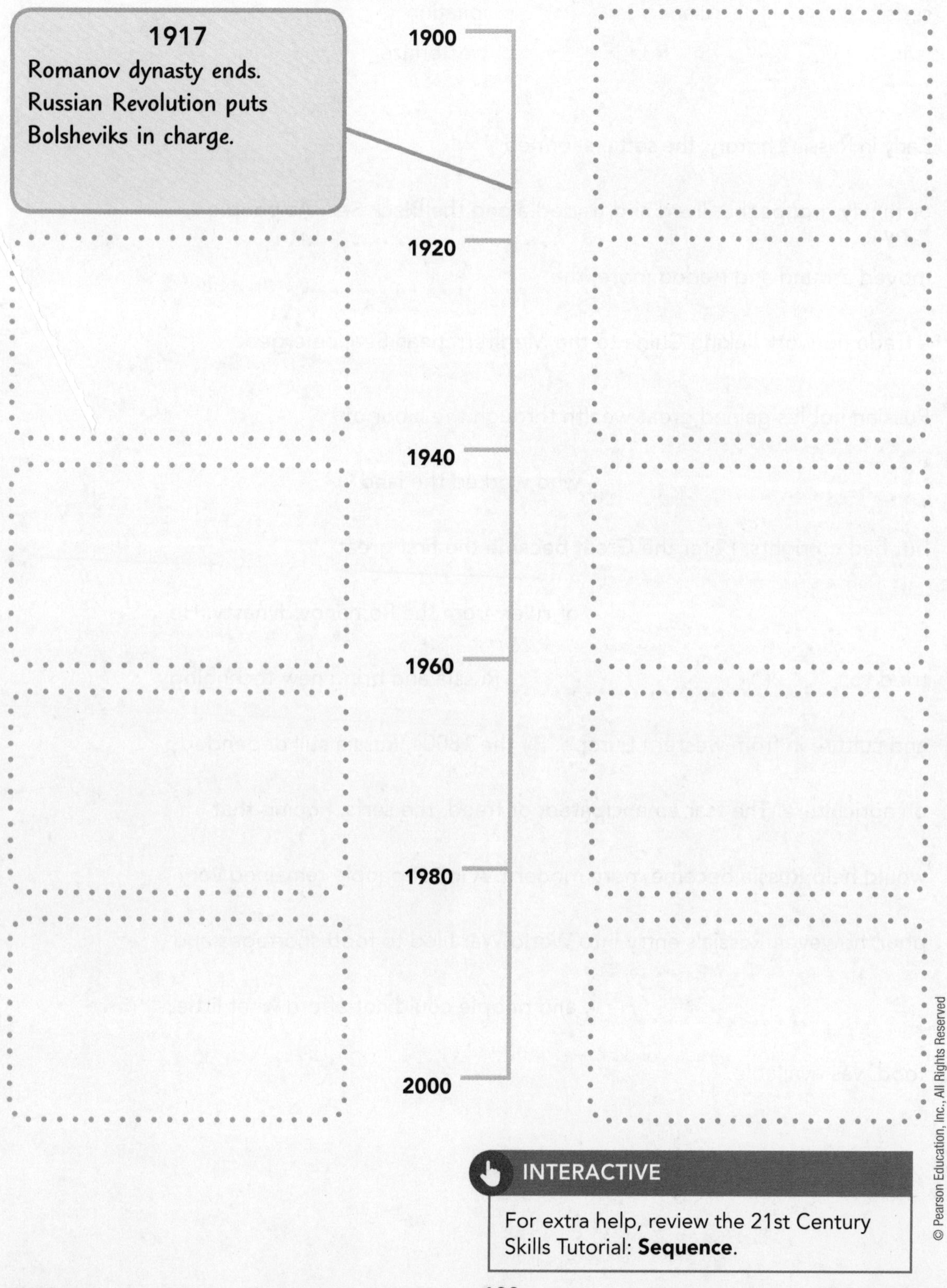

INTERACTIVE

For extra help, review the 21st Century Skills Tutorial: **Sequence**.

Practice Vocabulary

Sentence Revision **Revise each sentence so that the underlined vocabulary term is used logically. Be sure not to change the vocabulary term. The first one is done for you.**

1. The sanctions placed on Russia were intended to permit it to do whatever it wanted to Crimea.
   The sanctions placed on Russia were intended to get Russia to follow international law.

2. The development of communism meant that property was owned by individuals.

3. When the Soviet Union fell, an economic oligarchy was formed by the workers.

4. The Bolsheviks called for the tsars to control Russia.

5. The Cold War began because the Soviet Union and the United States disagreed about how to fight World War II.

6. Collectivization transferred ownership of farms to individuals.

Quick Activity Debate!

Hold a debate with a partner in which one of you supports the ideals of communism and the other supports the policies of glasnost and perestroika. Use the table to help you prepare for your debate. Be sure to come up with arguments and counterarguments.

I support:	
Arguments:	
Counterarguments:	
Summarizing Argument:	

Team Challenge! Create a T-chart with your whole class. Each student supporting communism writes a reason on one side of the chart, and each student supporting the policies of perestroika and glasnost writes a reason on the other side of the chart. Discuss the reasons that might make both arguments valid. Have you changed your opinion?

Take Notes

Literacy Skills: Draw Conclusions Use what you have read to complete the charts. For each factual statement, write three conclusions that explain the significance of the fact. The first one has been completed for you.

More people live in cities than in Siberia, where there are more natural resources.

Living in Siberia is difficult because of the cold climate, and people generally prefer to live in places with a milder climate.

In the Caucasus, there are many ethnic groups that sometimes clash.

INTERACTIVE

For extra help, review the 21st Century Skills Tutorial: **Draw Conclusions**.

Practice Vocabulary

Word Map Study the word map for the word *permafrost*. Characteristics are words or phrases that relate to the word in the center of the word map. Non-characteristics are words and phrases not associated with the word. Use the blank word map to explore the meaning of the word *taiga*. Then make a word map of your own for the word *tundra*.

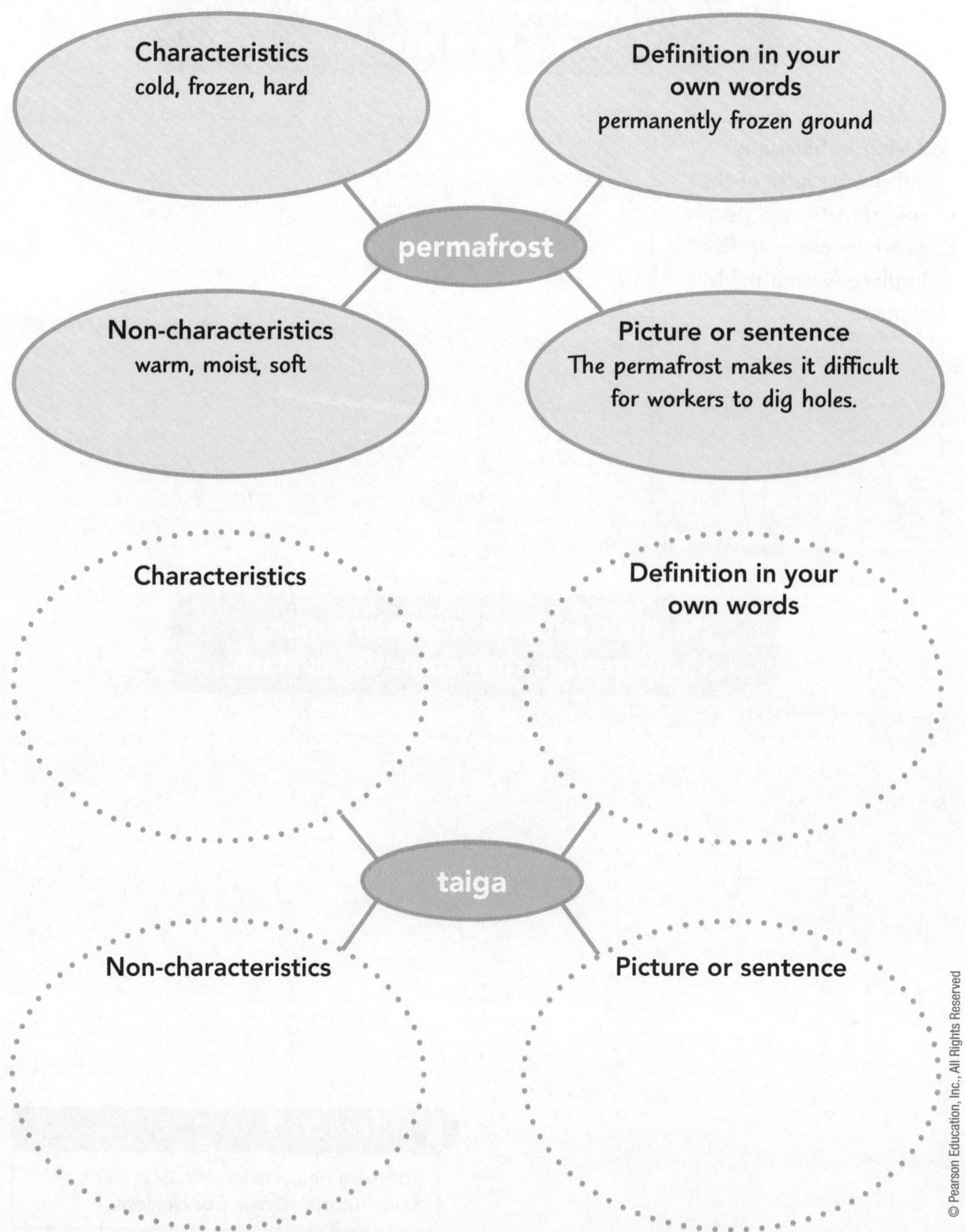

Take Notes

Literacy Skills: Use Evidence Use what you have read to complete the table. For each statement, provide three pieces of evidence from the text that explain why it is true. The first piece of evidence has been provided for you.

Statement	Evidence
Russia has an authoritarian government.	• Elections are not free and fair.
The effects of the Soviet Union continue to affect Russia's economy.	
Natural resources are critical parts of the economy for many former Soviet republics.	

INTERACTIVE

For extra help, review the 21st Century Skills Tutorial: **Identify Evidence**.

Practice Vocabulary

True or False? Decide whether each statement below is true or false. Circle T or F, and then explain your answer. Be sure to include the underlined vocabulary term in your explanation. The first one is done for you.

1. **T / F** Industrial goods are products or materials needed to make other products.
   True; An example of industrial goods is machinery made to produce paper.

2. **T / F** Having an authoritarian government means that the people govern themselves.

3. **T / F** Russia lacks reserves of gas, copper, and iron.

Quick Activity Categorize Governments

Since the fall of the Soviet Union, a few different types of government have emerged in the countries of Northern Eurasia. With a partner, use the table to categorize governments in Northern Eurasia. First identify the different forms of government. Then use the information in your text to list the countries that utilize each form of government.

Type of Government	Countries

Team Challenge! On a separate piece of paper, write what type of government you classified Russia as having and two reasons for doing so. Hang it up in your classroom. Did any teams classify it differently? Discuss the reasons there may be differences.

Take Notes

Literacy Skills: Identify Cause and Effect Use what you have read to complete the chart. For each cause provided for you, write an effect that might occur because of it. For each effect provided, write a major cause. The first one has been completed for you.

Cause		Effect
The Green Revolution involved heavy use of toxic fertilizers and pesticides that caused high levels of pollution across Russia.	→	Pesticides and fertilizers have killed fish and caused nearby communities to have high rates of cancer.
	→	The Aral Sea became too salty, the fish died, and the lake evaporated.
	→	Norilsk, a mining town, is one of the most polluted cities on the planet.
People who had been part of the Soviet government became leaders in new countries.	→	
Conflicts between ethnic groups persist across Central Asia.	→	
Corruption is a serious problem in many countries across Central Asia.	→	

INTERACTIVE

For extra help, review the 21st Century Skills Tutorial: **Analyze Cause and Effect**.

Practice Vocabulary

Sentence Builder **Finish the sentences below with a key term from this section. You may have to change the form of the words to complete the sentences.**

Word Bank

Green Revolution   militant   Aral Sea

1. A person who is aggressively active in a cause is called a

2. The term for the big increase in agriculture in the Soviet Union and other countries during the 1950s and 1960s is the

3. A body of water that has been destroyed by the effects of environmental damage is the

Writing Workshop Argument

As you read, build a response to this question: What role should citizens play in their government? The prompts below will help walk you through the process of turning your ideas into an essay presenting an argument.

Lesson 1 Writing Task: Introduce Claims Think about how Russia's history was affected by its citizens' role, or lack of a role, in government. Then, write a broad statement about what you think the role of citizens in government should be. You will develop this claim into a thesis statement for the argument you will write at the end of the topic.

Lessons 2 and 3 Writing Task: Support Claims Add support for the claim in your thesis from all of the lessons in this topic to the table below. For instance, how does the Soviet Union and its breakup, discussed in Lesson 2, support an argument for a strong or limited role for citizens in government? Does the cultural diversity of Northern Eurasia, discussed in Lesson 3, support a strong role for citizens? Adjust your thesis if the evidence you find pulls you in another direction.

Support from Lessons 1 and 2	
Support from Lesson 3	
Support from Lessons 4 and 5	

Lessons 4 and 5 Writing Task: Write an Introduction and Organize Your Essay Write an introductory paragraph in the first row of the table below that introduces your thesis and lays out what points you will make to support your argument. Then make a brief outline of your essay, including the order of your supporting points and addressing opposing claims. End with your strongest point.

Introduction	
Outline	

Writing Task: Using your introduction and outline above, write an argument that describes the role you believe citizens should have in their government. Support your claims with evidence from the text. Be sure to address opposing claims, and use transitional words or phrases to clarify the relationships between your ideas.

TOPIC 8

Africa Preview

Essential Question Who should benefit from a country's resources?

Before you begin this topic, think about the Essential Question by completing the following activities.

1. Think about the country where you live. What are some of your country's resources? Make a list of those resources. Circle the ones that you benefit from.

2. Preview the topic by skimming lesson titles, headings, and graphics. Then place a check mark next to the items that you predict the text will say have affected how people use resources in Africa. After you finish reading the topic, circle the predictions that were correct.

__varied environments	__trading empires	__Arab Spring
__religion	__city-states	__colonization
__ancient civilizations	__apartheid	__literacy rates
__infrastructure	__government	__Pan-Africanism

Map Skills

Using the political, physical, and climate maps from the Regional Atlas in your text, label the outline map with the places listed. Then color in climate regions and water. Make a key to define your coloring.

Cairo, Egypt	Monrovia, Liberia	Addis Ababa, Ethiopia
Cape Town, South Africa	Nairobi, Kenya	Lagos, Nigeria
Atlantic Ocean	Mediterranean Sea	Sahara
Red Sea	Lake Victoria	Nile River

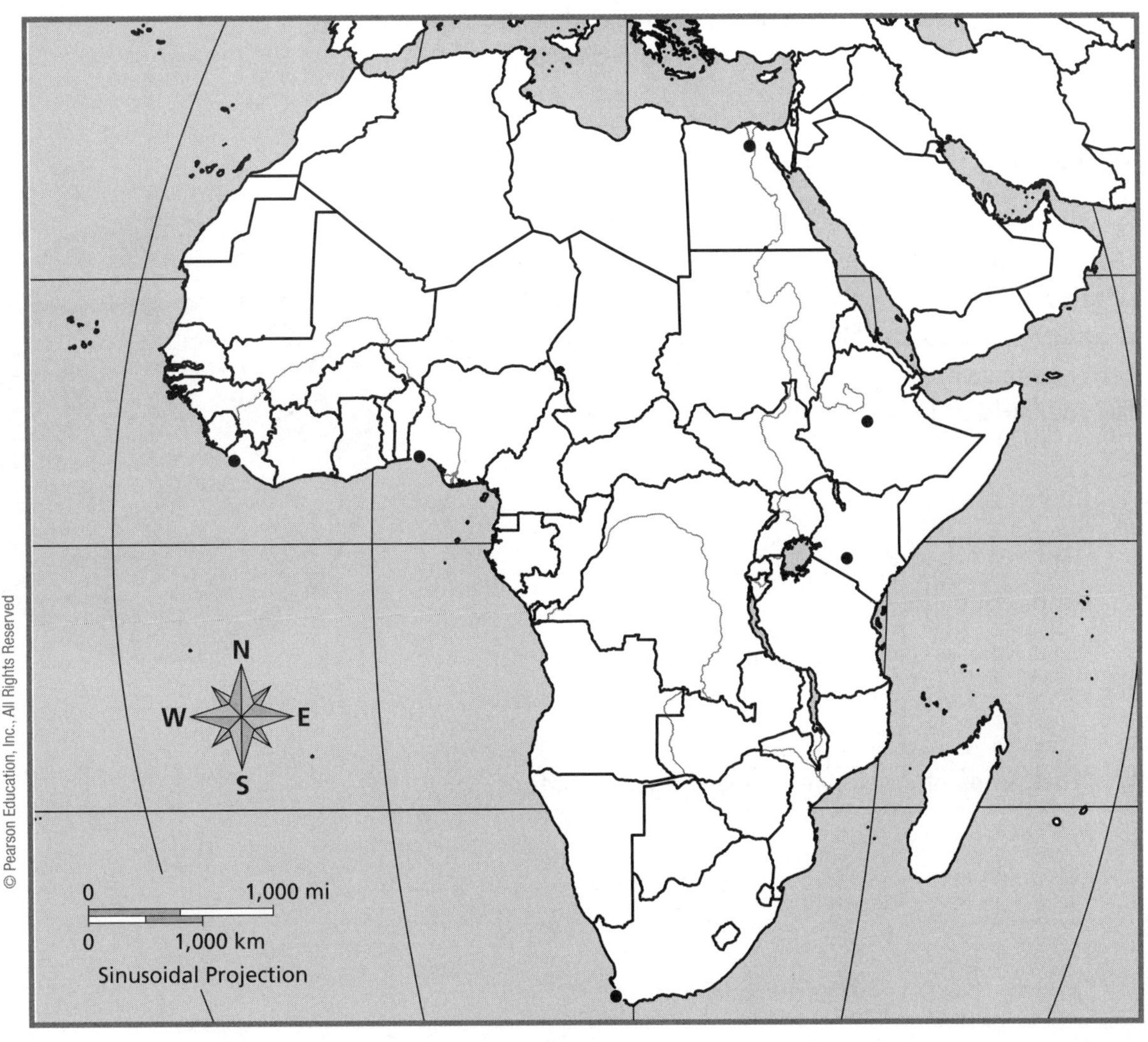

Discuss Nigeria's Oil Industry

On this Quest, you will investigate whether the oil industry in Nigeria benefits the country as a whole. You will assume the role of director of a nongovernmental organization (NGO). An NGO is a nonprofit organization, often a charity, that is independent from government. You will discuss the issue with other NGO directors.

1 Ask Questions

As you begin your Quest, keep in mind the Guiding Question: **Does the oil industry in Nigeria benefit the country as a whole?** and the Essential Question: **Who should benefit from a country's resources?** List questions that you need to ask in order to answer these questions. Two questions are filled in for you. Add at least two questions for each theme.

Theme Development

Sample questions:

What does development mean for a country?

What kinds of development does Nigeria need?

Theme Natural Resources

Theme Environment

Theme Economic Growth

Theme Wealth and Poverty

Theme My Additional Questions

 INTERACTIVE

For extra help with Step 1, review the 21st Century Skills Tutorial: **Ask Questions**.

2 Investigate

As you read about economic development in Africa, collect five connections from your text to help you answer the Guiding Question. Three connections are already chosen for you.

Connect to African Trading History

Lesson 3 East African City-States

Here's a connection! Who had control over natural resources and trade in premodern African empires and city-states?

Who do you think benefited from this control?

Connect to Imperialism

Lesson 4 European Rule

Here's another connection! Why were foreign companies the first to search for oil in Africa?

Who do you think benefited from their activities?

Connect to Political Challenges

Lesson 6 Comparing Three Economies

What does this connection tell you about how resource wealth affects politics and government in Africa?

What factors have kept Africans from benefiting from these resources?

It's Your Turn! **Find two more connections. Fill in the titles of your connections, then answer the questions. Connections may be images, primary sources, maps, or text.**

Your Choice | Connect to

Location in text

What is the main idea of this connection?

What does it tell about whether Nigeria's oil industry benefits the entire country?

Your Choice | Connect to

Location in text

What is the main idea of this connection?

What does it tell about whether Nigeria's oil industry benefits the entire country?

3 Examine Primary Sources

Examine the primary and secondary sources provided online or from your teacher. Fill in the chart to show how these sources provide further information about Nigeria's oil industry. The first one has been done for you.

Does the oil industry in Nigeria benefit the country as a whole?	
Source	**Yes or No? Why?**
Africa's Richest Man, Aliko Dangote, Is Just Getting Started	YES, *because it can help Nigeria become self-sufficient and attract foreign investment.*
The $20 Billion Hole in Africa's Largest Economy	
Top Ten Toxic Threats 2013: Niger River Delta, Nigeria	

INTERACTIVE

For extra help with Step 3, review the 21st Century Skills Tutorial: **Compare Viewpoints**.

4 Discuss!

Now that you have explored sources about the oil industry in Nigeria, you are ready to discuss with your fellow NGO directors the Guiding Question: Does the oil industry in Nigeria benefit the country as a whole? Follow the steps below, using the spaces provided to prepare for your discussion.

You will work with a partner in a small group of directors. Try to reach consensus, a situation in which everyone is in agreement, on the question. Can you do it?

1. **Prepare Your Arguments** You will be assigned a position on the question, either YES or NO.

   My position: ______________________

   Work with your partner to review your Quest notes from the Quest Connections and Quest Sources.

   - If you were assigned YES, agree with your partner on what you think were the strongest reasons from Okeowo.
   - If you were assigned NO, agree on what you think were the strongest reasons from *The Economist* and the Blacksmith Institute.

2. **Present Your Position** Those assigned YES will present their reasons and evidence first. As you listen, ask clarifying questions to gain information and understanding.

What is a clarifying question?	
These types of questions do not judge the person talking. They are only for the listener to be clear on what he or she is hearing.	
Example: **Can you tell me more about that?**	**Example:** **You said [x]. Am I getting that right?**

INTERACTIVE

For extra help with Step 4, review the 21st Century Skills Tutorial: **Participate in a Discussion or Debate.**

While the opposing side speaks, take notes on what you hear in the space below.

3. **Switch!** Now NO and YES will switch sides. If you argued YES before, now you will argue NO. Work with your same partner and use your notes. Add any claims, reasons, and evidence from the clues and sources. Those *now* arguing YES go first.

   When both sides have finished, answer the following:

Before **I started this discussion with other NGO directors, my opinion was that the oil industry in Nigeria**	***After*** **my discussion with other NGO directors, my opinion is that the oil industry in Nigeria**
__ benefits the country as whole. __ does not benefit the country as a whole.	__ benefits the country as whole. __ does not benefit the country as a whole.

4. **Point of View** Do you all agree on the answer to the Guiding Question?

   - __Yes
   - __No

   If not, on what points do you all agree?

Take Notes

Literacy Skills: Identify Main Ideas Use what you have read to complete the table. In each column write one main idea and at least two supporting details. The first one has been completed for you.

The study of early humans	African beginnings	How early hunter-gatherers lived
Main idea: Archaeologists study fossils and artifacts to learn about early humans.	**Main idea:**	**Main idea:**
Details: Remains like teeth and bones tell archaeologists what early humans ate and looked like. Artifacts like tools, pottery, and weapons tell how early humans lived.	**Details:**	**Details:**

Migration from Africa	Adapting to varied environments
Main idea:	**Main idea:**
Details:	**Details:**

INTERACTIVE

For extra help, review the 21st Century Skills Tutorial: **Identify Main Ideas and Details.**

Practice Vocabulary

Vocabulary Quiz Show Some quiz shows ask a question and expect the contestant to give the answer. In other shows, the contestant is given an answer and must supply the question. If the blank is in the Question column, write the question that would result in the answer in the Answer column. If the question is supplied, write the answer.

Question	Answer
1. What is a word used to describe the tools and skills that early humans developed to meet their needs and wants?	1.
2.	2. fossils
3.	3. pastoralism
4. What are ancient, human-made objects studied by archaeologists?	4.
5.	5. hunter-gatherers

Take Notes

Literacy Skills: Summarize Use what you have read to complete the chart. For each topic provided write at least two details. The first one has been started for you. Then write a brief summary of the lasting impact of Ancient Egypt and Kush.

Ancient Egypt	Kush
Government and society • Government was a bureaucracy run by the vizier, who reported to the pharaoh. • Society led by the pharaoh with an upper class, a middle class and a lower class.	**Interactions with Egypt**
Religion and pyramids	**Accomplishments of independent Kush**
Writing, science, and technology	**Trade**

Summary

INTERACTIVE

For extra help, review the 21st Century Skills Tutorial: **Summarize**.

Practice Vocabulary

Sentence Revision **Revise each sentence so that the underlined vocabulary word is used logically. Be sure not to change the vocabulary word. The first one is done for you.**

1. An official called a pharaoh worked for the Egyptian bureaucracy.
   The Egyptian bureaucracy was a system of officials who served the pharaoh.

2. Egyptians made mummies to commemorate the lives of the dead.

3. Egyptians developed a system of writing using hieroglyphics, drawings or symbols that represented the letters of the alphabet.

4. When Egypt conquered Kush, Kush received tribute from Egypt.

5. Narmer became the first pharaoh when he took over the Egyptian bureaucracy.

6. Scribes carved important documents into papyrus, a type of stone.

7. In ancient Egypt, the position of vizier was the head of the ruling dynasty.

Take Notes

Literacy Skills: Compare and Contrast Use what you have read to complete the chart. In each space write details about civilizations that developed in the region of Africa. The first detail has been completed for you.

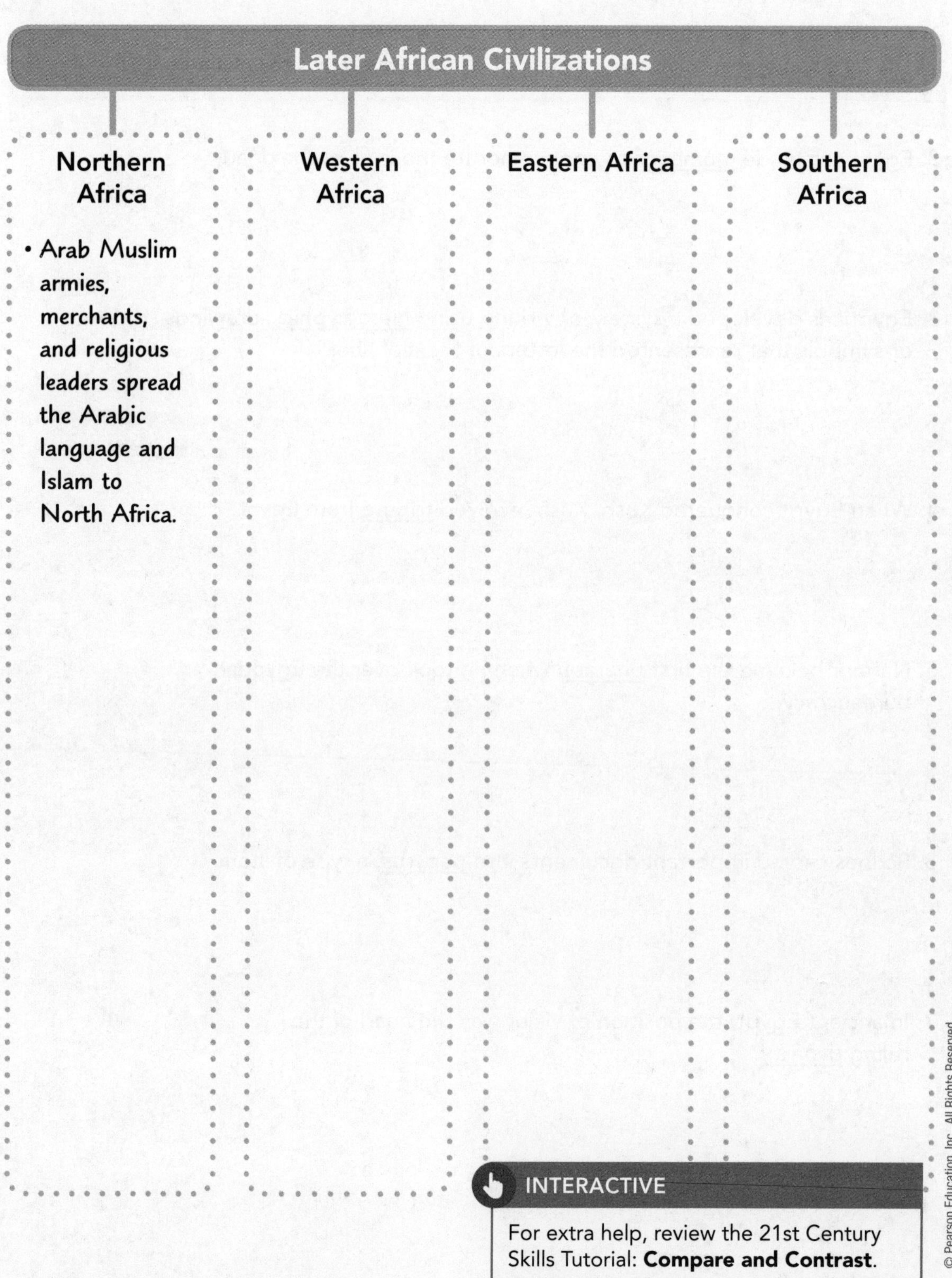

INTERACTIVE

For extra help, review the 21st Century Skills Tutorial: **Compare and Contrast**.

Practice Vocabulary

Words in Context **For each question below, write an answer that shows your understanding of the boldfaced key term.**

1. What role did **stonetowns** play in East African trade?

2. What were **steles**, and why were they built?

3. How did **monks** contribute to the rise of Christianity in Ethiopia?

Quick Activity African Trading Strategies

Suppose that you and a partner are African merchants in the year 1000. Together, discuss and list below what you would like to sell and buy in each region listed below, based on what you have learned about each of them in your text. You may not have enough information for one or two of the regions.

Kingdom or region	Main imports: things to sell there	Main exports: things to buy there
Muslim North Africa		
Kingdom of Ghana		
Christian Ethiopia		
Swahili city-States		
Southern Africa		

Team Challenge! Choose one of the regions in your list to represent with your partner. Find another pair of merchant students in your class representing a different region. With the other pair, discuss what you can sell them from your region, and what you can buy from their region.

Take Notes

Literacy Skills: Identify Cause and Effect Use what you have read to complete the charts. In each space write details about the effects of the causes provided. The first one has been completed for you.

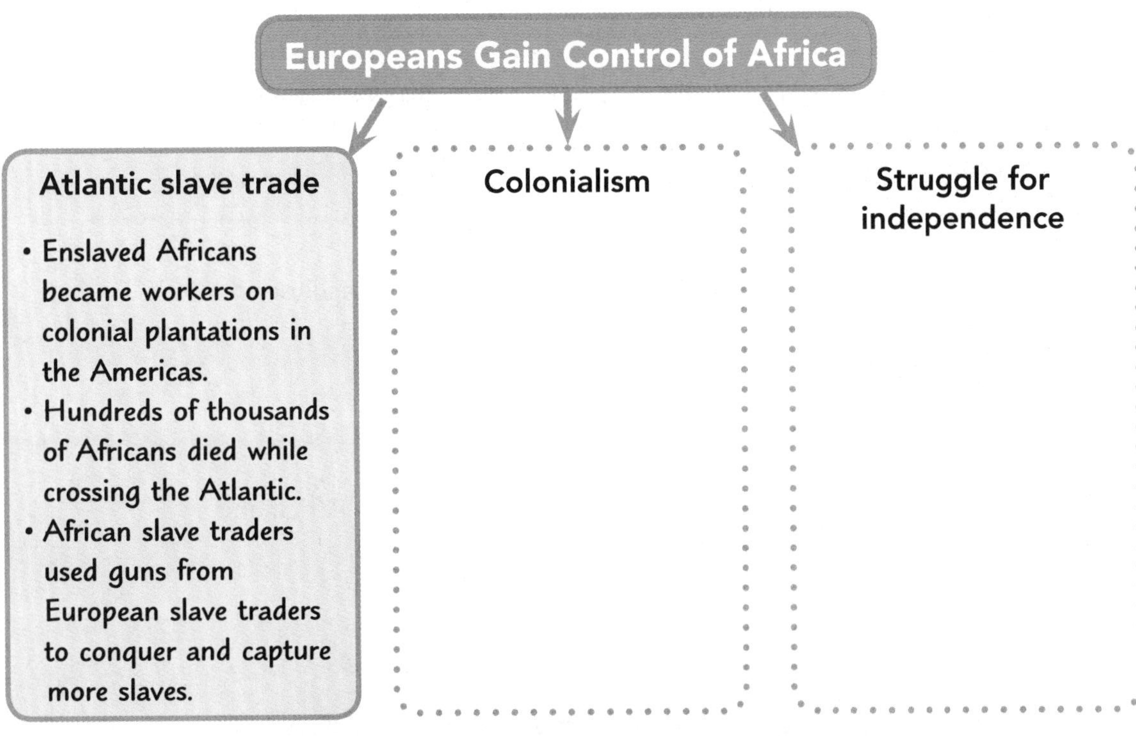

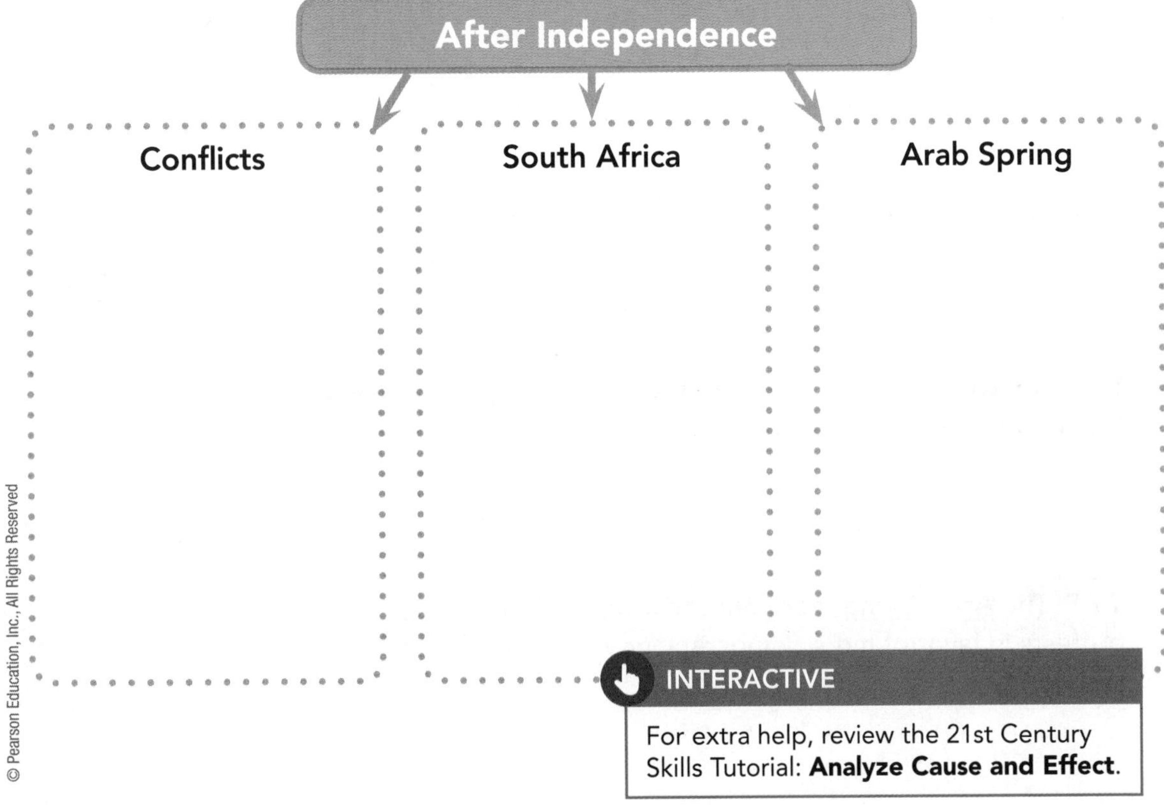

INTERACTIVE

For extra help, review the 21st Century Skills Tutorial: **Analyze Cause and Effect.**

Practice Vocabulary

True or False? Decide whether each statement below is true or false. Circle T or F, and then explain your answer. Be sure to include the underlined vocabulary term in your explanation. The first one is done for you.

1. **T / F** Colonialism is a policy by which one country seeks to trade with other areas.
   False; Colonialism is a policy by which one country seeks to rule other areas.

2. **T / F** Conflict between the Hutu and the Tutsi in Rwanda resulted in genocide.

3. **T / F** In 1994, Nelson Mandela became president of South Africa and enacted the government policy of apartheid.

4. **T / F** In the Atlantic slave trade, African traders brought enslaved Africans across the Atlantic and sold them to work on plantations in the Americas.

5. **T / F** Islamism is the main religion of North Africa.

6. **T / F** Kwame Nkrumah promoted the idea of Pan-Africanism, the belief that black Africans should unite.

7. **T / F** The Arab Spring movement that began in Tunisia sparked protests in favor of more democratic government in countries around the world.

Take Notes

Literacy Skills: Draw Conclusions Use what you have read to complete the table. Under each heading, write details from your text. Then, write a conclusion for each heading. The first one has been completed for you.

Supporting Details	Conclusion
Where Africans Live • Extremely dry and extremely wet areas are usually sparsely populated. • Cities have developed along rivers and coastlines where water routes make trade possible.	Climate and access to water affect where people live in Africa.
Environment and Culture	
Religion and Ethnicity	

INTERACTIVE

For extra help, review the 21st Century Skills Tutorial: **Draw Conclusions**.

Practice Vocabulary

Sentence Builder **Finish the sentences below with a key term from this section. You may have to change the form of the words to complete the sentences.**

Word Bank

Copts	indigenous
oasis	savanna

1. People or customs that have been present in a region since ancient times are

.

2. Park-like grasslands with scattered trees that can survive dry spells are known as

.

3. A place in the desert where water can be found is called a(n)

.

4. Members of an ancient Christian church who make up a religious minority in Egypt are

.

Take Notes

Literacy Skills: Use Evidence Use what you have read to complete the table. In each space write one or two details about each aspect of the country's economy. The first country has been completed for you. Then, use the evidence you have gathered to draw conclusions about how the different factors affect the economies and standards of living in these African countries.

Kenya	Nigeria	South Africa
Natural resources • rich soil for farming	Natural resources	Natural resources
Capital investment and entrepreneurship • capital investment $301/person in 2014 • more difficult to start a business than in South Africa	Capital investment and entrepreneurship	Capital investment and entrepreneurship
Literacy rate and GDP per capita • 78% literacy rate • GDP per capita $3,083 in 2015	Literacy rate and GDP per capita	Literacy rate and GDP per capita

Conclusions

INTERACTIVE

For extra help, review the 21st Century Skills Tutorial: **Identify Evidence**.

Practice Vocabulary

Matching Logic **Using your knowledge of the underlined vocabulary words, draw a line from each sentence in Column 1 to match it with the sentence in Column 2 to which it logically belongs.**

Column 1	Column 2
1. Some African countries are entering the outsourcing market by developing call centers.	When Pierre traveled from the Ivory Coast to Burkina Faso, he did not have to exchange currency.
2. One criticism of some African democracies is that widespread corruption prevents them from functioning properly.	The president of Equatorial Guinea has used his power and influence to enrich himself and control elections.
3. The CFA franc is linked to the euro and makes trade easier among the countries that use it.	Aisha lives in Kenya, but she is a customer service representative for a British company.

Take Notes

Literacy Skills: Analyze Text Structure Use what you have read to create an outline of the lesson. As you create your outline, pay attention to headings, subheadings, and key terms that you can use to organize the information. The first section of the outline has been completed for you.

I. Environmental Challenges
   A. Clean Water
      1. Lack of proper waste disposal contaminates water supplies and causes water-borne diseases like cholera.
      2. Lack of water for crop irrigation threatens Africa's food supply and agricultural exports.
   B.

INTERACTIVE

For extra help, review the 21st Century Skills Tutorial: **Take Effective Notes**.

Practice Vocabulary

Use a Word Bank **Choose one word from the word bank to fill in each blank. When you have finished, you will have a short summary of important ideas from the section.**

Word Bank

deforestation

desertification

nongovernmental organization (NGO)

Citizens of many African nations face environmental, political, and economic challenges that threaten stability and quality of life. One environmental challenge is __________, the change of fertile land to desert. Where livestock have overgrazed and people have cut down forests, land dries and becomes desert. Less usable land is left for farming and raising livestock, and the risk of famine increases. This process is sometimes due to __________, the loss of forest that occurs when so many trees are removed that they cannot grow back. Removing trees in large quantities puts land at risk for soil erosion, and rain often washes away soil nutrients. Cleared soil with poor nutrients results in smaller yields of lower quality crops.

As a result of these and other challenges, many Africans do not have regular access to adequate food. Foreign governments and privately operated __________ often provide aid to African nations to combat famines and other issues such as disease and poverty.

Quick Activity Identifying Africa's Challenges

In your reading, you have been introduced to some of the challenges facing Africa. Many of these challenges are widespread, affecting large areas and multiple countries. Working with a partner, list below at least four challenges facing Africa. For each challenge, list the main cause and at least one way that challenge is connected to other challenges facing Africa.

Team Challenge! **After the exercise is complete, discuss with your class how the challenges facing Africa are connected to one another. In the box below, write what you learned from the class discussion.**

Writing Workshop Explanatory Essay

As you read, build a response to this question: How have people benefited from Africa's resources? The prompts below will help walk you through the process.

Lesson 1 Writing Task: Gather Information Before you can begin crafting your essay, you must first gather information about the topic. In the space below, list ways early humans benefited from Africa's resources.

Lesson 2 Writing Task: Develop a Clear Thesis Based on what you have learned so far about resource use in Africa, write a thesis statement for your essay. Your thesis statement is a topic sentence that tells what your essay will prove, so it should briefly answer the question of who has benefited from Africa's resources. Write your thesis statement in the space below.

Lesson 3 Writing Task: Support Thesis With Details A well-written essay uses specific examples to provide support for the ideas it presents. As you read Lesson 3, look for examples of who benefited from Africa's resources. Record examples in the space below.

Lesson 4 Writing Task: Revise Your Thesis Consider what you have read about the role of resources in the colonization and independence of Africa. Use what you have learned to revise the thesis you wrote on the previous page.

Lessons 5 and 6 Writing Task: Pick an Organizing Strategy and Include Graphics Choosing an organizing strategy for your essay will help you communicate information in a way that clearly supports your thesis statement. For example, depending on your thesis, it may make sense to organize your essay chronologically or by topic. Use this table to organize your sections and the details you will include in each section. Create at least one table or graph to include in your essay on a separate sheet of paper.

Section	Details

Lesson 7 Writing Task: Write an Introduction In your opening, or introductory, paragraph, introduce the subject you are writing about and include your essay's thesis statement. Make your subject appealing to readers. Draft this paragraph on a separate piece of paper.

Writing Task Using your outline and the introduction you drafted, write a five-paragraph essay that answers the following question: Who has benefited from Africa's resources? Be sure to use some of the evidence you collected to support your claims. End your essay with a concluding paragraph that sums up your essay and points out the importance of the issues it raises.

TOPIC 9

Southwest Asia Through Time Preview

Essential Question How do values shape a culture?

Before you begin this topic, think about the Essential Question by completing the following activities.

1. Consider what you know about American culture and the values of the country. Write a list of ten values that have contributed to the culture of the United States of America. Circle the five values that you believe are especially important to our culture and rank them in order from most important (1) to fifth most important (5).

2. Preview the topic by skimming lesson titles, headings, and graphics. Then, below or on a separate sheet of paper, create a series of drawings that shows how the culture of Southwest Asia has changed over time.

Map Skills

Using the physical map in the Regional Atlas in your text, label the outline map with the places listed. Then color in water, mountains, and deserts.

- Black Sea
- Strait of Hormuz
- Elburz Mountains
- Mesopotamia
- Iranian Plateau
- Zagros Mountains
- Syrian Desert
- Arabian Peninsula
- Yemen Highlands
- Tigris River
- Euphrates River
- Persian Gulf
- Bosporus
- Anatolia
- Jordan River
- Rub' al-Khali

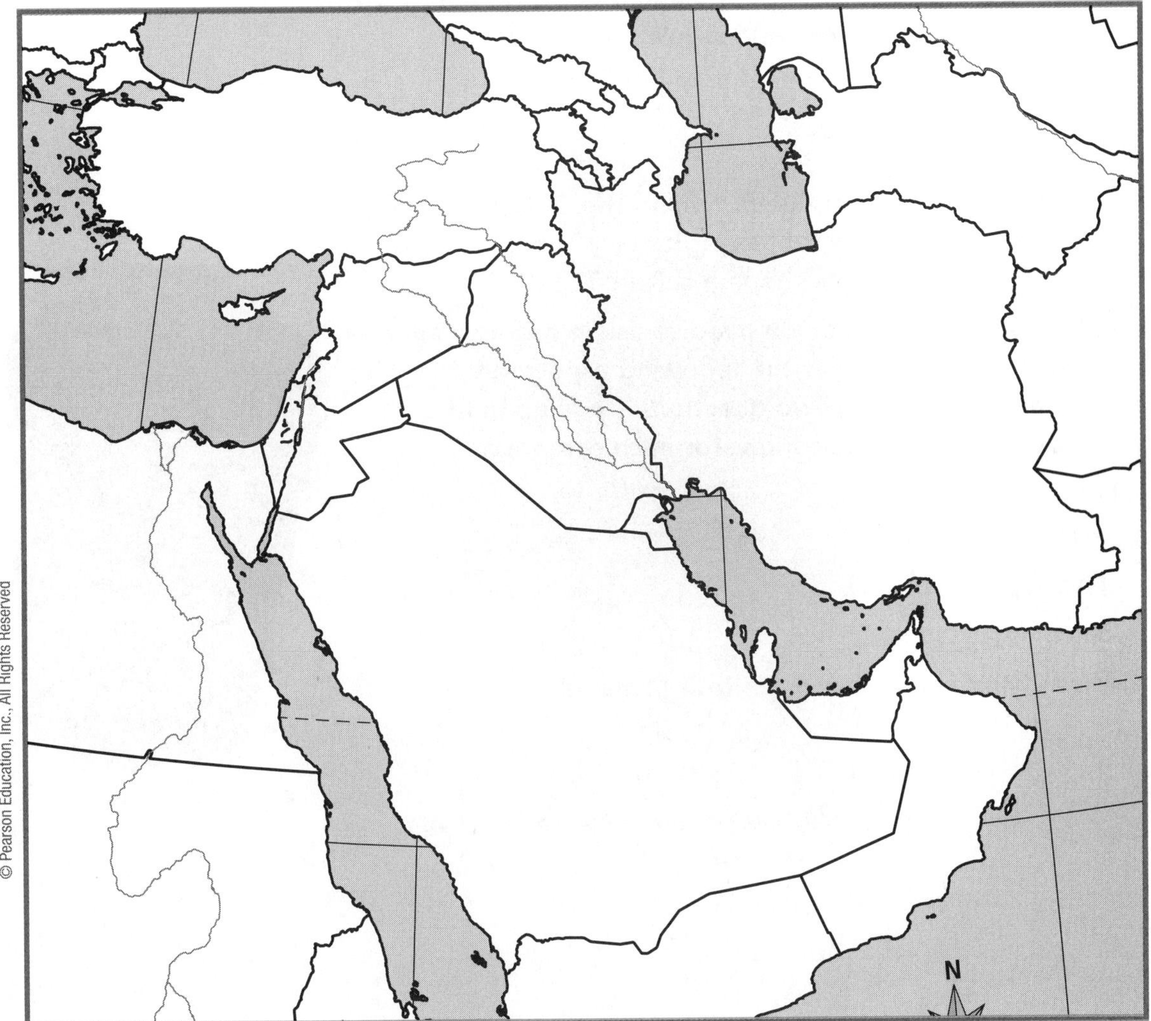

Establishing a Government

On this Quest, you need to determine how a government establishes legitimacy. You will examine sources related to different governments in Southwest Asia. At the end of the Quest you will write a report to a leader who is planning to form a new government for a country in Southwest Asia following a civil war.

1 Ask Questions

As you begin your Quest, keep in mind the Guiding Question: **How do governments establish legitimacy?** and the Essential Question: **How do values shape a culture?**

What other questions do you need to ask in order to answer these questions? Consider the following aspects of government legitimacy. Two questions are filled in for you. Add at least two questions for each category.

Theme Laws

Sample questions:

What types of laws contribute to legitimacy?

What types of laws could harm a government's legitimacy?

Theme Leadership

Theme Citizens' Rights

Theme Culture

Theme Popular Support

Theme My Additional Questions

 INTERACTIVE

For extra help with Step 1, review the 21st Century Skills Tutorial: **Ask Questions**.

2 Investigate

As you read about government legitimacy, collect five connections from your text to help you answer the Guiding Question. Three connections are already chosen for you.

Connect to the Establishment of Laws

Lesson 2 The Babylonian Empire

Here's a connection! How does Hammurabi's stated goal for his code of law establish his legitimacy as ruler?

Do you think he would have had less legitimacy if the code were written to protect the powerful?

Connect to Muslim Principles

Lesson 6 The Caliphs

Here's another connection! How did the caliphs establish their legitimacy?

How might later caliphs, who didn't have close ties to Muhammad, have established their legitimacy?

Connect to National Identity

Lesson 7 How Did Conflict Develop in Israel?

What does this connection tell you about why the founders of Israel declared independence?

After the Holocaust, why do you think Jews felt that an independent Israel would protect them?

It's Your Turn! **Find two more connections. Fill in the title of your connections, then answer the questions. Connections may be images, primary sources, maps, or text.**

Your Choice | Connect to

Location in text

What is the main idea of this connection?

What does it tell you about government legitimacy?

Your Choice | Connect to

Location in text

What is the main idea of this connection?

What does it tell you about government legitimacy?

3 Examine Primary Sources

Examine the primary and secondary sources provided online or from your teacher. Fill in the chart to show how these sources provide further information about government legitimacy. The first one has been completed for you.

Source	A key idea about government legitimacy is . . .
Hammurabi's Code	*protecting the oppressed*
Letter from Hussein bin Ali to Sir Henry McMahon	
Constitution of Turkey	
Israeli Declaration of Independence	
President Hassan Rouhani's Address to the United Nations	

INTERACTIVE

For extra help with Step 3, review the 21st Century Skills Tutorial: **Analyze Primary and Secondary Sources.**

4 Write Your Report

Now it's time to put together all of the information you have gathered and use it to write your report.

1. **Prepare to Write** You have collected connections and explored primary and secondary sources about government legitimacy. Look through your notes and decide which facts you want to highlight in your report. Record them here.

Facts

2. **Write a Draft** Using evidence from the textbook and the primary and secondary sources you explored in this Quest, draft your report about how a government establishes its legitimacy.

3. **Share with a Partner** Exchange your draft with a partner. Tell your partner what you like about his or her draft and suggest any improvements.

4. **Finalize Your Report** Revise your report. Correct any grammatical or spelling errors.

5. **Reflect on the Quest** Think about your experience completing this topic's Quest. What did you learn about government legitimacy? What questions do you still have about this topic? How will you answer them?

Reflections

INTERACTIVE

For extra help with Step 4, review the 21st Century Skills Tutorial: **Write an Essay**.

Take Notes

Literacy Skills: Identify Cause and Effect Use what you have read to complete the charts. In each box, enter a cause. The first one has been started for you.

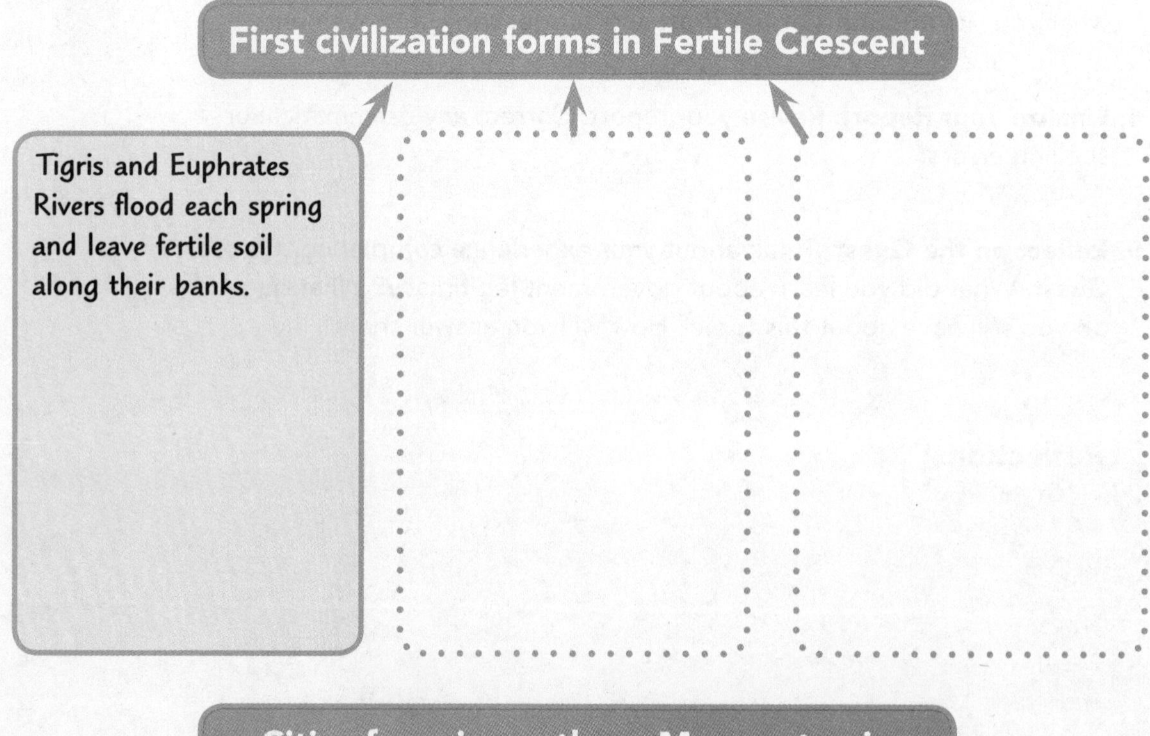

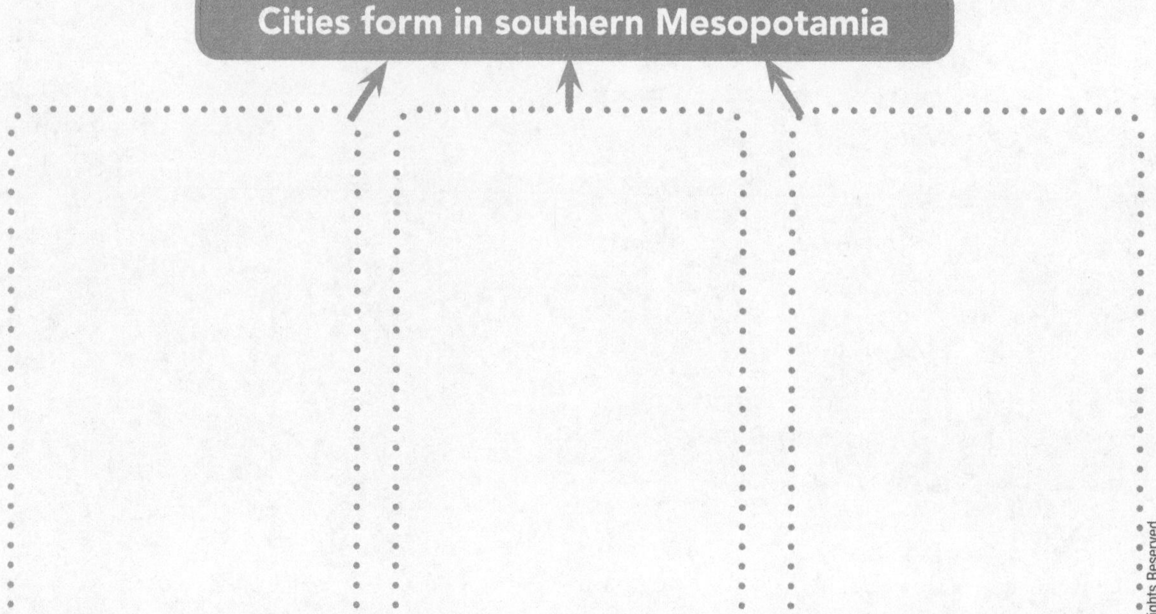

INTERACTIVE

For extra help, review the 21st Century Skills Tutorial: **Analyze Cause and Effect**.

Practice Vocabulary

Vocabulary Quiz Show **Some quiz shows ask a question and expect the contestant to give the answer. In other shows, the contestant is given an answer and must supply the question. If the blank is in the Question column, write the question that would result in the answer in the Answer column. If the question is supplied, write the answer.**

Question	**Answer**
1. What is the name given to the region between the Tigris and Euphrates Rivers?	1.
2. What is the term for an independent political unit that includes a city and its surrounding territory?	2.
3.	3. cuneiform
4.	4. irrigate
5.	5. Neolithic Revolution
6. What did early farmers do to change the growth of plants or behavior of animals so that they'd be useful for humans?	6.
7. What is the worship of many gods or deities?	7.

Quick Activity Draw a Social Pyramid

As Sumer grew, a social order developed, with each class having distinct roles in the society. Draw a pyramid to show how the different classes compared to one another.

Team Challenge! **After everyone in your class posts their drawings around the classroom, conduct a gallery walk. Then, engage in a discussion with your classmates about modern social orders. What categories of people are at the top of society today? In the middle? At the bottom? Is the order different if we rank by different attributes, such as wealth, power, and happiness?**

Take Notes

Literacy Skills: Compare and Contrast Use what you have read to complete the Venn diagram with similarities and differences. The first one has been started for you.

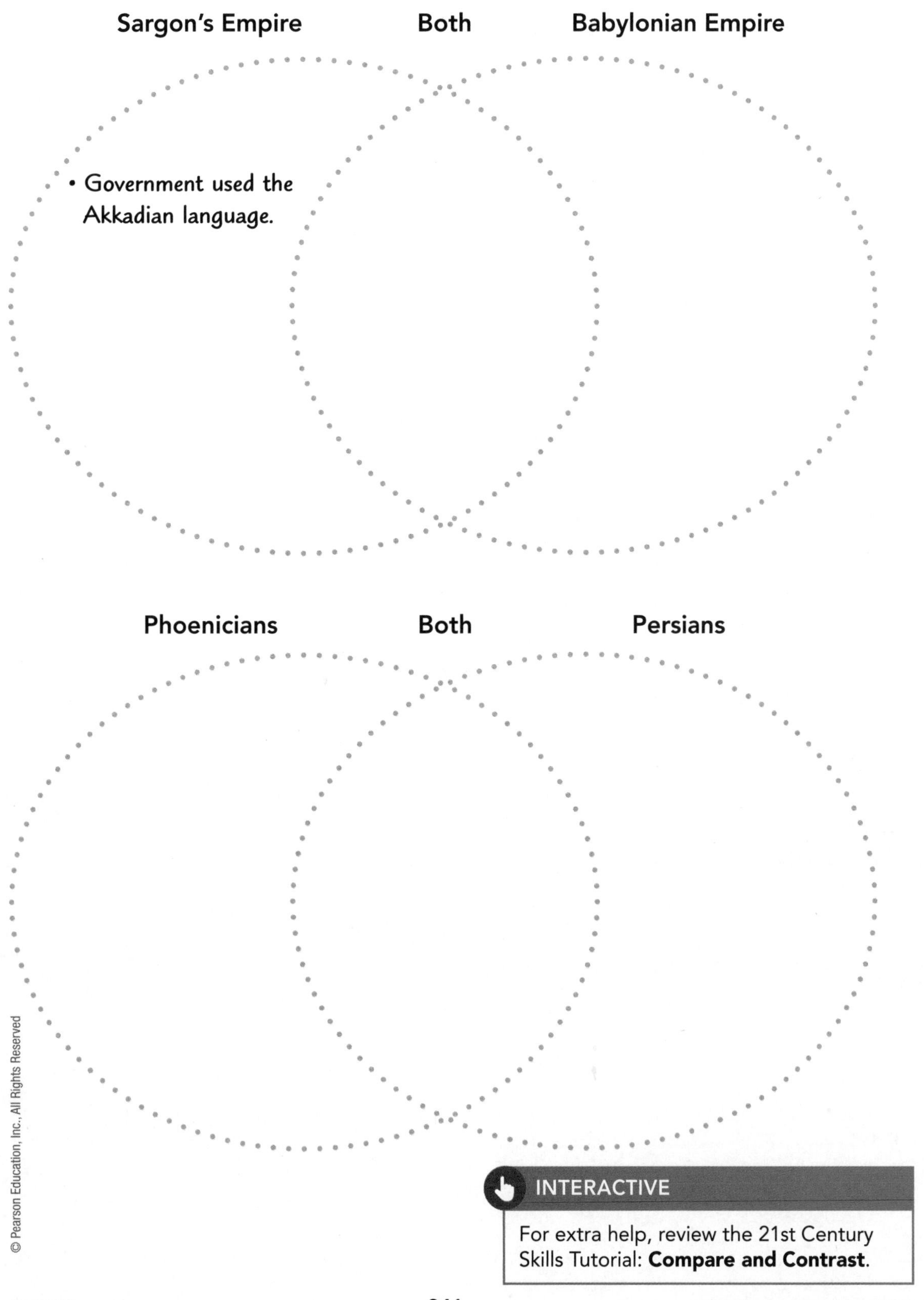

INTERACTIVE

For extra help, review the 21st Century Skills Tutorial: **Compare and Contrast**.

Practice Vocabulary

Words in Context **For each question below, write an answer that shows your understanding of the boldfaced key term.**

1. Who created the world's first **empires**?

2. What was the purpose of **Hammurabi's Code**?

3. What did the Phoenicians' skill in **navigation** help them do?

Take Notes

Literacy Skills: Summarize Use what you have read to complete the tables. In each space write three of the most important details from the section. The first one has been completed for you.

The Exodus	Important Details
Moses	• Moses asked the pharoah to free Israelites from slavery. Pharaoh said no. • According to the Hebrew Bible, God brought hardships to Egypt. • Pharaoh allowed Israelites to leave Egypt.
The Desert Experience	

The Importance of Law and Learning	Important Details
Laws, the Talmud, and Commentaries	
The Need to Study	

INTERACTIVE

For extra help, review the 21st Century Skills Tutorial: **Summarize**.

Practice Vocabulary

Use a Word Bank Choose one word from the word bank to fill in each blank. When you have finished, you will have a short summary of important ideas from the section.

Word Bank

covenant	Diaspora	rabbis	monotheism
Exodus	Torah	Talmud	ethics
Sabbath	commandments		

The ancient Israelites practiced __________ and believed that God wanted them to act according to __________. Most of what Jews believe about the origins of their religion comes from the __________, which says that God made a __________ with Abraham. The Israelites were enslaved by the Egyptian pharaoh, but he eventually allowed them to leave, in what is called the __________. According to Jewish belief, during the Israelites' journey from Egypt, God gave Moses laws that included a group of __________. Many years after Moses lived, Jewish __________ recorded and commented on the oral laws they believed came down from Moses in the __________. Jews observe the __________ as a weekly day of rest. In the __________, Jews were spread throughout the world.

Take Notes

Literacy Skills: Determine Central Ideas Use what you have read to complete the chart. In the top box, write the central idea. Then complete the lower boxes with missing details. Both charts have been started for you.

Under the Romans, different Jewish groups had different approaches to Judaism.

According to the Bible, a young Jewish religious teacher began to attract many followers in Judea.

The apostle Peter became a leader of a new church.

The first Christians still considered themselves Jews.

INTERACTIVE

For extra help, review the 21st Century Skills Tutorial: **Identify Main Ideas and Details.**

Practice Vocabulary

Use a Word Bank Choose one word from the word bank to fill in each blank. When you have finished, you will have a short summary of important ideas from the section.

Word Bank

epistles	parables	New Testament
apostles	crucifixion	conversion
Trinity	Gospels	resurrected

According to the Christian Bible, the Roman government had Jesus killed by __________, but God __________ him. The story of Jesus, his early followers, and their beliefs are described in the __________. Its first four books are referred to as the __________. They create a powerful portrayal of Jesus, who often presented his teachings in the form of __________. Other books follow, most of which are __________. They were largely written by the __________. Christians believe God exists in three forms, known as the __________. One apostle, named Paul, originally opposed Christianity, but he had an experience that led to his __________, a heartfelt change in one's opinions or beliefs.

Take Notes

Literacy Skills: Analyze Text Structure Use what you have read to complete the outline. Fill in the outline to summarize the main ideas of the lesson. The outline has been started for you.

I. How Did Islam Begin?

A. Mecca

1. Muhammad was born in Mecca, a religious center.
2. Mecca is the location of an important shrine, the Kabba.

B. Muhammad's Early Life

1. Muhammad was orphaned and raised by relatives.
2.
3.
4.

C. Preaching a New Message/The Hijra

1.
2.
3.
4.

D. Principles and Practices of Islam

1.
2.
3.
4.
5.

INTERACTIVE

For extra help, review the 21st Century Skills Tutorial: **Summarize**.

Practice Vocabulary

Use a Word Bank **Choose one word from the word bank to fill in each blank. When you have finished, you will have a short summary of important ideas from the lesson.**

Word Bank

Hijra	Quran	mosque	Bedouins
hajj	Kaaba	Sharia	Sunnah

Many ancient Arabs were nomads known as ______. Eventually, many were attracted to Mecca, where Muhammad was born. Mecca was a religious center and the location of an important shrine called the ______. Muslims believe the angel Gabriel brought messages from God to Muhammad, which were later written down in the ______. Muhammad and early Muslims eventually moved to Medina in the ______. There are many sources of Islamic thought. The ______ are traditions believed by Muslims to come from Muhammad and his associates. There are five pillars of Islam. The fifth pillar is the ______, the pilgrimage made by Muslims to the holy city of Mecca. Muslims worship in a place called a ______. Muhammad taught Muslims to follow what they believe to be God's laws, known as the ______.

Take Notes

Literacy Skills: Use Evidence Use what you have read to complete the table. In each column write details about the topic provided. The first one has been completed for you. Then, use the information you have gathered to draw a conclusion about the question provided.

The Arab Muslim Empire	The Caliphs	Crusaders and Mongols
• Arab Muslims conquered many different lands and established an empire. • Islam spread as the Arab Muslims built their empire. • Muslim warriors were able and devoted. • Muslims conquerors were relatively tolerant of Judaism and Christianity, but still discriminated.		

Conclusion: Why did Islam spread, and how were non-Muslims treated in Muslim empires?

INTERACTIVE

For extra help, review the 21st Century Skills Tutorial: **Identify Evidence**.

Practice Vocabulary

Words in Context **For each question below, write an answer that shows your understanding of the boldfaced key term.**

1. What is a **caliph** and how did the caliphates begin?

2. Who are **sultans** and what did they rule?

Take Notes

Literacy Skills: Sequence Use what you have read to complete the charts. Enter events in the sequence they occurred. The first one has been started for you.

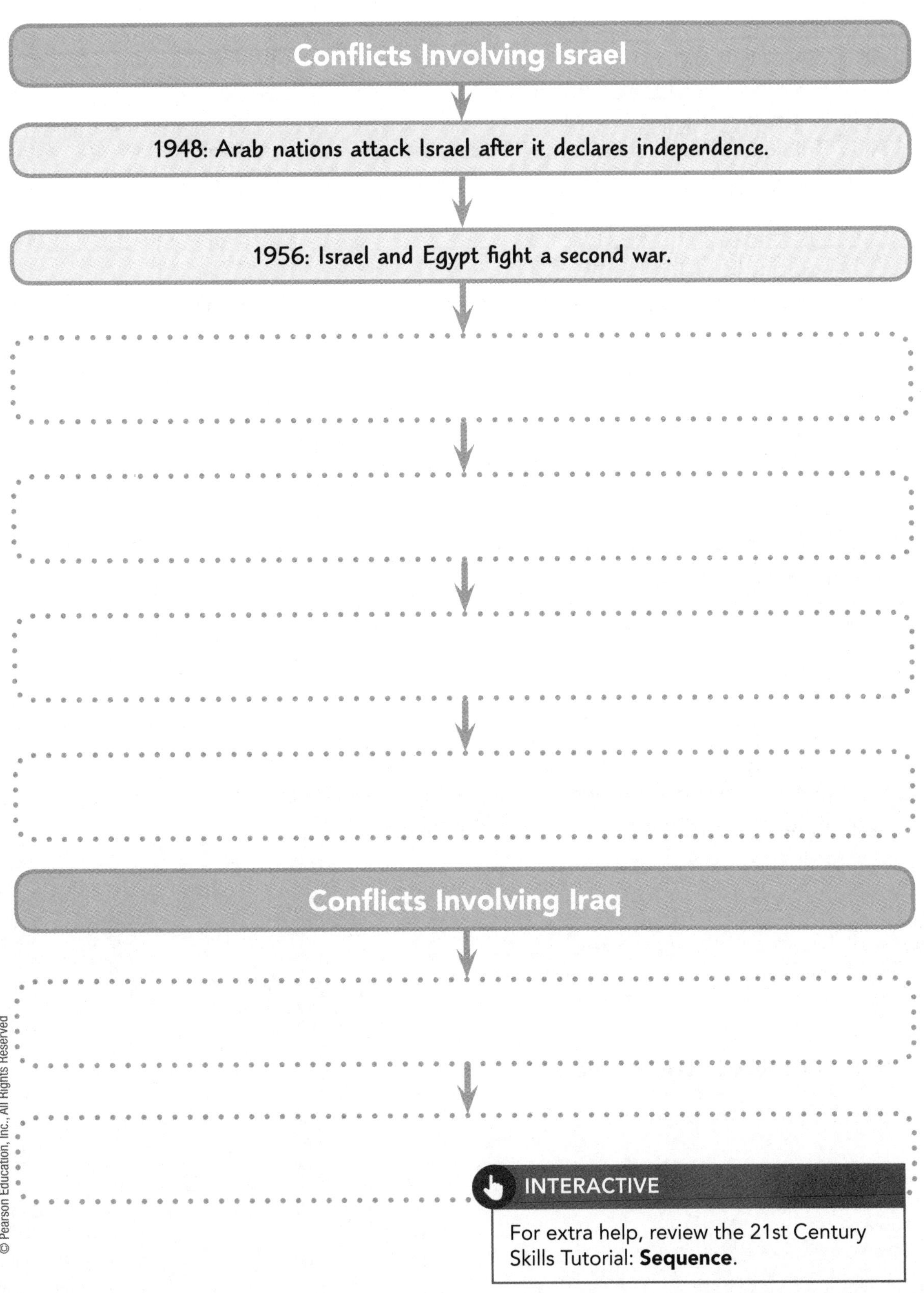

INTERACTIVE

For extra help, review the 21st Century Skills Tutorial: **Sequence**.

Practice Vocabulary

Sentence Revision **Revise each sentence so that the underlined vocabulary word is used logically. Be sure not to change the vocabulary word. The first one is done for you.**

1. After Britain and France defeated the Ottoman empire in World War I, they had new popular mandates over what are now Iran, Egypt, Saudi Arabia, Afghanistan, and Kuwait.
   After Britain and France defeated the Ottoman empire in World War I, they declared mandates over what are now Syria, Lebanon, Israel, Jordan, and Iraq.

2. After World War I, people worked with foreign powers to establish new nation-states in Southwest Asia.

3. The Jews of Europe endured very little anti-Semitism in the centuries preceding World War I.

4. Mustafa Kemal became the first president of the Turkish Republic, fighting for those who wanted to make it a secular state.

5. In the late 1800s, Jews in Europe formed a movement called Zionism to establish a Jewish state in Africa.

Quick Activity Southwest Asia Timeline

Write a timeline of major events that have occurred in Southwest Asia. Then write three or four sentences about the changes that have happened over time.

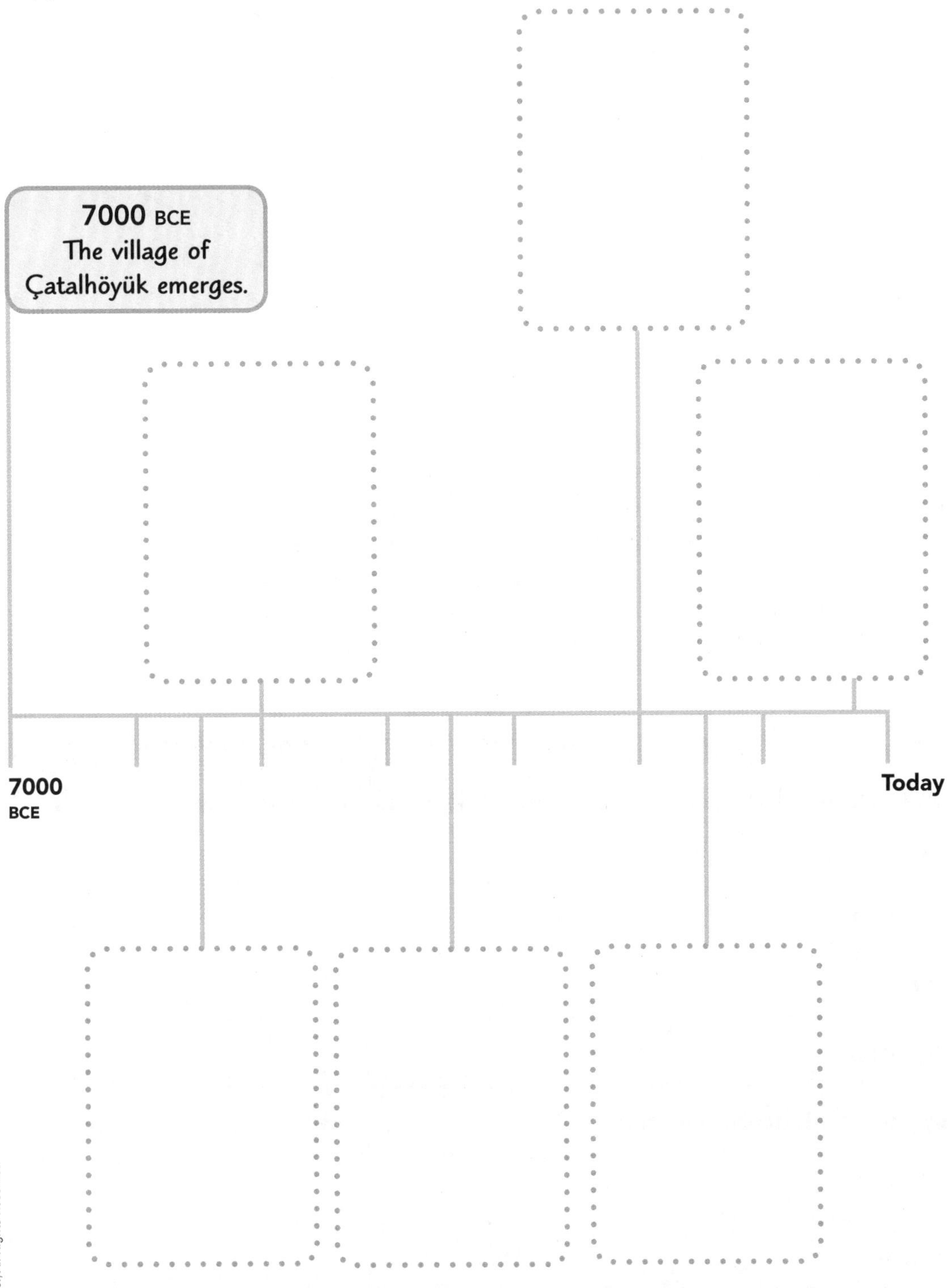

Team Challenge! **Compare your timeline to the ones that your classmates have created. How are they the same? How are they different? Have a group discussion about the reasons each of you selected the events on your timeline.**

Writing Workshop Research Paper

Select a culture from Southwest Asia and write a research paper exploring its values. The prompts below will help walk you through the process.

Lesson 1 Writing Task: Generate Questions to Focus Research Write two to four questions about Sumerian civilization. Start with this one: How was Sumerian civilization organized? What other features were important to Sumerian cultures or values?

Lessons 2 through 5 Writing Task: Support Ideas with Evidence For each lesson, take notes about the values of the cultures and people you've read about. Mark the check box when you complete the notes on each group. Then, on a separate piece of paper, write a paragraph that summarizes the values you think have been most important to the region over time.

Culture/People	Complete
Sumerian	☐
Babylonian	☐
Hittite	☐
Phoenician	☐
Assyrian and Neo-Babylonian	☐
Persian	☐
Israelite	☐
Christian	☐
Muslim	☐

Lesson 6 Writing Task: Develop a Clear Thesis Write a sentence that synthesizes and summarizes the information you have gathered about the values of cultures in Southwest Asia. This sentence will serve as the thesis statement, or central position, of your research paper.

Lesson 7 Writing Task: Write an Introduction Draft an introductory paragraph. Your first sentence should contain your thesis. Each of the next three sentences should introduce the topic of a paragraph in your essay. Your fifth sentence should conclude your introduction and transition to the next paragraph.

Writing Task Using your notes, write a research paper about a culture from Southwest Asia and the impact its values have had on it. When you write your paper, use a word processing program. When you are finished revising, use technology to publish your paper based on your teacher's instructions.

TOPIC 10

Southwest Asia Today Preview

Essential Question How should we handle conflict?

Before you begin this topic, think about the Essential Question by completing the following activities.

1. Think about the various historical conflicts that you have learned about (for example, wars in ancient Mesopotamia and World War I). List as many as you can remember and, next to each one, write the way that the conflict was resolved. Circle the resolutions you believe were most sensible.

2. Make a list of ways to resolve conflict, drawing on the resolutions to conflict you listed in the first exercise, your personal experience, and current events. Place an X next to the resolutions you think may be used to resolve conflict in Southwest Asia. After you finish reading the topic, circle the predictions that were correct.

Map Skills

Using the maps in the Regional Atlas in your text, label the outline map with the places listed. Use coloring to indicate the type of government of each nation. Create a key to define your coloring.

Iran	Baghdad	Riyadh	Israel	Tehran
Turkey	Saudi Arabia	Jerusalem	Syria	Lebanon
Iraq	Beirut	Istanbul	West Bank	Mecca

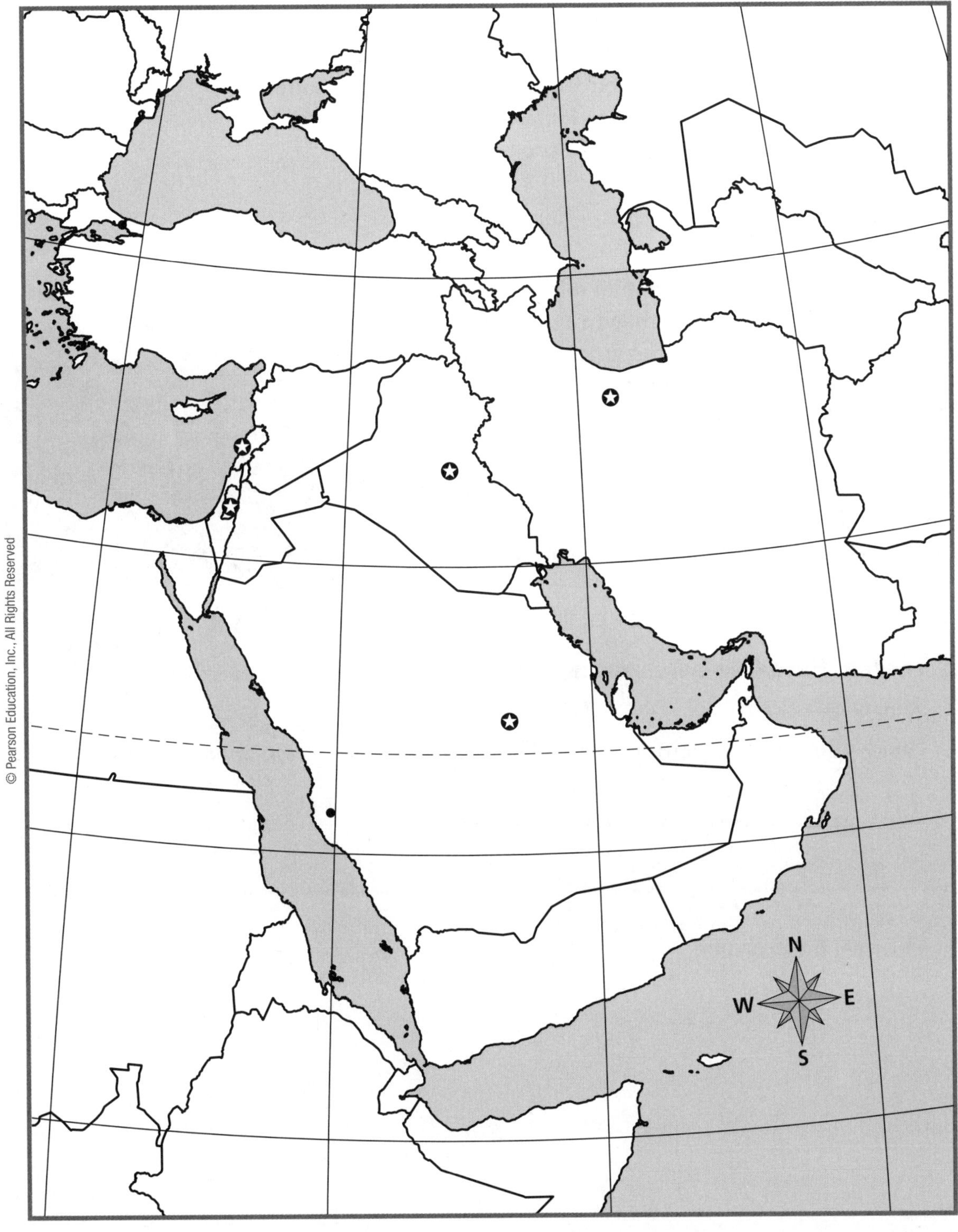

Plan a Youth Peace Summit

On this Quest, you and your classmates are planners for a peace summit. You will gather information about peace summits and conflicts in Southwest Asia by examining sources in your text and conducting your own research. At the end of the Quest, you will work together to make a plan for a youth peace summit that includes a schedule, a list of issues, and rules for productive dialogue. You will also create a flyer and a brochure to promote your summit.

1 Ask Questions

As you begin your Quest, keep in mind the Guiding Question: **How can people work together to overcome conflict?** Also, consider how people have responded to conflict throughout history, as part of your exploration of the Essential Question: **How should we handle conflict?**

What other questions do you need to ask in order to answer these questions? Consider the following aspects of life in Southwest Asia. Two questions are filled in for you. Add at least two questions for each category.

Theme Ethnic and Religious Differences

Sample questions:

Which ethnic and religious groups in Southwest Asia have major, ongoing disputes?

What are the reasons for their disagreements?

Theme Economics

Theme International Community

Theme History and Government

Theme My Additional Questions

INTERACTIVE

For extra help with Step 1, review the 21st Century Skills Tutorial: **Ask Questions**.

2 Investigate

As you read about Southwest Asia, collect five connections from your text to help you answer the Guiding Question. Three connections are already chosen for you.

Connect to Ethnicity

Lesson 1 A Region of Many Peoples

Here's a connection! Who are some of the ethnic and religious groups that live together in Southwest Asia?

Why might conflict arise between these ethnic and religious groups?

Connect to Fossil Fuels

Lesson 2 Geographic Sources Oil Dependence in Southwest Asia

Here's another connection! How can natural resources like oil lead to conflict?

How can conflicts over natural resources be resolved?

Connect to Lebanon's Constitution

Lesson 3 What Kinds of Democracy Exist in Southwest Asia?

How does Lebanon's constitution reflect compromise as a response to conflict?

What are other ways that governments can reach compromises to avoid conflict?

It's Your Turn! **Find two more connections. Fill in the title of your connections, then answer the questions. Connections may be images, primary sources, maps, or text.**

Your Choice | Connect to

Location in text

What is the main idea of this connection?

What does it tell you about ways to resolve conflict?

Your Choice | Connect to

Location in text

What is the main idea of this connection?

What does it tell you about ways to resolve conflict?

3 Conduct Research

Form teams based on your teacher's instructions. Meet to decide who will create each segment.

You will research only the segment for which you are responsible. Use the ideas in the connections to further explore the subject you have been assigned. Pick what aspect of the segment you will report about, and find sources about that subject.

Be sure to find valid sources and take good notes so you can properly cite your sources. Record key information about your segment and brainstorm ways to enhance your points with visuals.

Team Member	Segment	Key Information
	Ethnic and Religious Differences	
	Economics	
	International Community	
	History and Government	

INTERACTIVE

For extra help with Step 3, review the 21st Century Skills Tutorials: **Search for Information on the Internet** and **Avoid Plagiarism**.

4 Plan Your Youth Peace Summit

Now it's time to put together all of the information you and your teammates have gathered and compose your plan. First, meet as a team to discuss how each segment will be handled in the summit and in the promotional materials.

1. **Prepare to Plan** Review the research you've collected, and make sure the information you've gathered will help you plan the summit and create promotional materials. Begin by creating an agenda that includes a list of discussion topics related to your segment.

Agenda:

Ideas for visuals to include in flyers and brochures:

2. **Write a Draft Plan** Using evidence from your textbook and the sources you explored, write a detailed plan for discussing your segment at the peace summit. Be sure to include a sketch of your flyer and brochure designs. Include details from the evidence you've studied in this Quest.

3. **Share With a Partner** Exchange your plan and sketches with a partner. Tell your partner what you like about his or her drafts and suggest any improvements. Make revisions to your materials based on your partner's feedback. Correct any grammatical or spelling errors.

4. **Finalize Your Plan and Promotional Materials** Work with all your teammates to finalize your agenda and the promotional materials. Make sure that each segment is represented in the final products.

5. **Reflect on the Quest** Think about your experience completing this topic's Quest. What did you learn about peace summits as an approach to resolving conflicts? What questions do you still have about peace summits? How will you answer them?

Reflections

INTERACTIVE

For extra help with Step 4, review the 21st Century Skills Tutorial: **Work in Teams**.

Take Notes

Literacy Skills: Analyze Text Structure Use what you have read to complete the outline. Fill in the outline to summarize the main ideas of the lesson. The outline has been started for you.

I. A Region of Many Faiths

A. Sunnis, Shias, and Ibadis

1. Most people in Southwest Asia are Muslims who follow the Five Pillars of Islam.
2. Two main varieties of Islam are Sunni and Shia.
3.
4.
5.

B. Wahhabism and Islamism

1.
2.
3.
4.

INTERACTIVE

For extra help, review the 21st Century Skills Tutorial: **Summarize**.

Practice Vocabulary

Sentence Builder Finish the sentences below with a key term from this section. You may have to change the form of the words to complete the sentences.

Word Bank

Sharia	fundamentalism	Islamism
ethnic group	hijab	

1. Wahhabis think holy books should be taken literally, a type of belief called

2. Many women in the Arab world wear a veil that covers the head and chest, called a

3. A group of people who share a distinct language, culture, and identity is called an

4. Those who believe that government and society should reflect Islamic law practice

5. The government of Iran enforces strict observance of Islamic law, or

Take Notes

Literacy Skills: Summarize Use what you have read to complete the tables. Note two of the most important details from each section listed. The first section has been completed for you.

How Does Geography Affect Where People Live?	Important Details
Settlement in Southwest Asia	• Much of the region's population lives in the Fertile Crescent region. • Areas with moist climates have higher population densities.
Effects of Technology	
Effects of Resources	

Economies of Southwest Asia	Important Details
Economic Systems	
Investment and Living Standards	
Specialization and Trade	

INTERACTIVE

For extra help, review the 21st Century Skills Tutorial: **Summarize**.

Practice Vocabulary

Vocabulary Quiz Show **Some quiz shows ask a question and expect the contestant to give the answer. In other shows, the contestant is given an answer and must supply the question. If the blank is in the Question column, write the question that would result in the answer in the Answer column. If the question is supplied, write the answer.**

Question	**Answer**
1. What is the term for the removal of salt from sea water?	1.
2. What do you call the money or goods that are used to make products?	2.
3.	3. subsistence farming
4.	4. nationalize
5. What is the name for a place in the desert where water can be found?	5.

Quick Activity Economic Challenges

The people of Southwest Asia face many economic challenges. However, the challenges differ depending on the country. Use the information in the infographic and your reading to record in the chart the economic challenges these countries face.

ECONOMIC INDICATORS IN SOUTHWEST ASIA

	SAUDI ARABIA	TURKEY	ISRAEL
Entrepreneurship rank	36th*	28th*	21st*
Literacy rate	94.7%	95%	97.8%
GDP per capita	$53,430	$19,618	$36,822

Source: Global Entrepreneurial Development Institute, CIA World Factbook, World Bank

*Compared to 130 countries

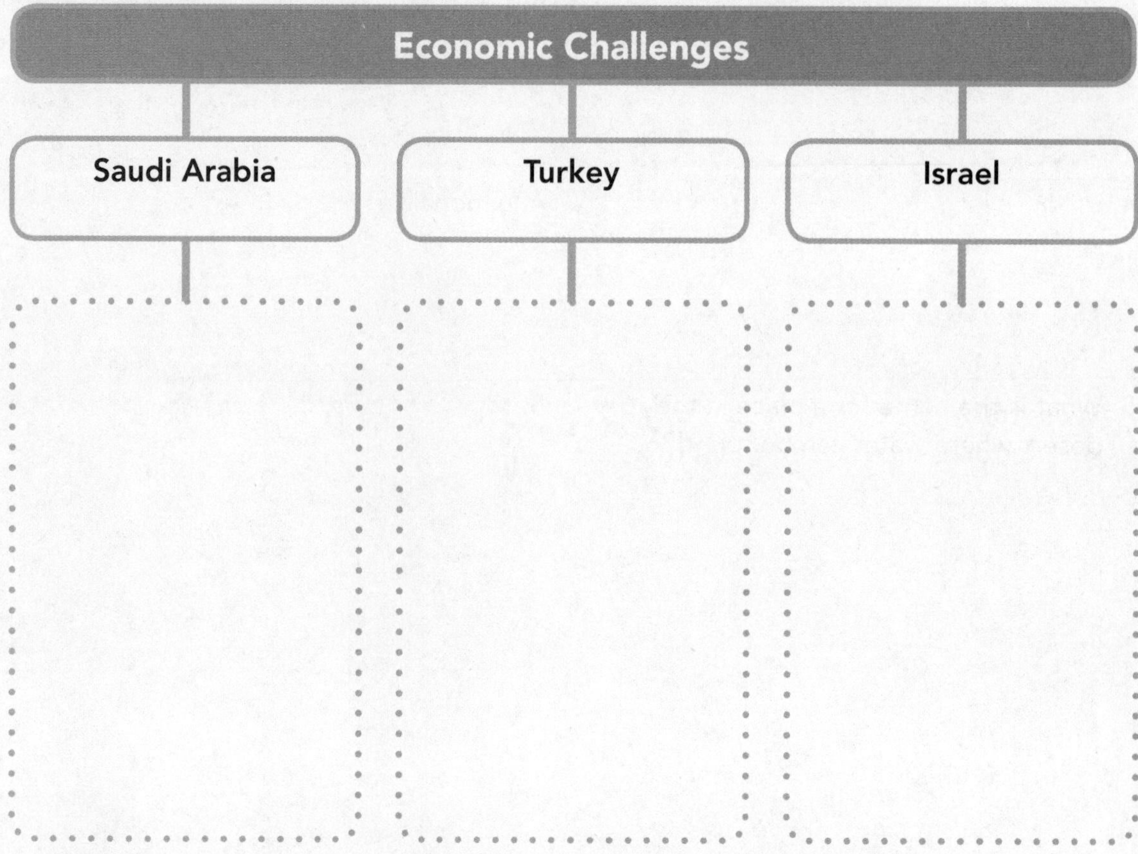

Team Challenge! Discuss with classmates the challenges that people in other Southwest Asian countries face. How are they similar to those faced by the people of Turkey, Israel, and Saudi Arabia? How are they different?

Take Notes

Literacy Skills: Classify and Categorize Use what you have read about governments in Southwest Asia in this lesson to complete the tables. Categorize the countries based on their governments. The first category has been completed for you.

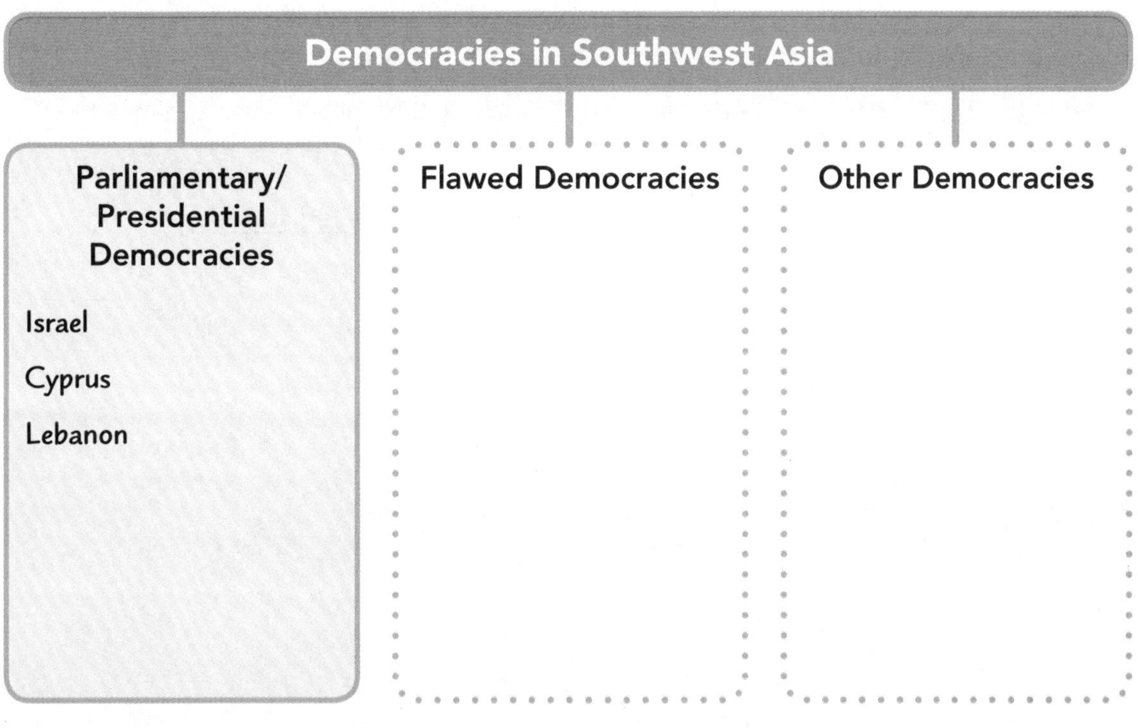

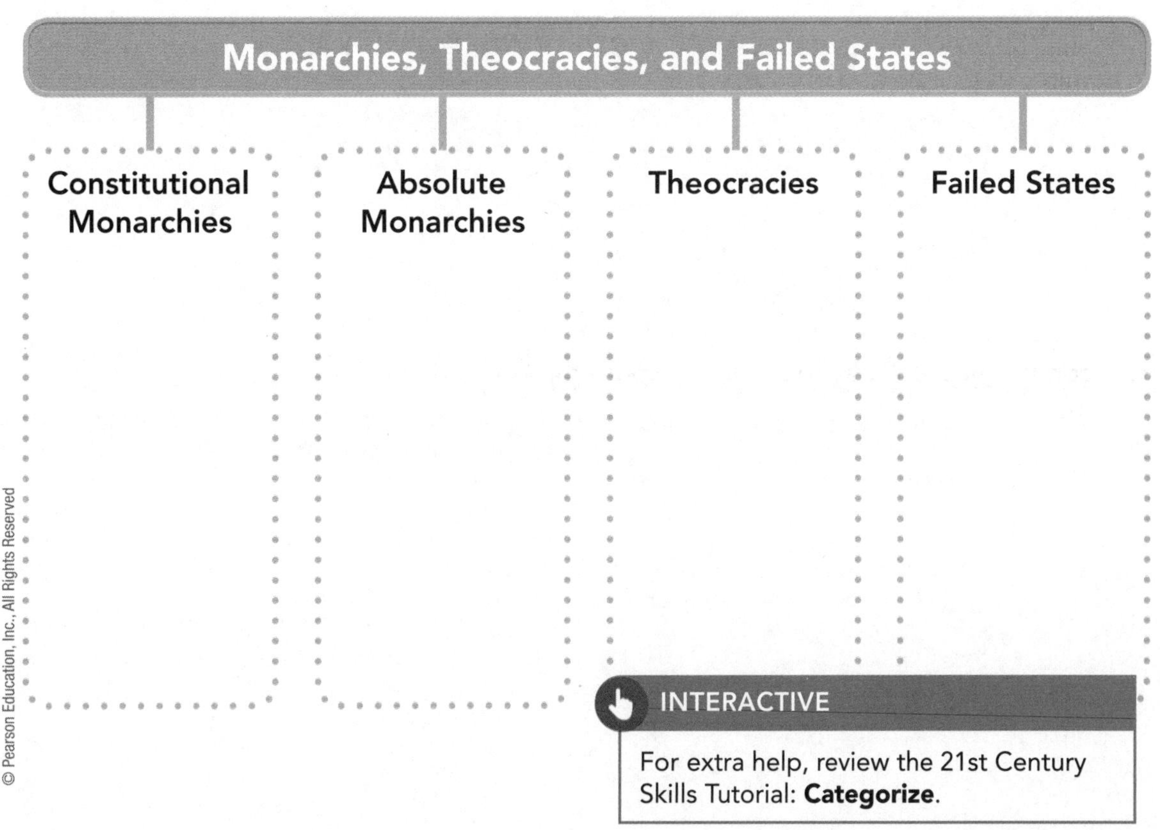

INTERACTIVE

For extra help, review the 21st Century Skills Tutorial: **Categorize**.

Practice Vocabulary

Sentence Revision **Revise each sentence so that the underlined vocabulary term is used logically. Be sure not to change the vocabulary term. The first one is done for you.**

1. Some people in Turkey favor a secular, or religious, government.
   Some people in Turkey favor a secular, or nonreligious, government.

2. Saudi Arabia and Lebanon are considered by many to be failed states.

3. Israel is a theocracy.

4. An authoritarian government is one in which power is held by a large number of people and groups.

5. A compromise is a way to settle a dispute through a decree.

Take Notes

Literacy Skills: Sequence Use what you have read to complete the charts. Enter events in the sequence in which they occurred. The first one has been started for you.

Conflict in Israel, West Bank, and Gaza

- During the Arab-Israeli War of 1967, Israel took control of the West Bank and Gaza.

Conflict in Syria

INTERACTIVE

For extra help, review the 21st Century Skills Tutorial: **Sequence**.

Practice Vocabulary

Words in Context For each question below, write an answer that shows your understanding of the boldfaced key term.

1. What happened during the First **Intifada** in the late 1980s?

2. Where did Israeli Jews build **Israeli settlements** in the 1970s and 1980s?

3. Why does the Islamic State call its state a **caliphate**?

Quick Activity Good Comparison?

The word *spring* has been used to describe peaceful revolutionary movements like the Arab Spring. Record some explanations for the use of this term in the graphic organizer below.

Characteristics of Peaceful Revolutions	Characteristics of Spring

Explanation for Use of *Spring* for These Movements

Team Challenge! **Think about whether the use of the term *spring* makes sense to describe these movements. All students who think it is an appropriate term should move to one area of the room, and all those who don't should move to the opposite side. Have a brief debate between the two sides. After the debate, any students who have changed their mind should move to the other side of the room.**

Writing Workshop Explanatory Essay

As you read, build a response to this question: What are the roots of conflict in Southwest Asia? The prompts below will help walk you through the process.

Lessons 1 and 2 Writing Task: Gather Information Gather information that helps answer the following questions. Be sure the information you record is logical and relevant. You will use it for the explanatory essay you will write at the end of the topic.

Question	Supporting Information
What religious and ethnic issues are the causes of conflict in the region?	
Are these conflicts within countries, between countries, or both?	
Why do these issues lead to conflict?	
What economic issues are or could be causes of conflict in Southwest Asia?	
Why do these issues lead to conflict?	
Are the conflicts being addressed?	

Lesson 3 Writing Task: Develop a Clear Thesis Write a sentence that synthesizes the information you have gathered about conflicts in Southwest Asia. What generalization can you make about the causes of conflict in the region? What can you say about how these conflicts are being addressed?

Lesson 4 Writing Task: Make an Outline Decide on the three or more main ideas you will present in your essay. For each main idea, write three or four details.

Main Idea

Main Idea

Main Idea

Writing Task Using the information you've gathered and the thesis you've written, answer the following question in a multi-paragraph explanatory essay: What are the roots of conflict in Southwest Asia?

TOPIC 11

South Asia Preview

Essential Question What should governments do?

Before you begin this topic, think about the Essential Question by completing the following activities.

1. List six ways that government impacts people's lives. Circle the one that you think has the most significant impact and write a sentence explaining why you think so.

2. Preview the topic by skimming lesson titles, headings, and graphics. Then make a drawing of something you expect to learn about.

Map Skills

Using the political and physical maps in the Regional Atlas in your text, label the outline map with the places listed. Then color in water, desert, and mountainous areas.

Ganges River	Bay of Bengal	Deccan Plateau	India
Dhaka	Kathmandu	Afghanistan	Indian Ocean
Islamabad	Bangladesh	New Delhi	Nepal
Himalayas	Mumbai	Pakistan	Indus River

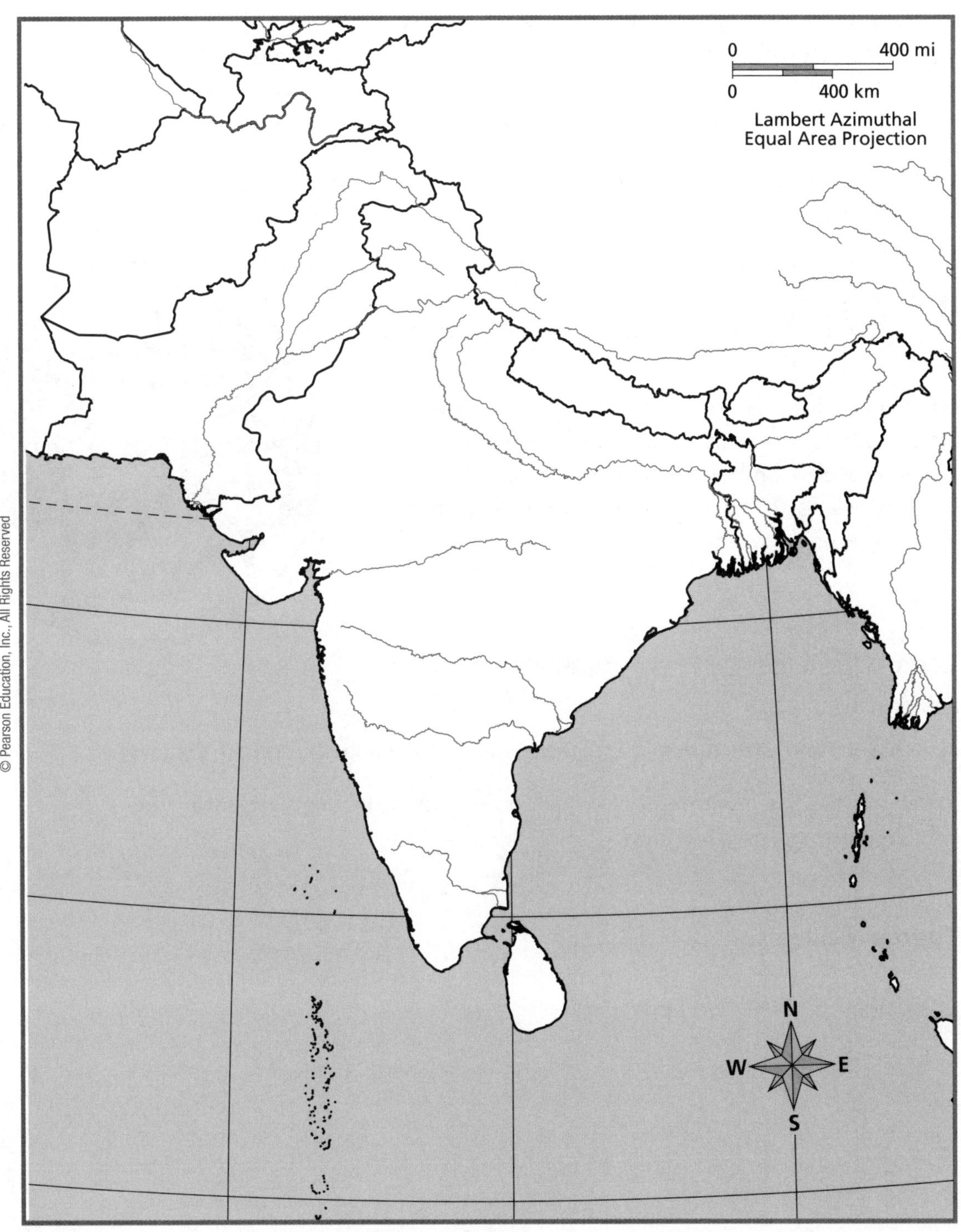

Comparing Economic Development

On this Quest, you will learn about the development of and challenges facing two of the most populous countries in the world, India and Bangladesh. You will examine sources related to their development. At the end of the Quest, you will write an essay comparing and contrasting the development of India and the development of Bangladesh.

1 Ask Questions

As you begin your Quest, keep in mind the Guiding Question: **How would you compare and contrast development in India and Bangladesh?** and the Essential Question: **What should governments do?**

What other questions do you need to ask in order to answer these questions? Consider the following points of comparison between the two countries. Two questions are filled in for you. Add at least two questions for each category.

Theme Transportation and Infrastructure

Sample questions:

How has the infrastructure in Bangladesh and India changed in recent decades?

What role has the government and business played in the improvement of the infrastructure in these countries?

Theme Education

Theme Health Care

Theme Employment

Theme Poverty

Theme My Additional Questions

 INTERACTIVE

For extra help with Step 1, review the 21st Century Skills Tutorial: **Ask Questions**.

Quest CONNECTIONS

2 Investigate

As you read about the development of and challenges facing India and Bangladesh, collect five connections from your text to help you answer the Guiding Question. Three connections are already chosen for you.

Connect to Infrastructure

Lesson 1 A Complex Civilization

Here's a connection! What kinds of developments took place in the ancient Indus Valley civilization?

How might these kinds of development be relevant today to people in underdeveloped areas of Bangladesh or India?

Connect to Economic Development

Lesson 4 European Colonialism

Here's another connection! How did the British develop South Asia during their colonial rule?

How did colonialism and gaining independence affect development in South Asia?

Connect to Employment

Lesson 6 Economies of South Asia

What does this connection tell you about development efforts that are underway in India and Bangladesh today?

How is investment in job-training programs in these countries leading to more employment?

It's Your Turn! **Find two more connections. Fill in the title of your connections, then answer the questions. Connections may be images, primary sources, maps, or text.**

Your Choice | Connect to

Location in text

What is the main idea of this connection?

What does it tell you about development in India and Bangladesh?

Your Choice | Connect to

Location in text

What is the main idea of this connection?

What does it tell you about development in India and Bangladesh?

3 Examine Primary Sources

Examine the primary and secondary sources provided online or from your teacher. Fill in the chart to show how these sources provide further information about development in India and Bangladesh. The first one is completed for you.

Source	This document provides details about . . .
Interview with India's Prime Minister Manmohan Singh	India's infrastructure, including roads, ports, airports, and irrigation
India Transportation	
Bangladesh's Transport System	
GDP, Occupations, and Education in India and Bangladesh	
Bangladesh Health System Review	

INTERACTIVE

For extra help with Step 3, review the 21st Century Skills Tutorial: **Analyze Primary and Secondary Sources**.

4 Write Your Essay

Now it's time to put together all of the information you have gathered and use it to write your essay.

1. **Prepare to Write** You have collected connections and explored primary and secondary sources about development in India and Bangladesh. Look through your notes and decide which facts you want to highlight in your essay. Record them here.

Facts

2. **Write a Draft** Using evidence from the information in the textbook and the primary and secondary sources you explored, write a draft of your essay. Be sure to write about development in both countries. Include details from the evidence in the material you've studied in this Quest.

3. **Share With a Partner** Exchange your draft with a partner. Tell your partner what you like about his or her draft and suggest any improvements.

4. **Finalize Your Report** Revise your essay based on the feedback you receive from your partner. Correct any grammatical or spelling errors.

5. **Reflect on the Quest** Think about your experience completing this topic's Quest. What did you learn about development in India and Bangladesh? What questions do you still have about these two countries? How will you answer them?

Reflections

INTERACTIVE

For extra help with Step 4, review the 21st Century Skills Tutorial: **Write an Essay**.

Take Notes

Literacy Skills: Analyze Text Structure Fill in the outline to summarize the main ideas of the lesson. The outline has been started for you.

I. An Advanced Civilization

A. Farming in the Indus Valley

1. Farmers built irrigation channels because monsoon rains were unreliable.

2. Farmers raised cattle, sheep, goats, and chickens.

B. Trade

1.

2.

C. Technology

1.

2.

3.

D. Indus Valley Mysteries

1.

2.

INTERACTIVE

For extra help, review the 21st Century Skills Tutorial: **Summarize**.

Practice Vocabulary

Sentence Revision **Revise each sentence so that the underlined vocabulary word is used logically. Be sure not to change the vocabulary word. The first one is done for you.**

1. The Maurya expressed their beliefs in a collection of hundreds of sacred hymns known as Vedas.
   The Indo-Aryans expressed their beliefs in a collection of hundreds of sacred hymns known as Vedas.

2. Guilds are individual merchants and craftpersons working in different businesses.

3. Over thousands of years, Buddhists have developed a social structure based on caste.

4. The principle of ahimsa states that hunting is acceptable if done humanely.

5. A person who has citizenship is an official who gives residents of a state civil and political rights and obligations.

6. Tolerance is an unwillingness to respect similar beliefs and customs.

7. Dalits belonged to a caste of people who do jobs such as banking and legislation.

Take Notes

Literacy Skills: Determine Central Ideas Use what you have read to complete the chart. In the top box, write the central idea. Then complete the lower boxes with missing details. Both charts have been started for you.

The Vedas are India's oldest religious texts.

Gurus began to think and talk about religious ideas.

Hindus believe that when a person dies the soul is reborn into a new body.

Hindus believe a person's karma determines how a person is reborn.

INTERACTIVE

For extra help, review the 21st Century Skills Tutorial: **Identify Main Ideas and Details.**

Practice Vocabulary

True or False? Decide whether each statement below is true or false. Circle T or F, and then explain your answer. Be sure to include the underlined vocabulary word in your explanation. The first one is done for you.

1. **T / F** Around 500 BCE, Hindu gurus stayed in their homes to think and talk about religious ideas.
   False. Around 500 BCE, Hindu gurus left their homes to live in the forest to think and talk about religious ideas.

2. **T / F** Dharma is a person's duty to do what is right for him or her.

3. **T / F** Reincarnation is the rebirth of a new soul in a new body.

4. **T / F** The first goal for Hindus is moksha, liberation from reincarnation.

5. **T / F** The Upanishads teach that all of the Gods that Indians worship are forms of Brahman.

6. **T / F** Hindus believe that the law of karma determines how a person is reborn.

Take Notes

Literacy Skills: Draw Conclusions Use what you have read to complete the charts. First, fill in details about the early and later life of the Buddha. Then write conclusions in the boxes above each set of details.

Siddartha's father, a king, shielded him from everything unpleasant and disturbing.

After Siddhartha left his father's palace, he saw people suffering, lived in poverty, and studied and meditated until he achieved enlightenment, or freedom from suffering.

As the Buddha taught, he gained many followers.

Buddha urged his followers to carry his teachings all over the Earth.

INTERACTIVE

For extra help, review the 21st Century Skills Tutorial: **Draw Conclusions**.

Practice Vocabulary

Vocabulary Quiz Show Some quiz shows ask a question and expect the contestant to give the answer. In other shows, the contestant is given an answer and must supply the question. If the blank is in the Question column, write the question that would result in the answer in the Answer column. If the question is supplied, write the answer.

Question	Answer
1. Which religious communities do Buddhists go to so that they have time to study and meditate?	1.
2. What is it called when a person reaches a state of perfect wisdom, free of suffering?	2.
3.	3. meditate
4.	4. bodhisattvas
5.	5. ascetic
6. What is the name of a state of blissful peace without desire or suffering?	6.
7. What do you call a person who seeks to spread his or her religion?	7.

Take Notes

Literacy Skills: Sequence Use what you have read to complete the chart. Enter events in the sequence in which they occurred. The first two have been completed for you.

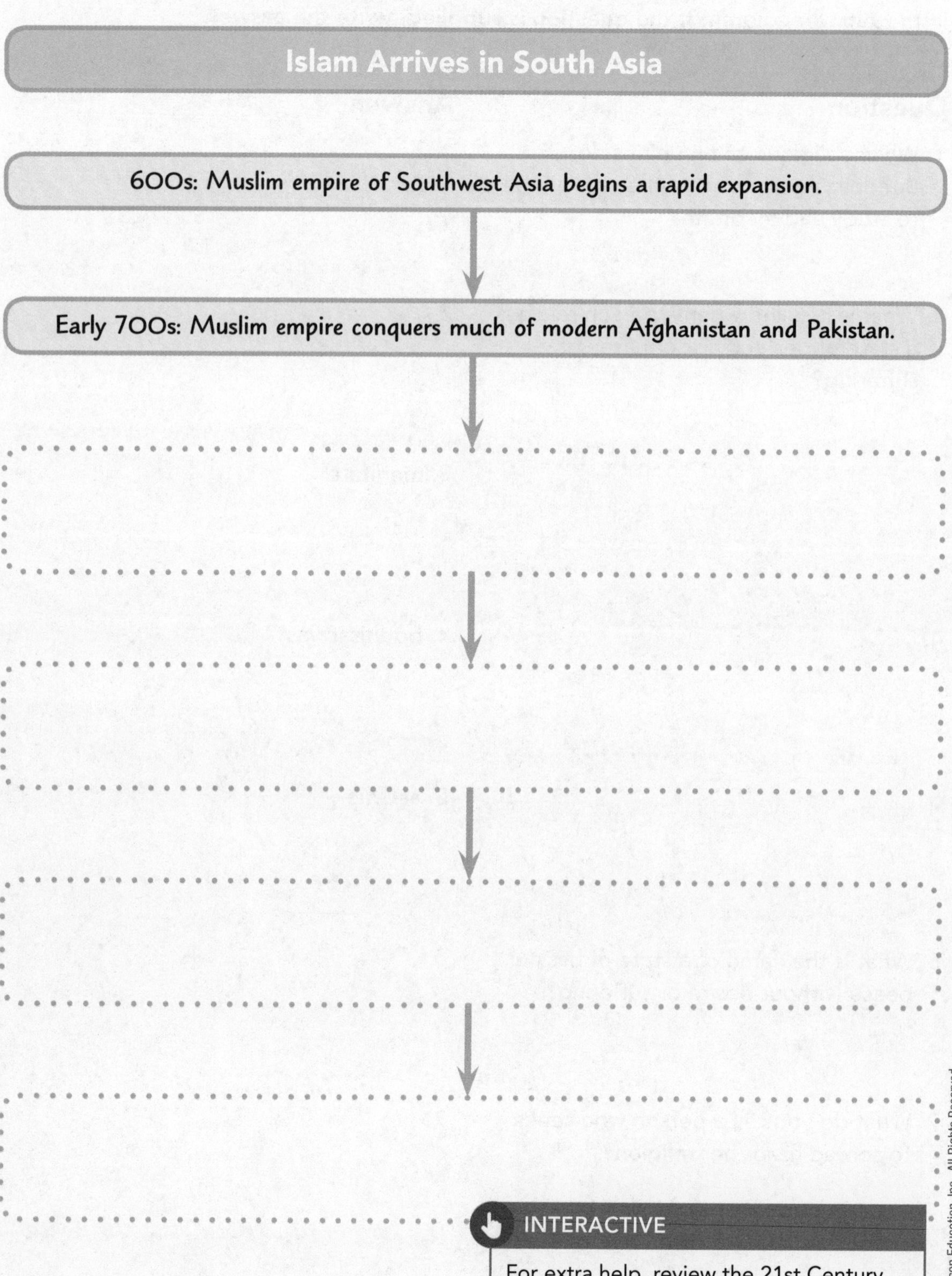

INTERACTIVE

For extra help, review the 21st Century Skills Tutorial: **Sequence**.

Practice Vocabulary

Sentence Builder **Finish the sentences below with a key term from this section. You may have to change the form of the words to complete the sentences.**

Word Bank

discrimination	partition	Punjab
nonalignment	nonviolent resistance	

1. Britain separated British India into two states through a process called

   ______________________.

2. Most Sikhs live in an area of northern India known as the

   ______________________.

3. The policy of avoiding alliance with the United States or Soviet Union during the Cold War was called

   ______________________.

4. Gandhi urged his followers to practice

   ______________________.

5. As the British considered withdrawing from South Asia in 1947, Muslims in the northwest feared they would face

   ______________________.

Quick Activity South Asia Historical Figures

What were the major contributions of key figures in South Asian history? With a partner, brainstorm as many notable figures as you can, indicating their country and the important contributions they made.

Key Figure and Country	Major Contributions

Team Challenge! Decide on the person you think had the most influence on South Asia. Write your answer on a sticky note and post it in the classroom. Appoint a classmate to group the answers. Who received the most votes? Why?

Take Notes

Literacy Skills: Use Evidence Use what you have read to complete the table. In each column write details about the topic provided. The first column has been completed for you. Then, use the information you have gathered to draw a conclusion based on the question provided.

Where Do South Asians Live?	Religion in South Asia	Ethnic Diversity
Topography has been a significant factor in how South Asia has been settled. People live where rainfall supports agriculture. Large numbers of the region's people live in humid, temperate climate regions. Coastal areas have excellent harbors, which has helped trade. Few people live in areas with an arid climate.		

Why does South Asia have a lot of diversity?

INTERACTIVE

For extra help, review the 21st Century Skills Tutorial: **Support Ideas With Evidence**.

Practice Vocabulary

Words in Context For each question below, write an answer that shows your understanding of the boldfaced key term.

1. What landforms are considered part of a nation's **topography**?

2. What impact do **monsoons** have on the climate of South Asia?

Take Notes

Literacy Skills: Compare and Contrast Use what you have read to complete the Venn diagram with similarities and differences. The first entry has been completed for you.

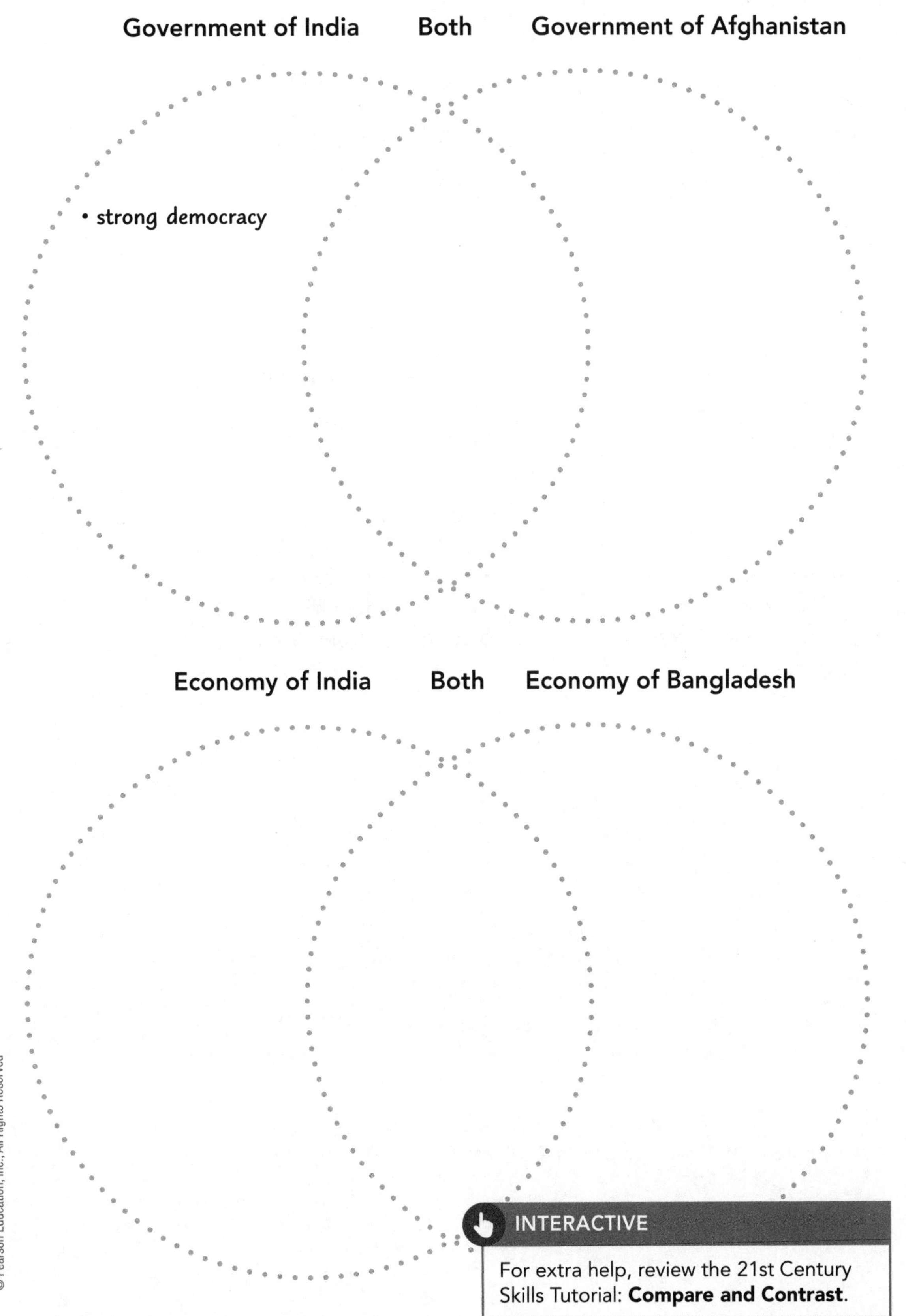

INTERACTIVE

For extra help, review the 21st Century Skills Tutorial: **Compare and Contrast**.

Practice Vocabulary

Matching Logic **Using your knowledge of the underlined vocabulary terms, draw a line from each sentence in Column 1 to match it with the sentence in Column 2 to which it logically belongs.**

Column 1	Column 2
1. India has a federal system similar to the United States.	Companies in the United States have hired foreign firms or workers.
2. People in Bangladesh have benefited from microlending.	Power is divided among national, state, and local governments.
3. India's economy and its workforce have benefited from outsourcing.	Banks have made small loans to people with their own small businesses.

Quick Activity Microloans

Microloans are small loans made to help people start or run their own small business. A business might use a microloan to purchase tools, equipment, or perhaps livestock to produce food. The questions below will help you gather the information a bank would require if you were to apply for a microloan. Begin by deciding the type of small business for which you need a loan.

Name of Business

What does the business do?

How much money would you like to borrow?

What will you use the microloan for?

How will you earn the money to pay back the loan?

Team Challenge! With a partner, role play applying for a microloan with a banker. Partners should decide whether they will grant you the loan and the reasons for their decision. Then switch roles.

Take Notes

Literacy Skills: Identify Cause and Effect Use what you have read to complete the charts. In each response box, enter a cause that led to the effect listed in each top box. The first one has been started for you.

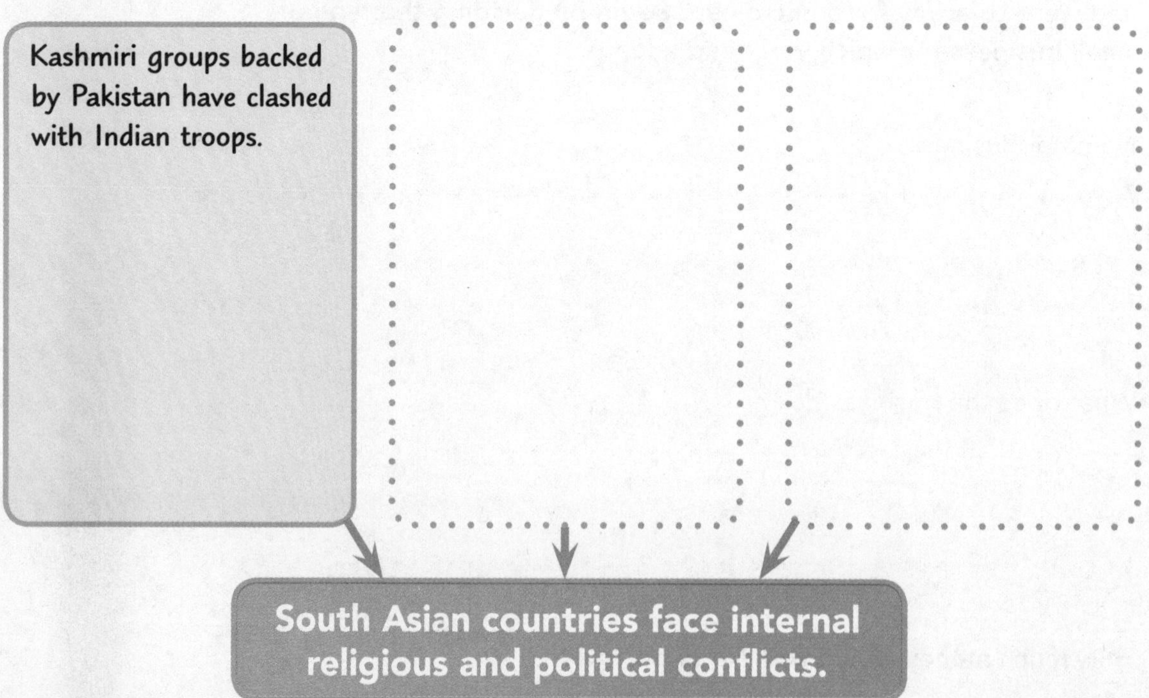

South Asian countries face environmental challenges.

INTERACTIVE

For extra help, review the 21st Century Skills Tutorial: **Analyze Cause and Effect**.

Practice Vocabulary

Word Map Study the word map for the word *sexism*. Characteristics are words or phrases that relate to the word in the center of the word map. Non-characteristics are words and phrases not associated with the word. Use the blank word map to explore the meaning of the word *regulation*.

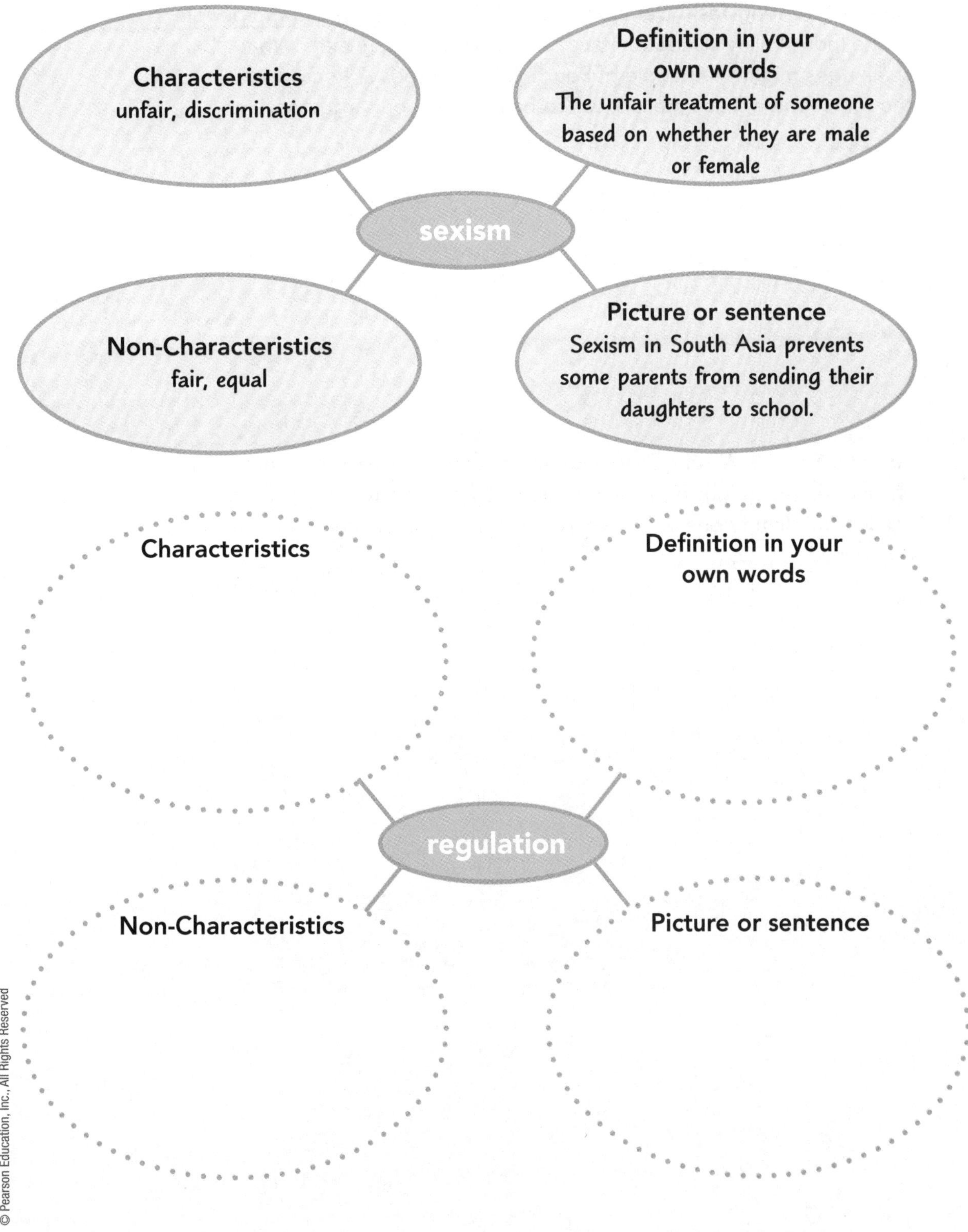

Writing Workshop Argument

Write an argument, or a persuasive essay, about one or more challenges facing South Asia and steps that can be taken to meet that challenge. The prompts below will help walk you through the process.

Lesson 1 Writing Task: Generate Ideas What challenges did the people of the Indus Valley civilization face, and how were they met? What challenges might the people of South Asia face today? Record your thoughts. You will use these ideas to help shape your argument.

Lessons 2 and 3 Writing Task: Generate Ideas Brainstorm a list of challenges that might face the people of South Asia today. For each challenge, identify one or two possible ways the challenge could be addressed.

Lessons 4, 5, and 6 Writing Task: Gather Evidence Review the ideas that you generated about challenges facing South Asia and possible ways to meet those challenges. Circle two or three in your chart on the previous page that interest you. Then, gather evidence that you can use to persuade a reader that the challenges you've identified merit attention and that the solutions you're recommending will meet the challenge. List your evidence in the space below.

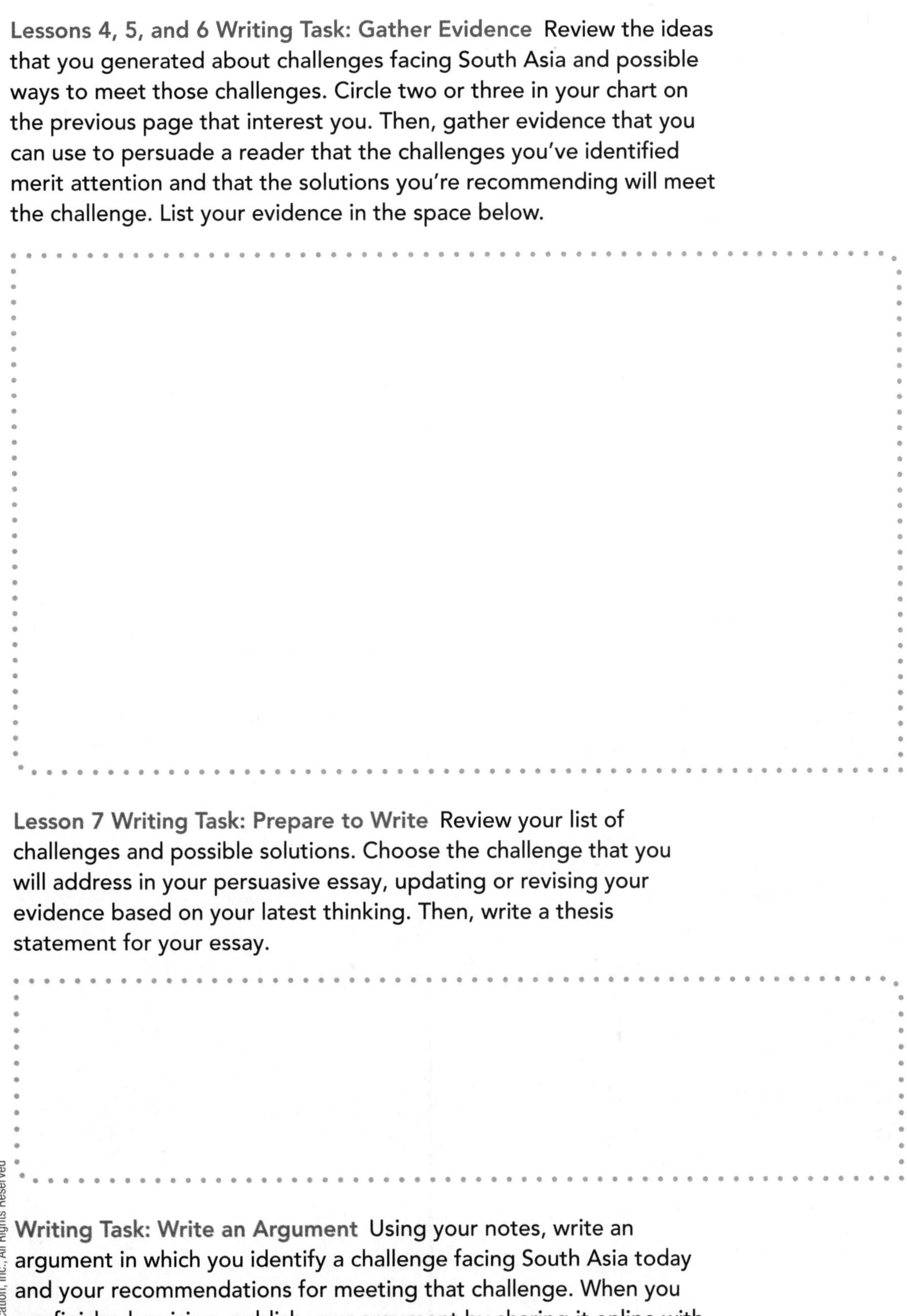

Lesson 7 Writing Task: Prepare to Write Review your list of challenges and possible solutions. Choose the challenge that you will address in your persuasive essay, updating or revising your evidence based on your latest thinking. Then, write a thesis statement for your essay.

Writing Task: Write an Argument Using your notes, write an argument in which you identify a challenge facing South Asia today and your recommendations for meeting that challenge. When you are finished revising, publish your argument by sharing it online with your classmates.

TOPIC 12

East Asia Preview

Essential Question What are the costs and benefits of technology?

Before you begin this topic, think about the Essential Question by completing the following activities.

1. List two positive aspects and two negative aspects of technology.

Map Skills

Using the political and physical maps in the Regional Atlas in your text, label the outline map with the places listed. Then color in water and areas with climates too dry (arid and semiarid) or too cold (tundra and subarctic) for most crops.

Seoul	Beijing
North China Plain	Plateau of Tibet
Huang River	Tokyo
South China Sea	Chang River
Pearl River Delta	Taklimakan Desert
Gobi	Taiwan
Japan	China
North Korea	South Korea
Manchurian Plain	

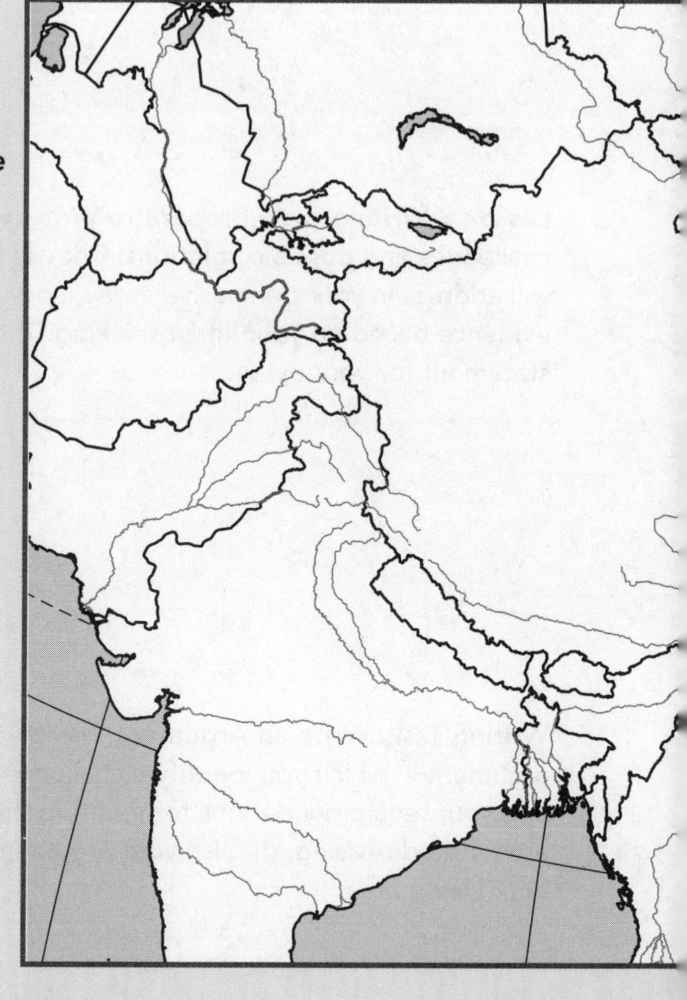

2. Preview the topic by skimming lesson titles, headings, and graphics. Then place a check mark next to the uses of technology that you think will play an important role in the growth of East Asia. After you finish reading the topic, circle the predictions that were correct.

__building dikes
__mining for gold
__producing silk
__purifying water
__building cities in deserts
__creating weapons from iron
__building the Great Wall
__sailing across oceans
__inventing the crossbow
__creating the Grand Canal

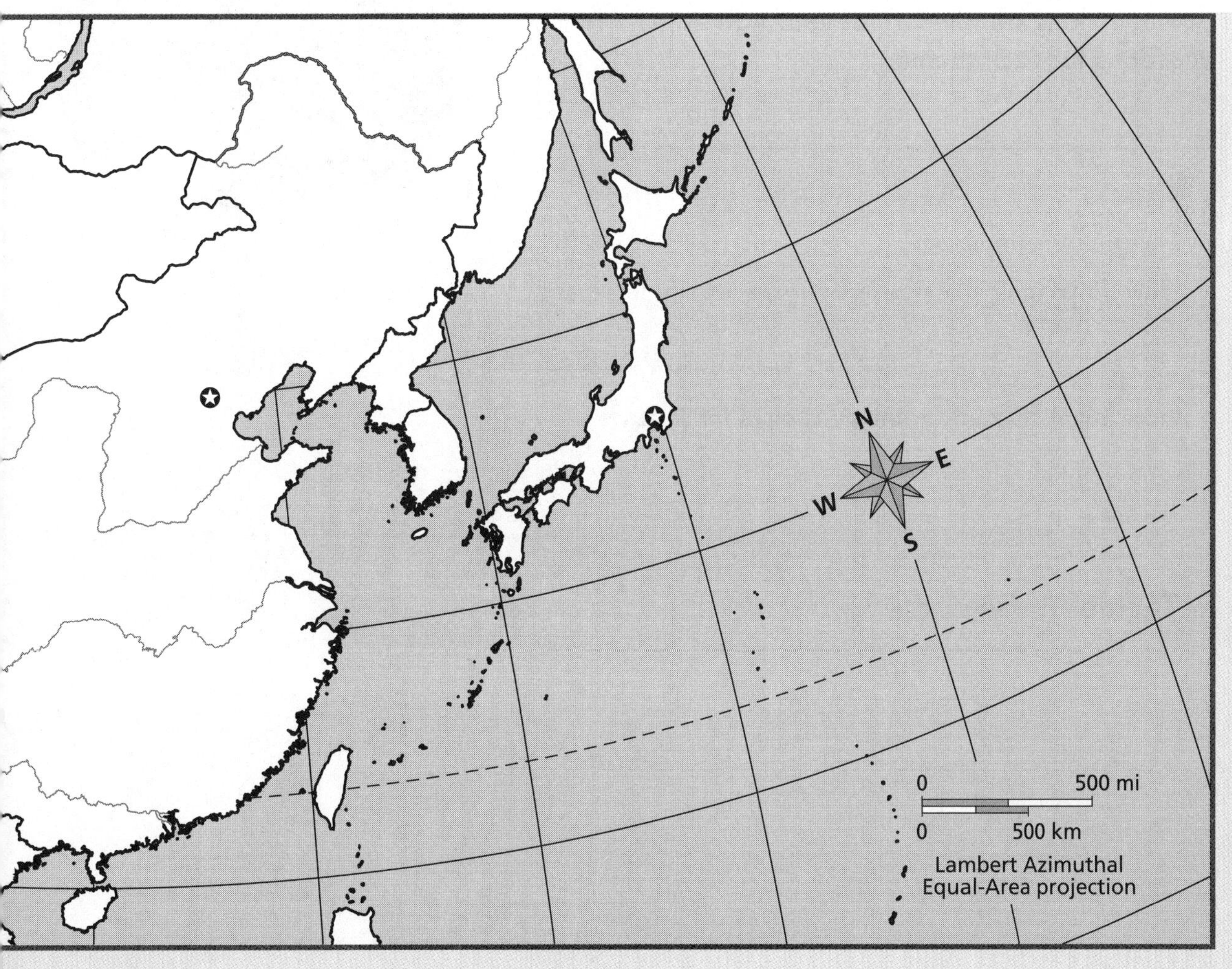

Debate Nuclear Power for Japan

On this Quest, you will explore sources and gather information about Japan's geography and the country's energy needs. You will take on the role of an engineer on an international team of experts. You will examine sources on Japan's geography and energy needs and then participate in a discussion with other experts about the Guiding Question.

1 Ask Questions

As you begin your Quest, keep in mind the Guiding Question: **Given the geography of Japan, should the country depend on nuclear energy?** and the Essential Question: **What are the costs and benefits of technology?**

To help you get started, consider the following themes. Two questions are filled in for you. Add at least two questions for each theme.

Theme Human-Environment Interaction

Sample questions:

How do tectonic plates affect human activity in Japan?

How might they affect energy choices for Japan?

Theme Technology

Theme Energy Supply and Needs

Theme Economics

Theme Environmental Concerns

Theme My Additional Questions

INTERACTIVE

For extra help with Step 1, review the 21st Century Skills Tutorial: **Ask Questions**.

2 Investigate

As you read about East Asia, collect five connections from your text to help you answer the Guiding Question. Three connections are already chosen for you.

Connect to Environmental Hazards

Lesson 1 How Did Government Emerge in China?

Here's a connection! Why was it important for early Chinese rulers to control the Huang River?

Were their efforts to control the river successful? Why or why not?

Connect to Energy Requirements

Lesson 5 Economies of East Asia

Here's another connection! What energy resources does China have? Identify at least two.

Why are sources of energy important for economic growth and development?

Connect to the Fukushima Disaster

Lesson 6 What Environmental Challenges Does the Region Face?

Here's another connection! What environmental hazards led to the Fukushima disaster?

How do you think the disaster at Fukushima has affected Japan's energy policy?

It's your turn! **Find two more connections. Fill in the title of your connections, then answer the questions. Connections may be images, primary sources, maps, or text.**

Your Choice | Connect to

Location in text

What is the main idea of this connection?

What does it tell about whether Japan should rely on nuclear power?

Your Choice | Connect to

Location in text

What is the main idea of this connection?

What does it tell about whether Japan should rely on nuclear power?

3 Examine Primary Sources

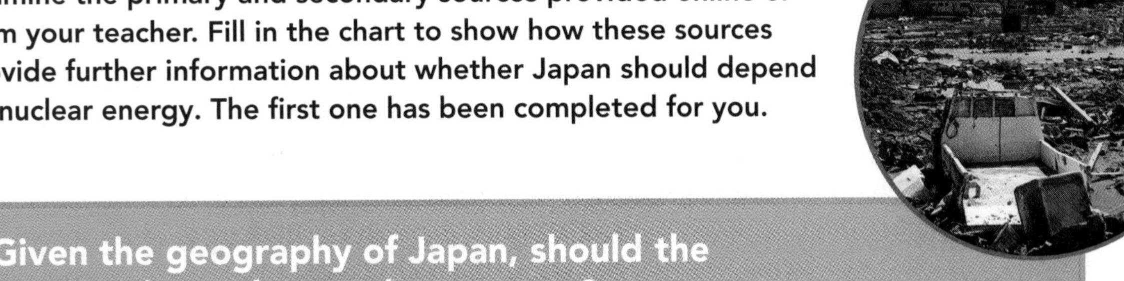

Examine the primary and secondary sources provided online or from your teacher. Fill in the chart to show how these sources provide further information about whether Japan should depend on nuclear energy. The first one has been completed for you.

Given the geography of Japan, should the country depend on nuclear energy?	
Source	**Yes or No? Why?**
Japanese Earthquake Renews Nuclear Energy Safety Concerns	NO, because Japan's history of earthquakes increases the risk of another nuclear accident.
The Calm Before the Wave	
Japan's Largest Nuclear Power Station Moves to Center of Reactor Restart Efforts	
Fukushima's Lessons in Climate Change	

INTERACTIVE

For extra help with Step 3, review the 21st Century Skills Tutorial: **Compare Viewpoints**.

4 Discuss

Now that you have researched issues surrounding energy and Japan's physical geography, you are ready to discuss with fellow experts the Guiding Question: Given the geography of Japan, should the country depend on nuclear energy? Follow the steps below, using the spaces provided to prepare for your discussion.

You will work with a partner in a small group of experts. Try to reach consensus, a situation in which everyone is in agreement, on the question. Can you do it?

1. **Prepare Your Arguments** You will be assigned a position on the question either YES or NO.

   My position: ____________________

   Work with your partner to review your Quest notes from the Quest Connections and Quest Sources.

   - If you were assigned YES, agree with your partner on what you think were the strongest arguments from Yurman and Lynas.
   - If you were assigned NO, agree on what you think were the strongest arguments from Grinberg and Folger.

2. **Present Your Position** Those assigned YES will present their arguments and evidence first. As you listen, ask clarifying questions to gain information and understanding.

What is a clarifying question?	
These types of questions do not judge the person talking. They are only for the listener to be clear on what he or she is hearing.	
Example: **Can you tell me more about that?**	**Example:** **You said [x]. Am I getting that right?**

INTERACTIVE

For extra help with Step 4, review the 21st Century Skills Tutorial: **Participate in a Discussion or Debate**.

While the opposite side speaks, use the space below to take notes on what those speakers say.

3. **Switch!** Now NO and YES will switch sides. If you argued YES before, now you will argue NO. Work with the same partner and use your notes. Add any arguments and evidence from the clues and sources. Those *now* arguing YES go first.

When both sides have finished, answer the following:

Before **I started this discussion with other experts, my opinion was**	***After*** **I completed this discussion with other experts, my opinion was**
_____Japan should depend on nuclear energy.	_____Japan should depend on nuclear energy.
_____Japan should not depend on nuclear energy.	_____Japan should not depend on nuclear energy.

4. **Point of View** Do you all agree on the answer to the Guiding Question?

- _____Yes
- _____No

On what points do you all agree?

Take Notes

Literacy Skills: Analyze Text Structure Use what you have read to complete the outline. Add details to explain the activities of early Chinese dynasties. Some entries are completed for you.

I. Prehistory and early history
- Small kingdoms formed near Huang River.

II. Zhou Dynasty

III. Qin Dynasty

IV. Han Dynasty

INTERACTIVE

For extra help, review the 21st Century Skills Tutorial: **Summarize**.

Practice Vocabulary

Sentence Revision **Revise each sentence so that the underlined vocabulary term is used correctly. Be sure not to change the vocabulary term. The first one is done for you.**

1. The Great Wall runs north and south along China's northern border.
   The Great Wall runs west and east along China's northern border.

2. The Shang claimed that the Mandate of Heaven gave them the right to rule.

3. According to Legalism, moral values are necessary to create social order.

4. The trade routes that crossed the Pacific Ocean are known as the Silk Road.

5. People from early Korean civilizations most likely belonged to clans, or groups of tribal states.

6. A system of government employees mainly selected for their political connections is known as civil service.

7. Acupuncture involves the use of surgery to cure sickness and stop pain.

Take Notes

Literacy Skills: Compare and Contrast Use what you have read to complete the Venn diagram. List the qualities specific to Confucianism and Daoism, as well as those shared by both. The first quality has been provided for you.

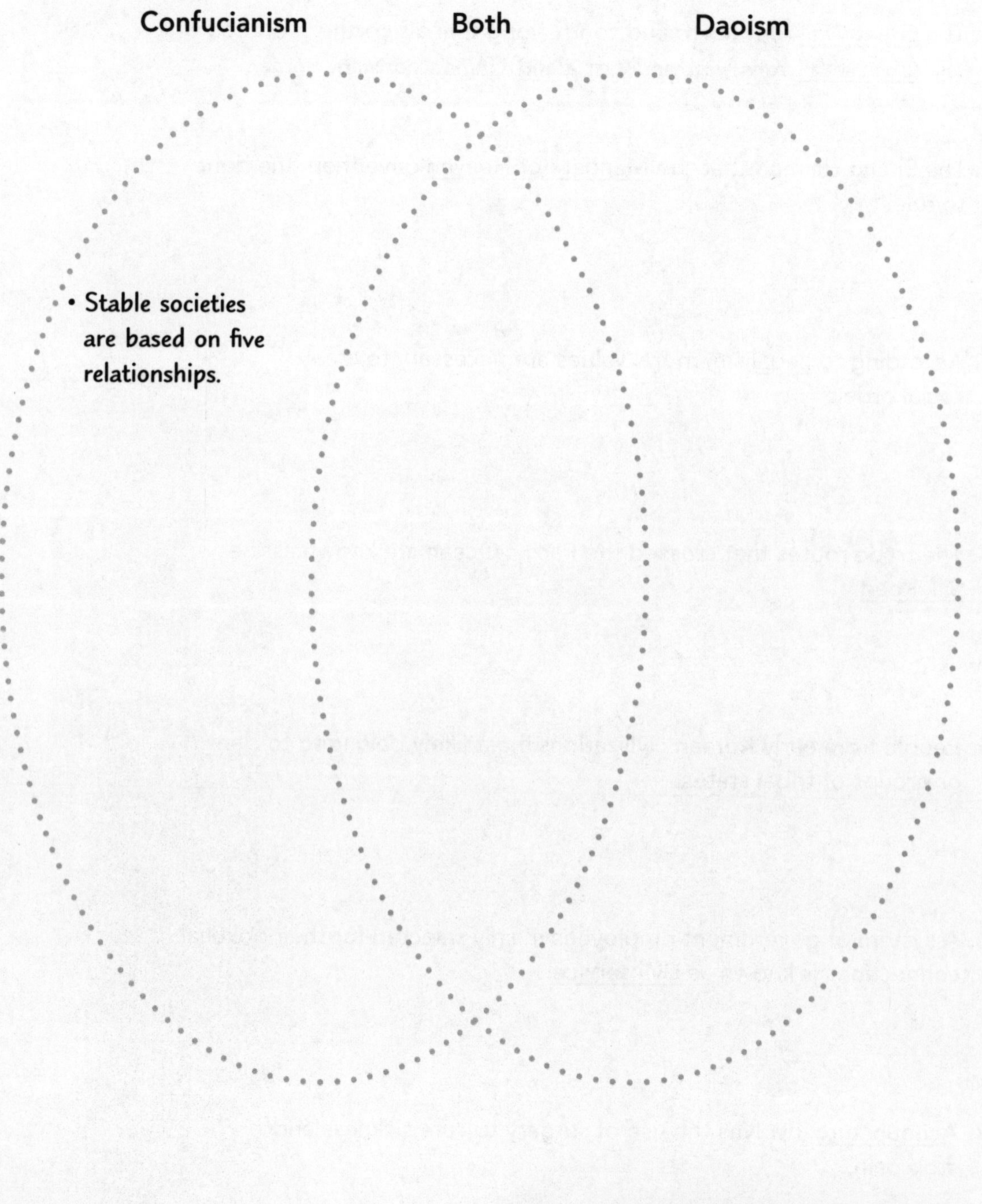

INTERACTIVE

For extra help, review the 21st Century Skills Tutorial: **Compare and Contrast**.

Practice Vocabulary

Sentence Builder **Finish the sentences below with a key term from this section. You may have to change the form of the words to complete the sentences.**

Word Bank

philosophy	Confucianism
filial piety	Daoism

1. The Chinese philosophy of following the natural way of the universe and emphasizing a simple, natural way of life is known as

   .

2. The Chinese belief system promoting the ideal of a stable, orderly society based on five types of human relationships is called

   .

3. Children who devote themselves to their parents are practicing

   .

4. An approach to knowledge, the world, and how to live one's life is known as a

   .

Take Notes

Literacy Skills: Sequence In each box, list an event from East Asia's history since the 1200s in the order it occurred, starting at the top. The first one has been completed for you.

Important events in East Asia's history since the 1200s

The Mongol conquest of China led to increased trade with other parts of Asia.

INTERACTIVE

For extra help, review the 21st Century Skills Tutorial: **Sequence**.

Practice Vocabulary

Words in Context **For each question below, write an answer that shows your understanding of the boldfaced key term.**

1. What is a major characteristic of Japan's traditional religion, **Shinto**?

2. What does **tribute** show about the relationship between two countries?

3. How is a **bureaucracy** run?

4. What was the **Meiji Restoration**?

Quick Activity Trade in China

With a partner or small group, discuss how trade has affected China over time. Based on what you have read so far and what you know about China today, think about the various ways trading with other nations has affected China in the past and present. Has China been helped or harmed by trade, or by the absence of trade? What kind of products did China produce in the past, and what does it produce now? How has trade changed the Chinese economy over time?

Products and issues that have affected Chinese trade	How the product or issue changed life in China

Team Challenge! Use the table to list products and issues that have affected Chinese trade, and explain how each product or issue changed life in China. Compare and contrast lists with a partner.

Take Notes

Literacy Skills: Determine Central Ideas Use what you have read to complete the concept maps about living in East Asia. Characteristics are words or phrases that relate to the concept in the center of the diagram. Non-characteristics are ideas that contrast with, or are opposed to, the concept. The first one has been started for you.

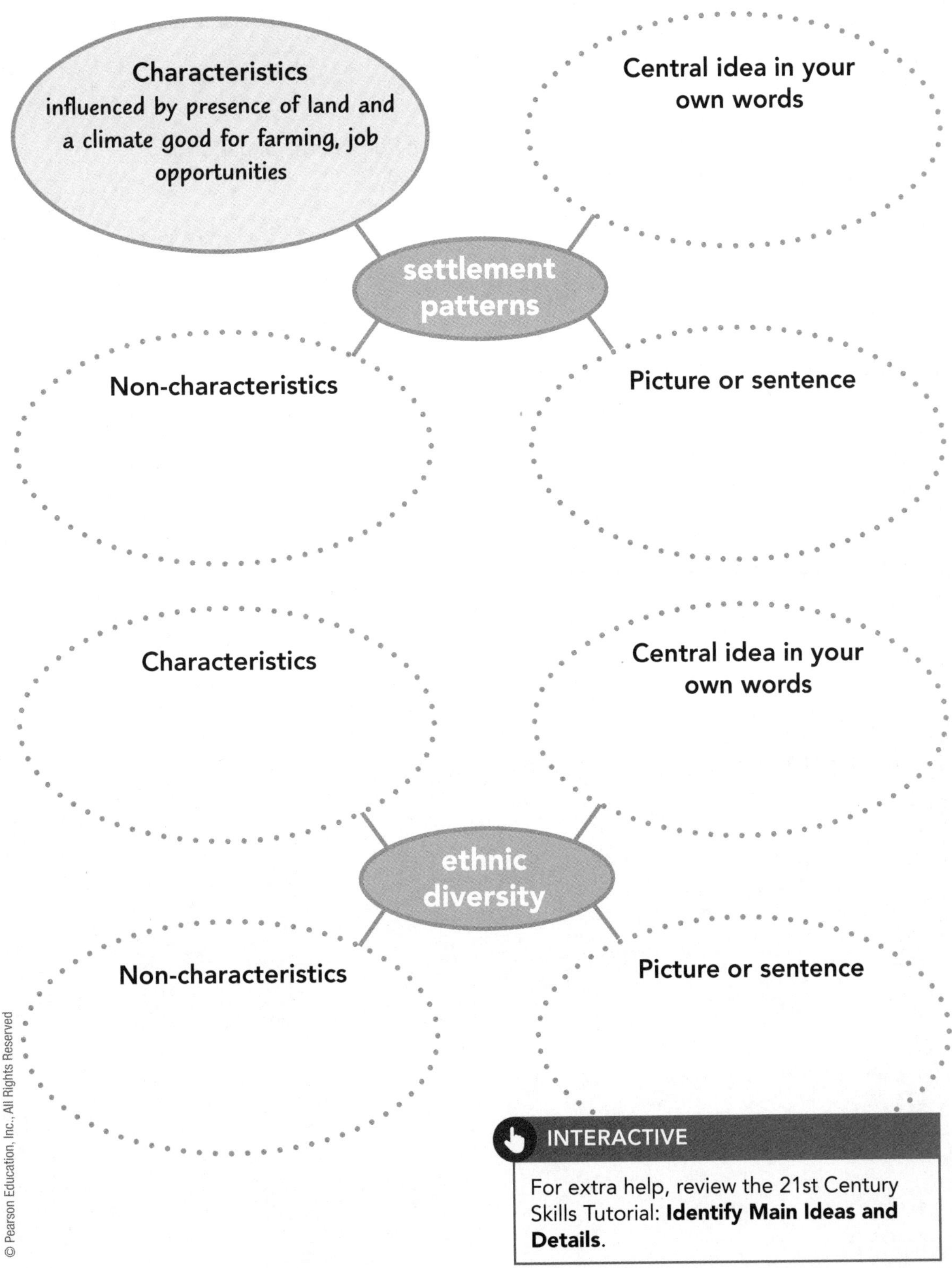

INTERACTIVE

For extra help, review the 21st Century Skills Tutorial: **Identify Main Ideas and Details.**

Practice Vocabulary

Sentence Builder **Finish the sentences below with a key term from this section. You may have to change the form of the words to complete the sentences.**

Word Bank

arable	indigenous
homogenous	steppe

1. The Japanese ethnic group makes up more than 98 percent of Japan's population, making the country relatively ethnically ______.

2. Taiwan has several ethnic groups that are ______.

3. The dry grassland in Mongolia is known as ______.

4. Only about 15 percent of China's land is ______.

Take Notes

Literacy Skills: Classify and Categorize Use what you have read to complete the chart. Under each heading, record the features that categorize the governments and economies of North Korea, South Korea, and Japan. The first one has been started for you.

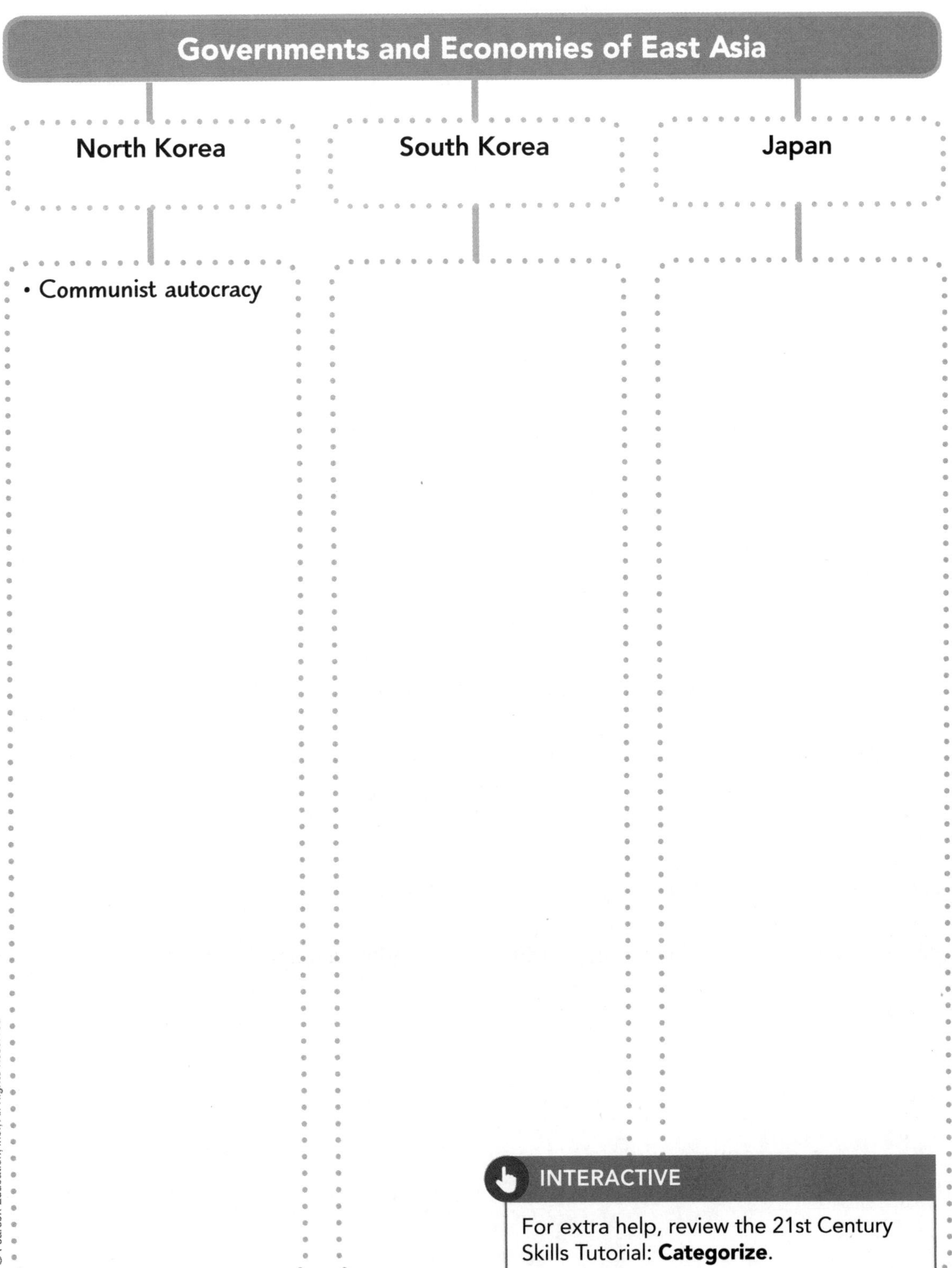

INTERACTIVE

For extra help, review the 21st Century Skills Tutorial: **Categorize**.

Practice Vocabulary

Use a Word Bank **Choose one word from the word bank to fill in each blank. When you have finished, you will have a short summary of important ideas from the section.**

Word Bank

veto
malnutrition
hydroelectric power
autocracy
sanctions

East Asian countries differ in their political philosophies. Like China, North Korea is a(n) __________, meaning the government wields unlimited power over citizens. Mongolia is more democratic. The Mongolian president has the power to __________ laws passed by the legislature. Countries in East Asia also differ in how they produce electricity. Mongolia uses a lot of coal for energy, while China relies greatly on both coal and __________. Economies differ across the region as well. China's shift away from a command economy led to rapid economic growth. North Korea's command economy has had poor results. In addition, North Korea's economy has been hindered by __________ that have limited its ability to trade with other nations. North Korea's struggles also include a low per capita GDP and deaths resulting from __________.

Take Notes

Literacy Skills: Use Evidence Use what you have read to complete the table. Gather evidence that supports the statement given. The first one has been started for you, but you should add more evidence to it.

Statement	Evidence
East Asia faces serious economic challenges.	• Low pay leads to poor economic growth because of low levels of consumption.
There are significant political issues in East Asia.	
East Asia has environmental problems.	

INTERACTIVE

For extra help, review the 21st Century Skills Tutorial: **Support Ideas with Evidence**.

Practice Vocabulary

Matching Logic Using your knowledge of the underlined vocabulary words, draw a line from each sentence in Column 1 to match it with the sentence in Column 2 to which it logically belongs.

Column 1	Column 2
1. A 400-mile-long reservoir now extends behind Three Gorges Dam.	Four tectonic plates meet in the region and are slowly moving together.
2. Underwater earthquakes can cause tsunamis that slam into the towns along the shores of Japan.	More than 1 million people had to be moved because their homes were flooded by the project.
3. Japan's problematic demography threatens economic growth.	The number of babies born each year is lower than the number of people retiring, so the number of workers is falling.

Quick Activity The Effects of Technology on East Asia

With a partner or small group, discuss how technology has affected these aspects of life in East Asia: economy, transportation, daily life, and environment. Which technologies have had the greatest impact? Are these technologies helpful or harmful?

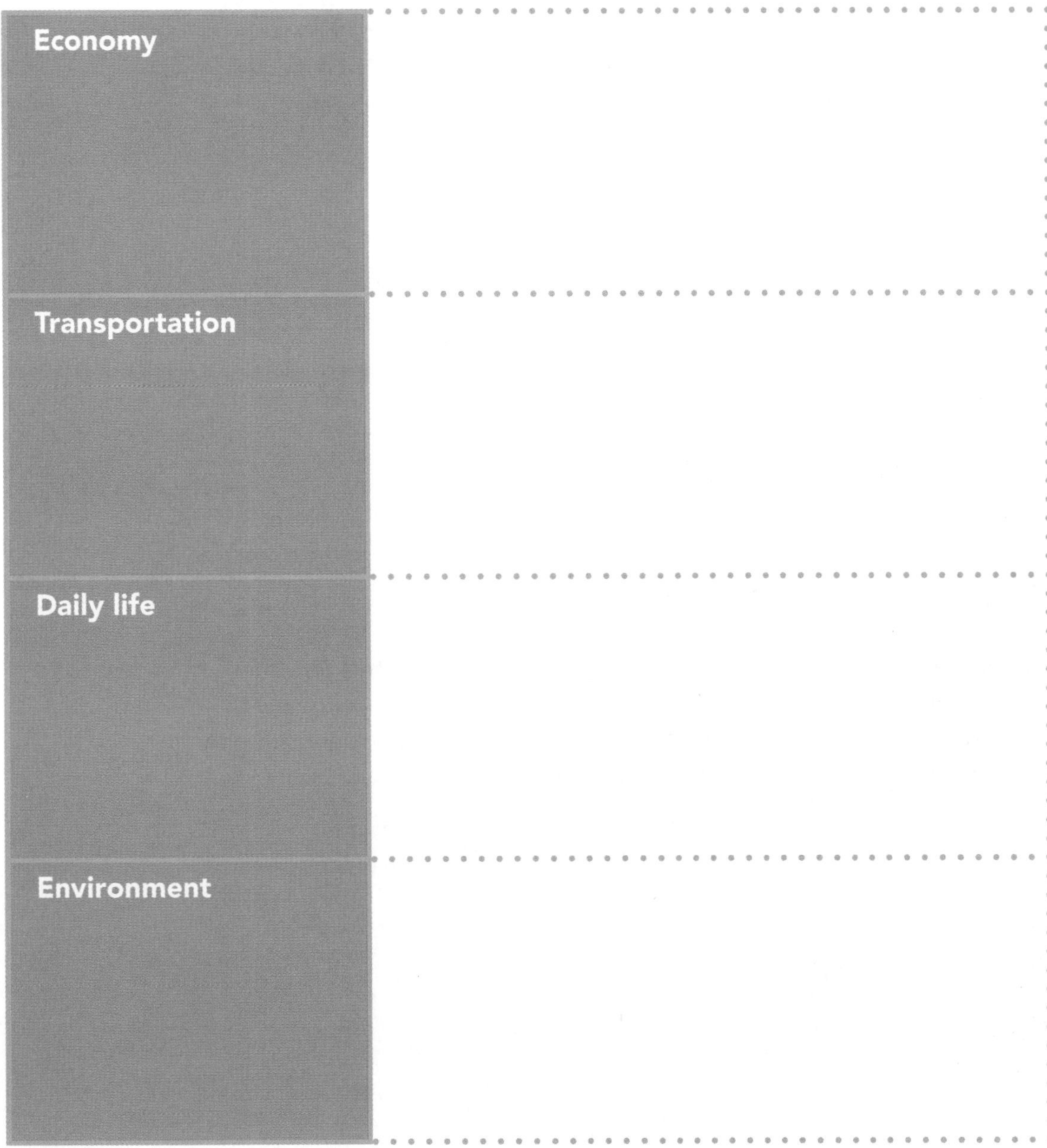

Team Challenge! With a partner, review your notes and choose the technological change that you agree was most harmful to life in East Asia. Then, choose the technological change you agree was most helpful. Create a poster to communicate your choices and hang it on the classroom wall. Walk around the room with your partner and look at your classmates' choices. How are their choices similar to or different from yours?

Writing Workshop Research Paper

As you read, build a response to this question: What are the costs and benefits of technology in East Asia? The prompts below will help walk you through the process of researching and writing an essay on this question.

Lesson 1 Writing Task: Generate Questions to Focus Research Based on what you read in Lesson 1, write two questions that you have about the costs and benefits of technology in East Asia. Think about how technology can solve problems of daily life and also create new problems.

Lesson 2 Writing Task: Find and Use Credible Sources Search for reliable sources that you can use for your research paper and cite at least three of them on a separate piece of paper.

Lesson 3 Writing Task: Support Thesis With Details Based on your research so far, write a thesis statement that summarizes your view of the costs and benefits of technology in East Asia. Then, list at least one detail that supports your thesis from each of your cited sources.

Lesson 4 Writing Task: Support Ideas With Evidence List evidence from your reading or research connecting the use of technology in East Asia to population growth and migration. Be sure to include examples of both the costs and benefits of technology.

Lesson 5 Writing Task: Choose an Organizing Strategy Decide how you will structure your research paper and create an outline for your structure here. Think about transition words that you may use to link your main ideas and paragraphs.

Lesson 6 Writing Task: Write an Introduction On a separate piece of paper, draft your introductory paragraph, including your thesis statement. Use this opportunity to revise or refine your thesis. Introduce each of your main points. Finish with a concluding sentence that helps transition to your first body paragraph.

Writing Task What are the costs and benefits of technology in East Asia? Answer the question in a research paper with at least three body paragraphs, plus introductory and concluding paragraphs. Be sure to support each point you make with the evidence you've collected, and cite your sources. You may wish to have someone review your draft to provide feedback before writing your final paper. You may use that feedback as you revise and finish your paper.

TOPIC 13

Southeast Asia Preview

Essential Question What role should people have in their government?

Before you begin this topic, think about the Essential Question by completing the following activities.

1. List some roles citizens have in government in your region, including at the local, state, and national levels. Circle the two methods of participation that you believe are most important for people to pursue.

Map Skills

Using the political and physical maps in the Regional Atlas in your text, label the outline map with the places listed. Then color in the countries and areas of water.

Brunei	Mekong River
Cambodia	Myanmar
East Timor	Philippines
Indian Ocean	Singapore
Indonesia	South China Sea
Irrawaddy River	Strait of Malacca
Malaysia	Thailand
Malay Peninsula	Vietnam

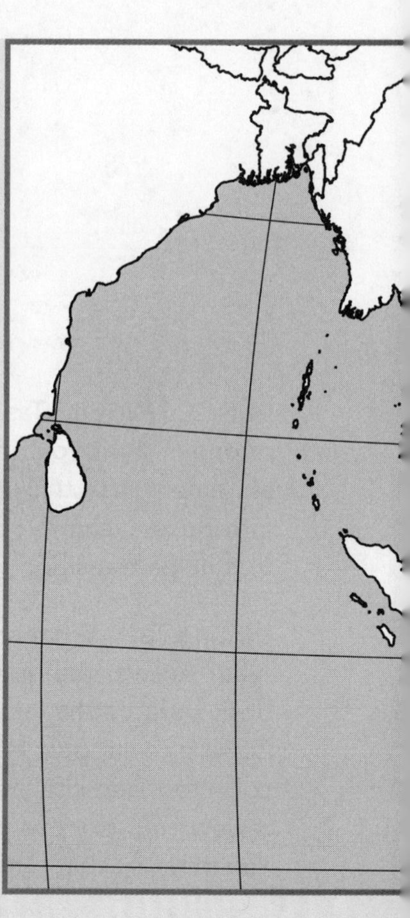

2. Preview the topic by skimming lesson titles, headings, and graphics. Then place a check mark next to the entries that you predict the text will say affect the roles that people in Southeast Asia have in their governments. After you finish reading the topic, circle the predictions that were correct.

__colonial rule	__Vietnam War	__Ring of Fire
__growing cities	__China	__skilled labor
__military governments	__education	__cultural diversity
__nationalism	__trade	

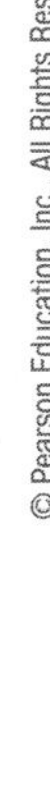

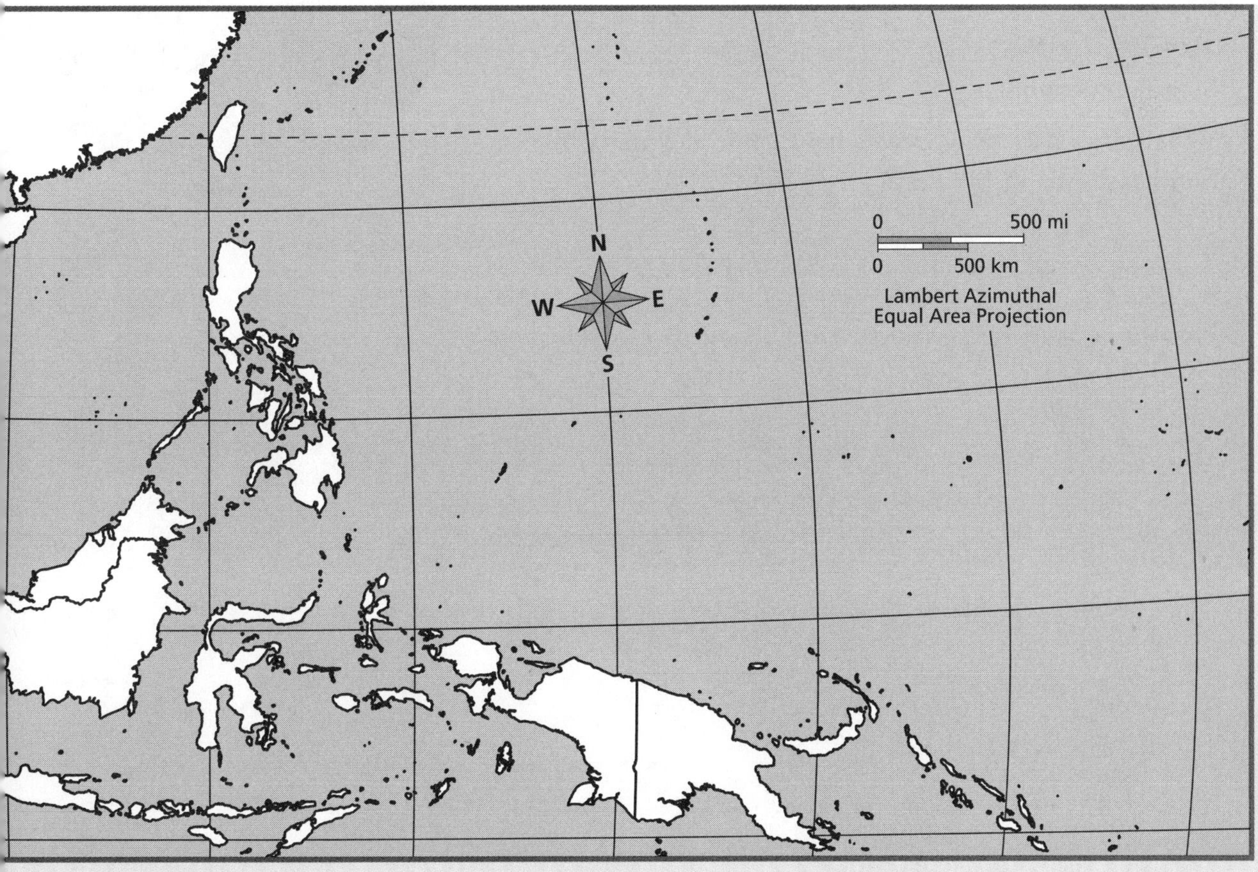

Studying Cultural Connections

On this Quest, you need to find out how the blending of cultures has shaped Southeast Asia. You will examine sources to find examples of how specific cultures have interacted with Southeast Asian countries and contributed to cultural diversity in the region. At the end of the Quest you will write an informative essay explaining your observations and drawing a conclusion on the Guiding Question.

1 Ask Questions

As you begin your Quest, keep in mind the Guiding Question: **How has contact with other cultures affected Southeast Asia?** and the Essential Question: **What role should people have in their government?**

What other questions do you need to ask in order to answer these questions? Consider the following aspects of life in Southeast Asia. Two questions are filled in for you. Add at least two questions for each category.

Theme History

Sample questions:

What other nations or people have controlled parts of Southeast Asia in the past?

How have Southeast Asian cultures changed since independence?

Theme Trade and Economics

Theme Ethnic Diversity

Theme Religious Diversity

Theme My Additional Questions

 INTERACTIVE

For extra help with Step 1, review the 21st Century Skills Tutorial **Ask Questions**.

2 Investigate

As you read about Southeast Asia, collect five connections from your text to help you answer the Guiding Question. Three connections are already chosen for you.

Connect to European Colonists

Lesson 1 How Did Westerners Affect the Region?

Here's a connection! Read about the arrival of European explorers in Southeast Asia and the conquest of much of the region by European powers. How did the arrival of Europeans impact native Southeast Asian cultures?

What aspects of European culture were brought to Southeast Asia?

Connect to Diversity

Lesson 3 Cultural Diversity in Southeast Asia

Here's another connection! Read about the presence of ethnic minorities in Southeast Asia and examine the infographic. How have religious and ethnic minorities changed the culture of their countries over time?

How have the cultures of ethnic minorities been changed by contact with other cultures? Use the Minangkabau of Indonesia as an example.

Connect to Modern Influences

Lesson 5 Political and Economic Challenges

What does this connection tell you about how other countries and cultures continue to influence Southeast Asia today?

Why might countries that are physically far from the region, like the United States, voice support for the countries of Southeast Asia in their disputes over territory with China?

It's Your Turn! Find two more connections. Fill in the title of your connections, then answer the questions. Connections may be images, primary sources, maps, or text.

Your Choice | Connect to

Location in text

What is the main idea of this connection?

What does it tell you about how contact with other cultures has affected Southeast Asia?

Your Choice | Connect to

Location in text

What is the main idea of this connection?

What does it tell you about how contact with other cultures has affected Southeast Asia?

③ Examine Primary Sources

Examine the primary and secondary sources provided online or from your teacher. Fill in the chart to show how the sources provide further information about cultural influence in Southeast Asia.

Source	Details About Cultural Influence
A Map of Trade Routes in the mid-1300s	Traders from India and China and elsewhere came to Southeast Asia, exchanging goods, ideas, and beliefs throughout all three regions.
Buddhism in Southeast Asia	
India-Southeast Asian Relations: An Overview	
Vietnam's Declaration of Independence	
Myanmar's Complex Transformation: Prospects and Challenges	

INTERACTIVE

For extra help with Step 3, review the 21st Century Skills Tutorials: **Analyze Primary and Secondary Sources** and **Read Charts, Graphs, and Tables**.

4 Write Your Informative Essay

Now it's time to put together all of the information you have gathered and use it to write your essay.

1. **Prepare to Write** You have collected connections and explored primary and secondary sources that describe the influences that other cultures have had on Southeast Asia. Look through your notes and decide which observations you want to include in your essay and what conclusions you have come to about the subject. Record them here. Then write a thesis statement that expresses your view on the subject.

Observations and Conclusions

Thesis Statement

2. **Write a Draft** Using evidence from the connections you found and the sources you explored, write a draft of your essay. Your essay should state your answer to the Guiding Question, **How has contact with other cultures affected Southeast Asia?** Be sure to include an introductory paragraph that builds on your thesis statement and a concluding paragraph that summarizes your ideas.

3. **Share with a Partner** Exchange your draft with a partner. Tell your partner what you like about his or her draft and suggest any improvements.

4. **Finalize Your Essay** Revise your essay. Be sure to incorporate your partner's suggestions and correct any grammatical or spelling errors. Your final essay should be typed or neatly handwritten.

5. **Reflect on the Quest** Think about your experience completing this topic's Quest. What did you learn about cultural influences in Southeast Asia? What questions do you still have about cultural diversity in this region? How will you answer them?

Reflections

INTERACTIVE

For extra help with Step 4, review the 21st Century Skills Tutorial: **Write an Essay**.

Take Notes

Literacy Skills: Sequence **Use what you have read to complete the timeline. For each time period, write at least one key event from Southeast Asia's history and connect it to its appropriate place on the timeline. The first one has been completed for you. Connect each event to the appropriate place on the timeline.**

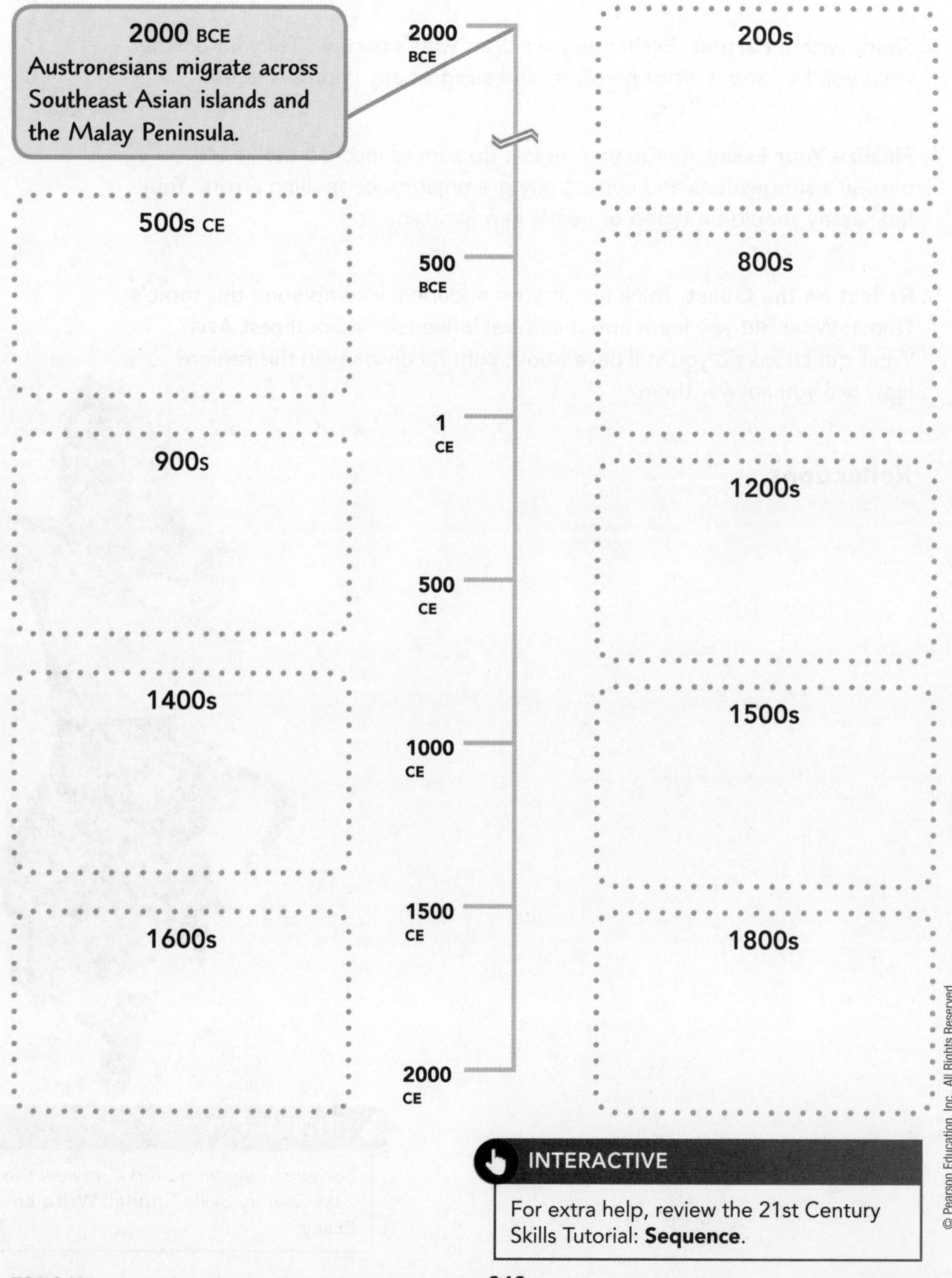

INTERACTIVE

For extra help, review the 21st Century Skills Tutorial: **Sequence**.

Practice Vocabulary

Matching Logic **Using your knowledge of the underlined vocabulary terms, draw a line from each sentence in Column 1 to match it with the sentence in Column 2 to which it logically belongs.**

Column 1	Column 2
1. During the 1800s, Indochina came under French control.	Many Chinese people have migrated to Southeast Asian countries, bringing their language and cultural identity with them.
2. The Khmer created a powerful empire by conquering surrounding peoples.	The Southeast Asian peninsula includes the countries of Cambodia, Laos, and Vietnam.
3. Southeast Asia is home to many ethnic groups.	These types of monarchies are headed by a sultan.
4. In the 1400s, sultanates spread across Southeast Asia.	For several centuries, the British controlled many different territories on several continents.

Take Notes

Literacy Skills: Analyze Text Structure **Use what you have read to complete the outline of the lesson's text. As you create your outline, pay attention to headings, subheadings, and key terms that you can use to organize the information. The first section has been started for you.**

I. World War II and Independence
   A. World War II
      1. Japan invaded and occupied most of Southeast Asia.
      2. Resistance groups in Southeast Asian countries fought against Japan.
   B. Independence

INTERACTIVE

For extra help, view the 21st Century Skills Tutorial: **Take Effective Notes**.

Practice Vocabulary

Vocabulary Quiz Show **Some quiz shows ask a question and expect the contestant to give the answer. In other shows, the contestant is given an answer and must supply the question. If the blank is in the Question column, write the question that would result in the answer in the Answer column. If the question is supplied, write the answer.**

Question	**Answer**
1.	1. Vietnam War
2. What term describes countries that have political and economic systems in which the state owns all property and the government makes all economic decisions?	2.
3.	3. Cold War
4. What do you call the sudden seizure of a government that is usually accomplished by force?	4.
5.	5. containment

Quick Activity Create a Timeline

Using your text as a reference, determine the date or date range of the events in the table below. Then, number them in the order in which they occurred from oldest to most recent.

Event	Year(s)	Order
East Timor wins independence from Indonesia.		
Paris Peace Accords are signed, formally ending Vietnam War.		
Vietnam declares independence from France.		
Military governments come to power in Myanmar and Thailand.		
Vietnam War begins.		
Hun Sen becomes president of Cambodia.		
Khmer Rouge gains power in Cambodia and kills a quarter of the country's people.		
United States grants independence to Philippines.		

Team Challenge! Form groups of eight. Have each group member choose a number between one and eight. Write the event corresponding to your number on a sticky note or note card. Create a blank timeline of Southeast Asia, 1940 to present on the board. Place your event on the timeline where it belongs to create a timeline about Southeast Asia after 1940.

Take Notes

Literacy Skills: Summarize Use what you have read to complete the table. In each column, write details about a specific aspect of diversity in Southeast Asia. The first detail has been added for you. Then write a summary statement about cultural diversity in Southeast Asia.

Ethnic Diversity	Religious Diversity	Cultural Blending
• Burmese, Thai, and Lao ethnic groups migrated to Southeast Asia from the north.		

Summary

INTERACTIVE

For extra help, review the 21st Century Skills Tutorial: **Summarize**.

Practice Vocabulary

Words in Context For each question below, write an answer that shows your understanding of the boldfaced key term.

1. Why is the Mekong River **delta** in Vietnam an area of high population density?

2. How have **indigenous** Southeast Asian ethnic groups been affected by other cultures?

3. How does the **terrain** affect where people live in Southeast Asia?

Take Notes

Literacy Skills: Classify and Categorize Use what you have read to complete the chart. In each space write details about Southeast Asia related to the category. The first one has been completed for you.

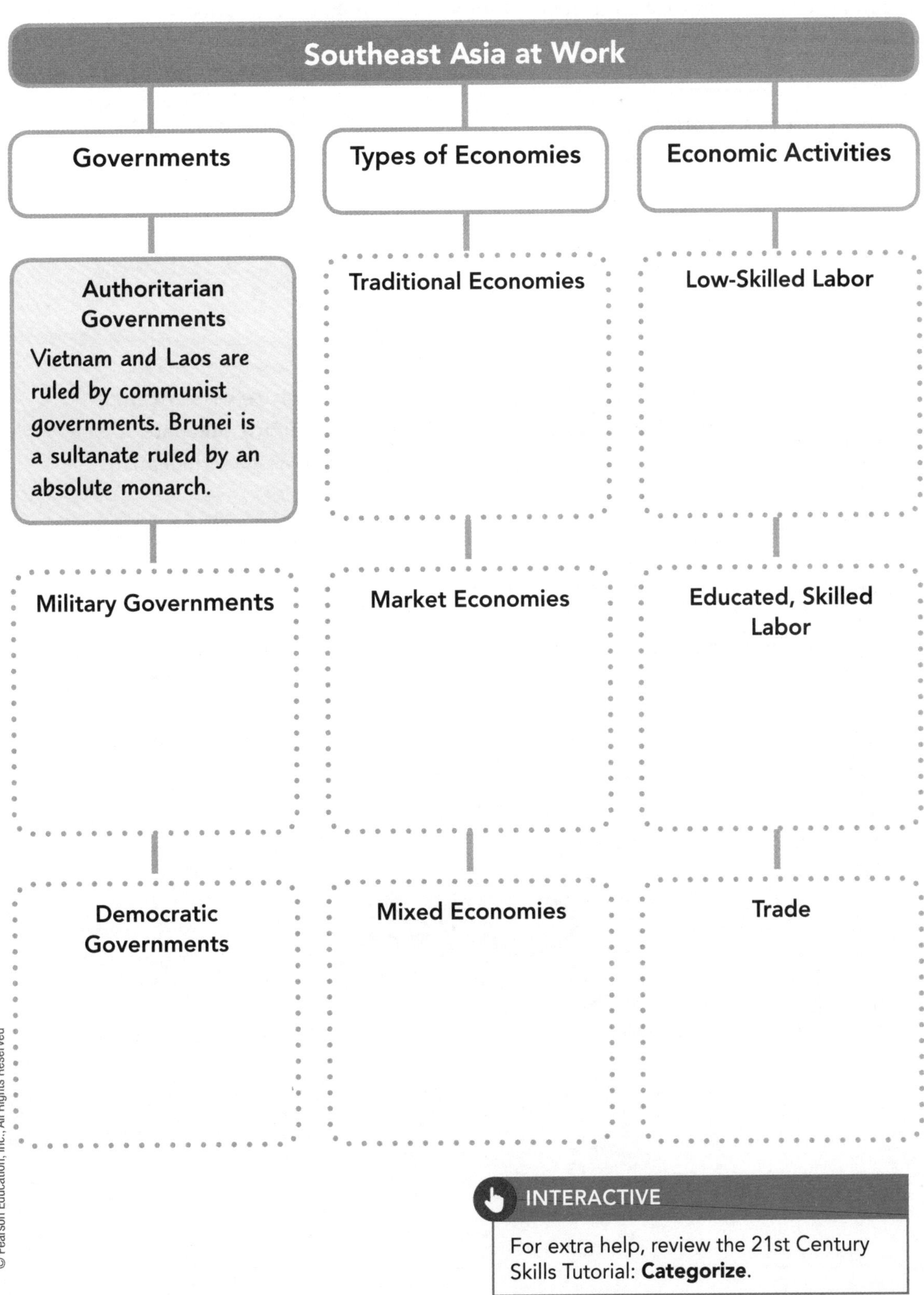

INTERACTIVE

For extra help, review the 21st Century Skills Tutorial: **Categorize**.

Practice Vocabulary

Word Map Study the word map for the term *absolute monarchy.* Characteristics are words or phrases that relate to the word in the center of the word map. Non-characteristics are words and phrases not associated with the word. Use the blank word map to explore the meaning of the term *exchange rate.* Then make a word map of your own for the word *semiconductor.*

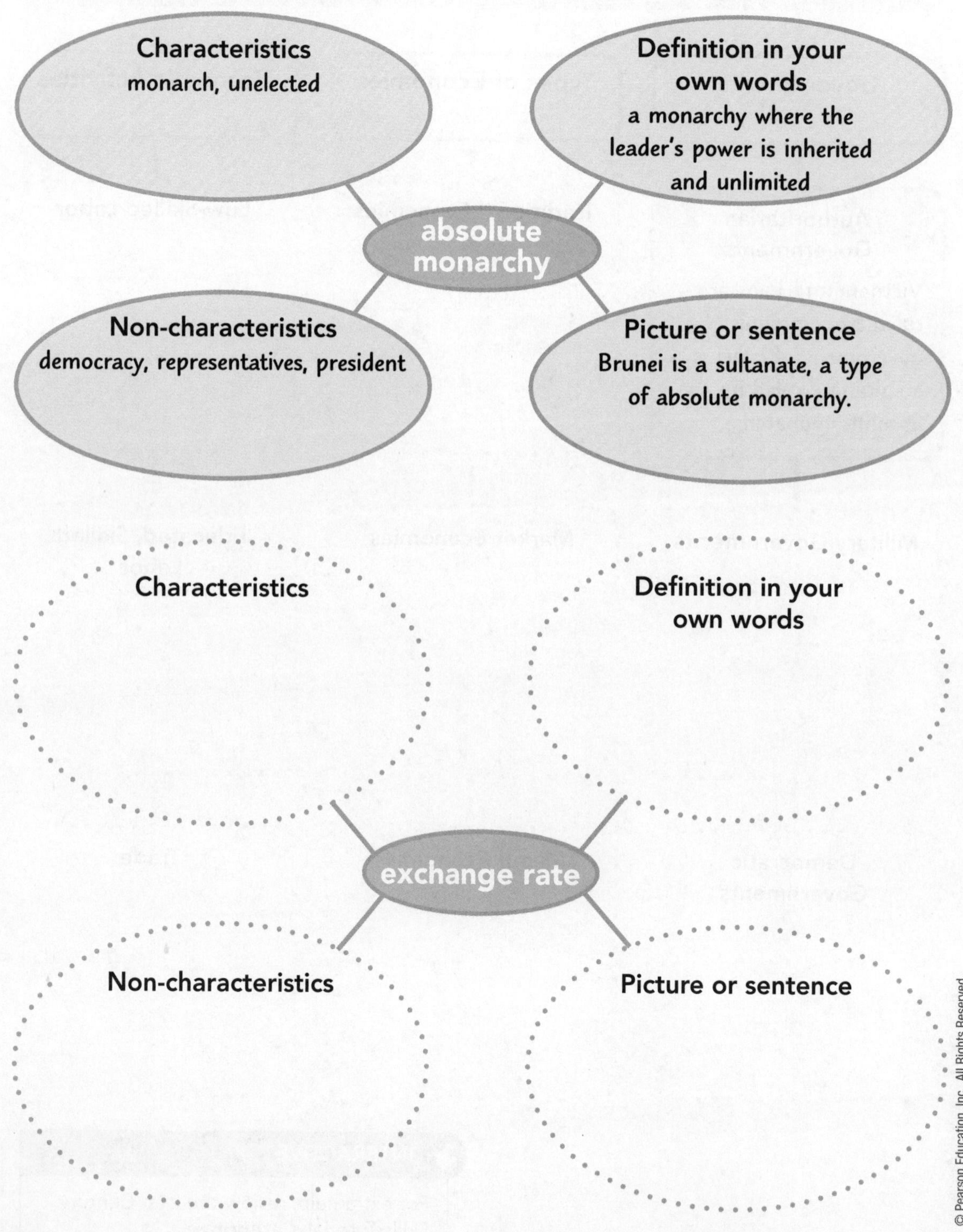

Quick Activity Roles in Government

With a partner, examine the photo of a political rally in Thailand. Think about the Essential Question: What role should citizens have in their government? How does this photo illustrate the role of citizens in the government of Thailand?

Team Challenge! With a partner, choose another Southeast Asian country. Based on what you have learned, answer the Essential Question about the country you selected. Take notes in the space below, and prepare to share your thoughts with the class.

Take Notes

Literacy Skills: Use Evidence Use what you have read to complete the chart. List evidence from the text about the types of challenges facing Southeast Asia. The first one has been started for you. Then use the evidence you have gathered to draw a conclusion about one or more of the challenges facing the region.

Environmental Challenges	Political and Economic Challenges
• Climate change that could raise global sea levels threatens densely populated low-lying areas.	

Conclusion

INTERACTIVE

For extra help, review the 21st Century Skills Tutorial: **Identify Evidence**.

Practice Vocabulary

Sentence Builder **Finish each sentence below with a key term from this section. You may have to change the form of the terms to complete the sentences.**

Word Bank

incentive
trade barrier
typhoon

1. A tax that makes it more expensive to import goods is an example of a(n)

2. Something of value that encourages people to behave a certain way is a(n)

3. A destructive tropical cyclone similar to a hurricane is a(n)

Writing Workshop Explanatory Essay

As you read, build a response to this question in the context of Southeast Asia: How have citizens' roles in the government changed over time? At the end of the topic you will write an explanatory essay. The prompts below will help walk you through the process.

Lesson 1 Writing Task: Narrow Your Topic It's impossible to explain all the changes in five paragraphs! So, narrow the topic before writing. Consider focusing on a single country or comparing and contrasting two countries. Record your focus.

Lesson 2 Writing Task: Develop a Clear Thesis Write a sentence expressing your main conclusion about how the role of citizens in Southeast Asian governments has changed over time. This will be the thesis statement for your essay.

Lesson 3 Writing Task: Support Thesis with Details Add details from each of the lessons you have read so far that support your thesis. If you have trouble supporting your thesis, you may need to revise it.

Lesson 4 Writing Task: Draft Your Essay Use the following table to organize your essay. Start with an introduction that includes your thesis, followed by key points that support that thesis. End with a conclusion that ties together the main ideas of your essay. Draft your essay on a separate piece of paper.

Introduction	
Key Point 1	
Key Point 2	
Key Point 3	
Conclusion	

Lesson 5 Writing Task: Revise Revise your draft. Look for ways to improve your essay. Make sure that your thesis is well supported and that your writing is clear and accurate. Be sure to check spelling, grammar, and punctuation.

Writing Task Finalize your explanatory essay that addresses the question: **How have citizens' roles in Southeast Asian governments changed over time?**

TOPIC 14

Australia and the Pacific Preview

Essential Question How much does geography affect people's lives?

Before you begin this topic, think about the Essential Question by completing the following activities.

1. List five ways that geography affects your everyday life. Circle the one that you think has the most significant impact.

Map Skills

Using the political and physical maps in the Regional Atlas in your text, label the outline map with the places listed. Add symbols to indicate where the capital cities are located.

Pacific Ocean
Indian Ocean
Papua New Guinea
French Polynesia
Solomon Islands
Port Moresby
Melanasia
Polynesia
Simpson Desert
Tasmania
Southern Ocean
Australia
New Zealand
Fiji
Canberra
Wellington
Micronesia
Great Dividing Range
Great Sandy Desert

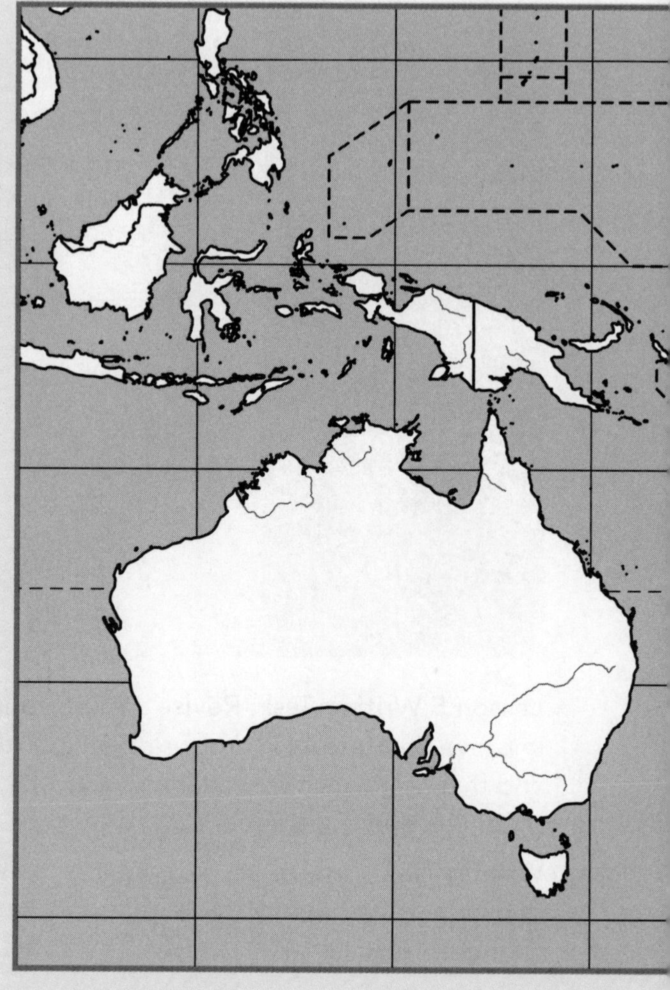

2. Preview the topic by skimming lesson titles, headings, and graphics. Then place a check mark next to the entries that you predict will be ways the text says geography affects people living in Australia and the Pacific today. After you finish reading, circle the predictions that were correct.

__colonialism
__Aboriginal culture
__research in Antarctica
__tourism
__immigration
__climate change
__Polynesian navigation
__coral bleaching
__exploration

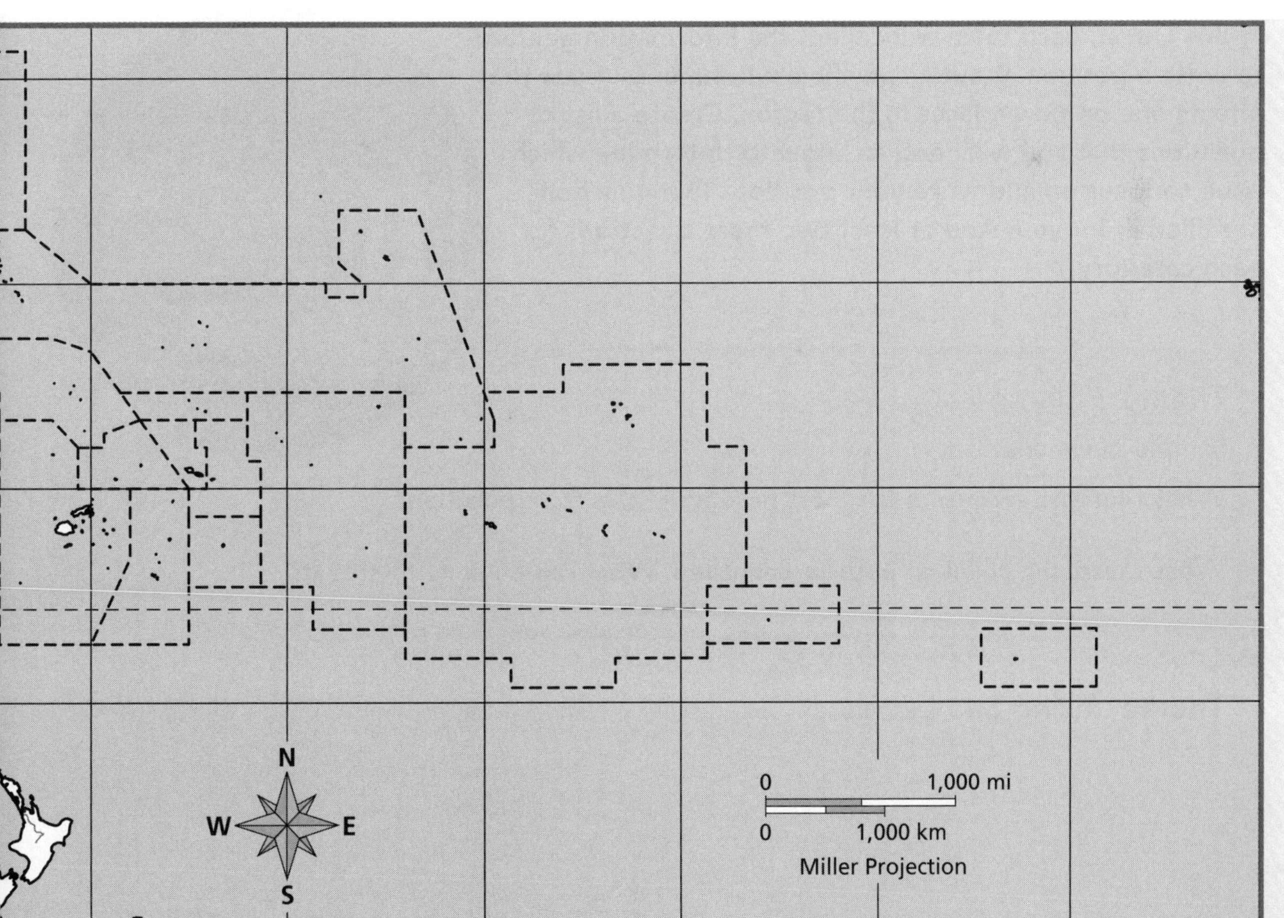

Write a Petition to Encourage Environmental Action

On this Quest, you are one of a group of citizens from Australia and the Pacific islands who are working to address an environmental issue in the region. You will gather information about an environmental issue by examining sources in your text and by conducting your own research. At the end of the Quest, you will write a petition to officials to convince them to take action to help prevent further environmental damage.

1 Ask Questions

As you begin your Quest, keep in mind the Essential Question: **How much does geography affect people's lives?**

In this Quest, each team will collect the information needed to write a petition about a specific environmental issue that affects one or more places in the region. Create a list of questions that you will need to know to determine which issue to focus on and write your petition. Two questions are filled in for you. Add at least two more questions for each category.

Theme Pollution

Sample questions:

What countries experience the most negative effects from pollution?

What causes the pollution in these countries? What can be done to stop it?

Theme Rising Sea Levels

Theme Drought

Theme Coral Bleaching

Theme Overfishing

Theme My Additional Questions

 INTERACTIVE

For extra help with Step 1, review the 21st Century Skills Tutorial: **Ask Questions**.

2 Investigate

As you read about Australia and the Pacific, collect five connections from your text to help you answer the Essential Question. Three connections are already chosen for you.

Connect to Early Cultures

Lesson 1 Early Cultures of Melanesia and Micronesia

Here's a connection! Read about Australia's first people and the early cultures of Melanesia and Micronesia. Look at the settlement map in your text. What solutions did early people of the region find to the problem of populations outgrowing available resources?

Did the solution work on a long-term basis?

Connect to Resources

Lesson 4 Economies of Australia and New Zealand

Here's another connection! Read about the importance of natural resources such as coal to the economy of Australia. Briefly research the environmental impact and economic benefits of coal mining. What are the costs and benefits of coal mining in Australia?

In what circumstances do environmental concerns outweigh economic benefits, and vice versa?

Connect to Climate Change and Antarctica

Lesson 6 Exploration and Research in Antarctica

What does this connection tell you about how climate change threatens the unique environments of Antarctica?

What solution was implemented for the problem of a hole in the ozone layer? Was it effective?

It's Your Turn! **Find two more connections. Fill in the title of your connections, then answer the questions. Connections may be images, primary sources, maps, or text.**

Your Choice | Connect to

Location in text

What is the main idea of this connection?

What does it tell you about an environmental issue in Australia and the Pacific?

Your Choice | Connect to

Location in text

What is the main idea of this connection?

What does it tell you about an environmental issue in Australia and the Pacific?

3 Conduct Research

Form teams based on your teacher's instructions. Meet to decide which issue you will choose to focus on. Then split up the research jobs by team members, filling out the chart below as a group.

Be sure to find valid, recent sources and take good notes so you can properly cite your sources. Record key information about your theme and brainstorm ways to incorporate it into your petition.

Environmental issue:

Areas to Research	Findings	Sources
Countries affected		
Audience for petition		
Data illustrating the issue		
Causes of issue		
Possible solutions		

4 Write Your Petition

Now it's time to put together all of the information your team has gathered and write your petition.

1. **Prepare to Write** Now that you have gathered information about the problem, the team should consider the advantages and disadvantages of each possible solution. Write a thesis sentence that briefly identifies the environmental issue, explains why it is a problem, and summarizes your call to action.

2. **Create an Outline** As a team, create an outline for your petition. Plan how you will describe the environmental issue, the economic and cultural significance of the issue, which data you will include and in what format to incorporate (maps, charts, graphs, and infographics are especially helpful), and the solution you are suggesting. Remember, your goal is to convince your audience to act!

Audience

Problem

Causes

Support from Research

Solution / Call to Action

3. **Write a Draft** Write a draft of the petition. You may choose to have each team member write about the part of the issue they researched, or have one person write the draft based on a summary of the other team members' notes. Be sure to stay focused on creating a powerful call to action to address the environmental problem. Remember to be respectful to your audience. If possible, present some of your data in a visual way.

4. **Review and Revise** Compile your group's draft. Work together to refine your introduction so that it is as effective as possible. Then work on a conclusion that sums up the need for action and the potential benefits of your proposal. Correct any grammatical or spelling errors. Then, create a final, revised version of your petition.

5. **Share With Others** Make a copy of the petition for each group member. Over the course of a week, each individual will present the petition to classmates, family, or other closely known people, clarifying that it is for a school project. Ask whether they would be willing to sign it if they were a resident of the region. Keep a record of how many say yes and how many say no, and note the reasons why.

6. **Reflect** After you have completed your petition and shared it with others, reflect on what you have learned. Discuss ways that you could evaluate the effectiveness of your petition in the real world. Discuss how the group worked together and what you could have done more effectively.

Reflection

INTERACTIVE

For extra help, review the 21st Century Skills Tutorials: **Organize Your Ideas, Support Ideas With Evidence**, and **Publish Your Work**.

Take Notes

Literacy Skills: Summarize Use what you have read to complete the chart. In each space, write details about the settlement of and early cultures in that part of the region. Then use the details you have gathered to write a brief summary of what you have learned. The first entry has been started for you.

Australia's First Peoples	Early Cultures of Melanesia and Micronesia	Polynesia's Great Navigators
• People migrated to Australia 60,000 years ago by crossing land bridges when ocean levels were lower		

Summary

INTERACTIVE

For extra help, review the 21st Century Skills Tutorial: **Summarize**.

Practice Vocabulary

Sentence Builder **Finish the sentences below with a vocabulary term from this section. You may have to change the form of the words to complete the sentences.**

Word Bank

Aborigine	marae
Maori	Polynesian

1. The original inhabitants of New Zealand and the Cook Islands are the

   ______________________.

2. Huge canoes powered by oars and sails that could travel hundreds of miles across the open ocean were built by the

   ______________________.

3. A rich oral tradition of songs and chants preserves the history, legends, religious beliefs, and knowledge of the Australian

   ______________________.

4. An enclosed area of land that functions as the center of Maori culture is a

   ______________________.

Quick Activity Take a Journey!

With a partner, examine this photo of a traditional-style boat similar to the boats used by the people who settled the Pacific Islands.

Imagine that you are living in the Pacific Islands and will be traveling on a traditional boat similar to the one shown, to a new home on an island you've never seen. The journey could take several weeks, and the boat does not have a lot of room. What will you take with you? What will you leave behind? With your partner, brainstorm about which items you would take with you and what things you would not need. Be prepared to explain your answers in a class discussion!

Items for Journey

Team Challenge! Gather in groups and assess what skills or practical knowledge you have that would help your group survive traveling a long distance across the ocean together. For example, how many of you know how to swim, fish, and paddle? What skills and practical knowledge are missing from your group that would be useful to learn before embarking on such a journey? Who is interested in learning each of those skills?

Take Notes

Literacy Skills: Sequence Use what you have read to complete the chart. In each space write a significant event and the date when the event occurred. The first entry has been completed for you.

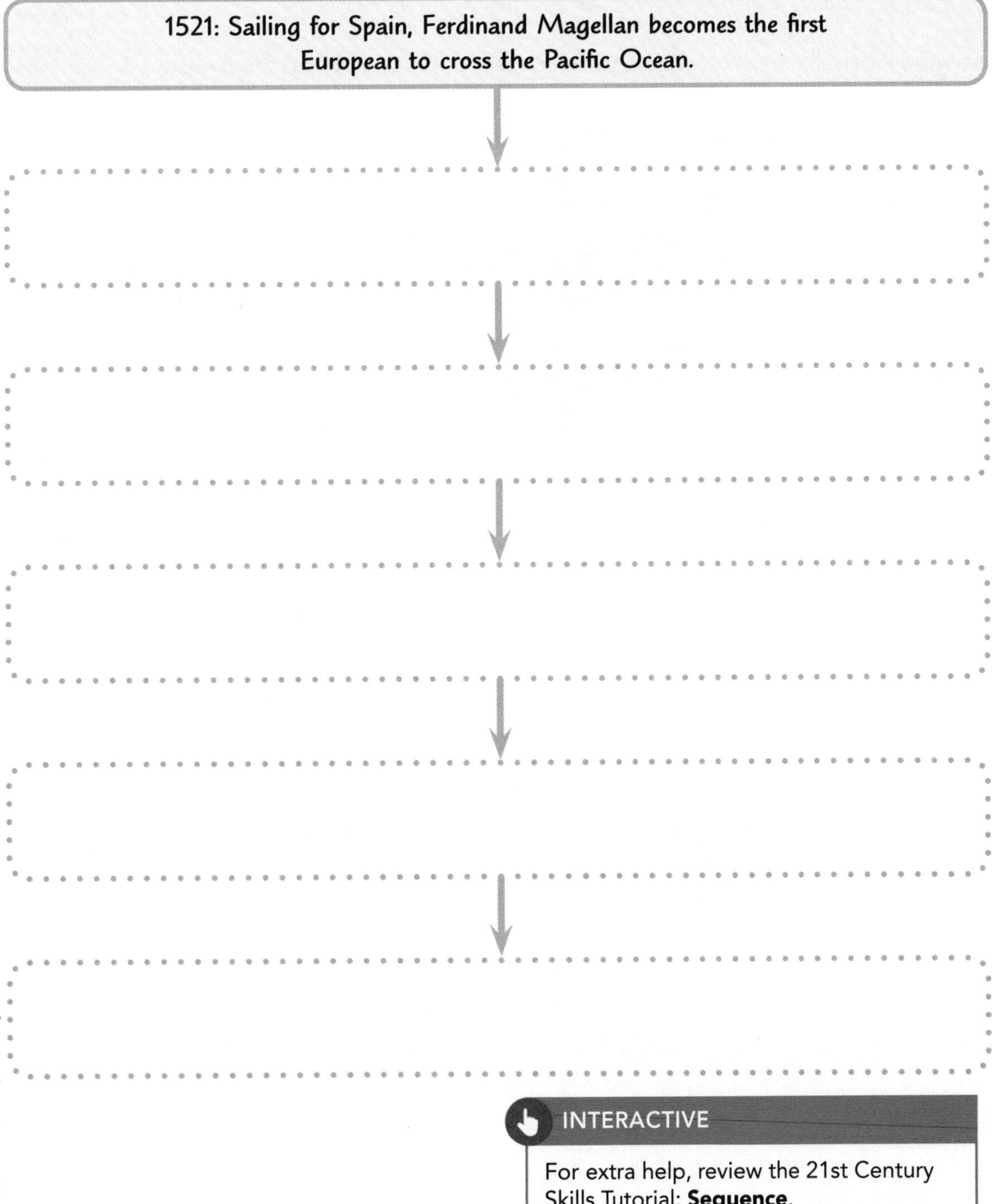

INTERACTIVE

For extra help, review the 21st Century Skills Tutorial: **Sequence**.

Practice Vocabulary

Use a Word Bank **Choose a word from the word bank to fill in each blank. When you have finished, you will have a short summary of important ideas from the lesson.**

Word Bank

assimilation dependency dominion penal colony

British influence in Australia and the Pacific began when James Cook claimed Australia and New Zealand for Britain in 1770. In 1788, the British sent a fleet with nearly 1,000 settlers. Many settlers were convicts sent to form a ______________. The settlers' arrival disrupted the lives of the Aborigines and Maori who had lived in Australia and New Zealand for thousands of years. In Australia, the British forced Aborigines off their land and forced the ______________ of Aboriginal children to British culture. Aboriginal rights were ignored, and Aborigines did not receive the same quality of services as Europeans. In 1901, Australia became a ______________ of Britain, and in the 1940s became fully independent. It was an era of independence for many other colonized areas, too. However, some colonies did not become completely independent. American Samoa, for example, is a self-governing territory, or ______________, of the United States.

Take Notes

Literacy Skills: Draw Conclusions Use what you have read to complete the chart. In each column write details about settlement patterns and cultural characteristics in the area specified. The first detail has been added for you. Then use the information you have gathered to draw a conclusion about population patterns and cultural characteristics in Australia and the Pacific.

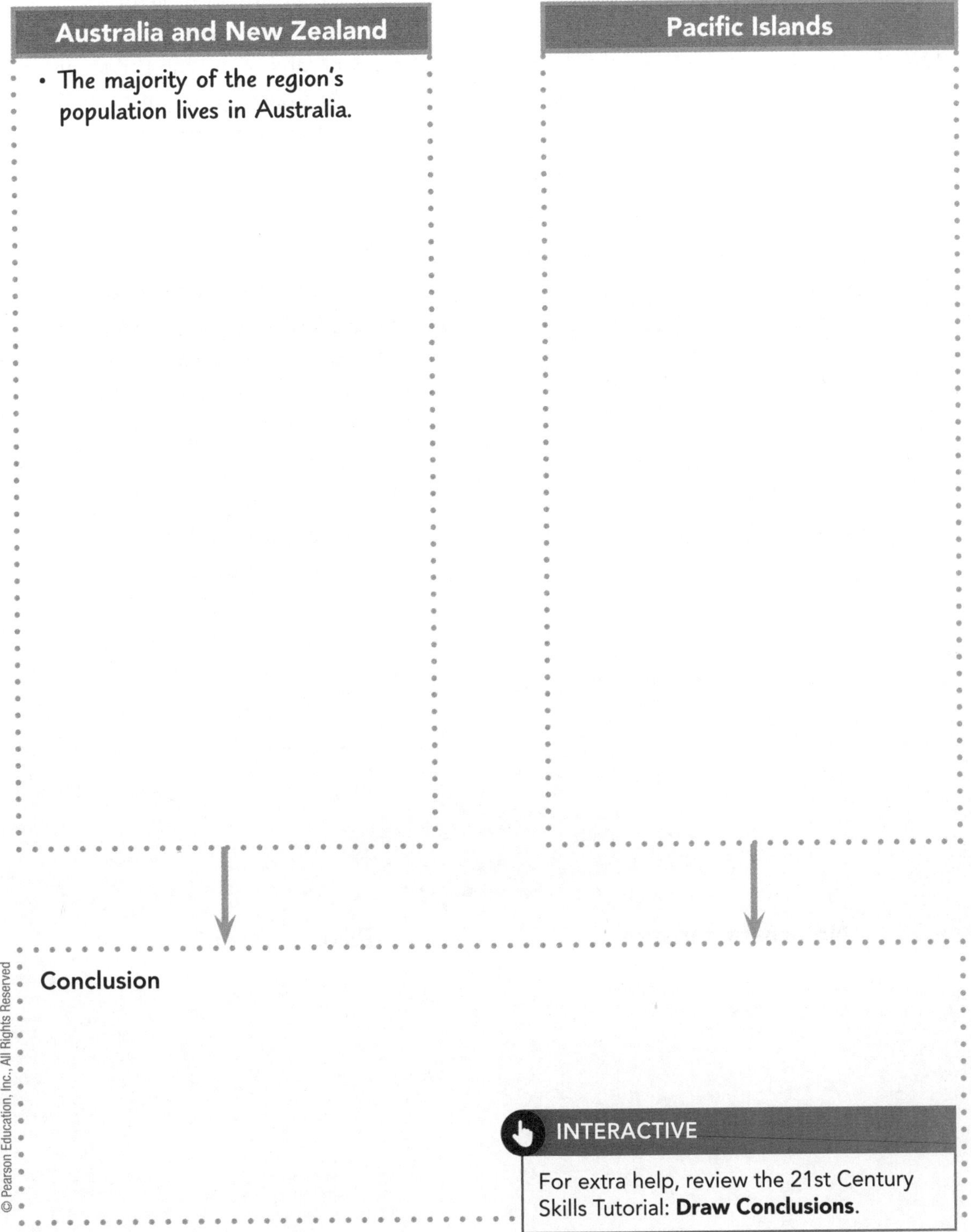

INTERACTIVE

For extra help, review the 21st Century Skills Tutorial: **Draw Conclusions**.

Practice Vocabulary

Word Map Study the word map for the word *station*. Characteristics are words or phrases that relate to the word in the center of the word map. Non-characteristics are words and phrases not associated with the word. Use the blank word map to explore the meaning of the term *pidgin language*.

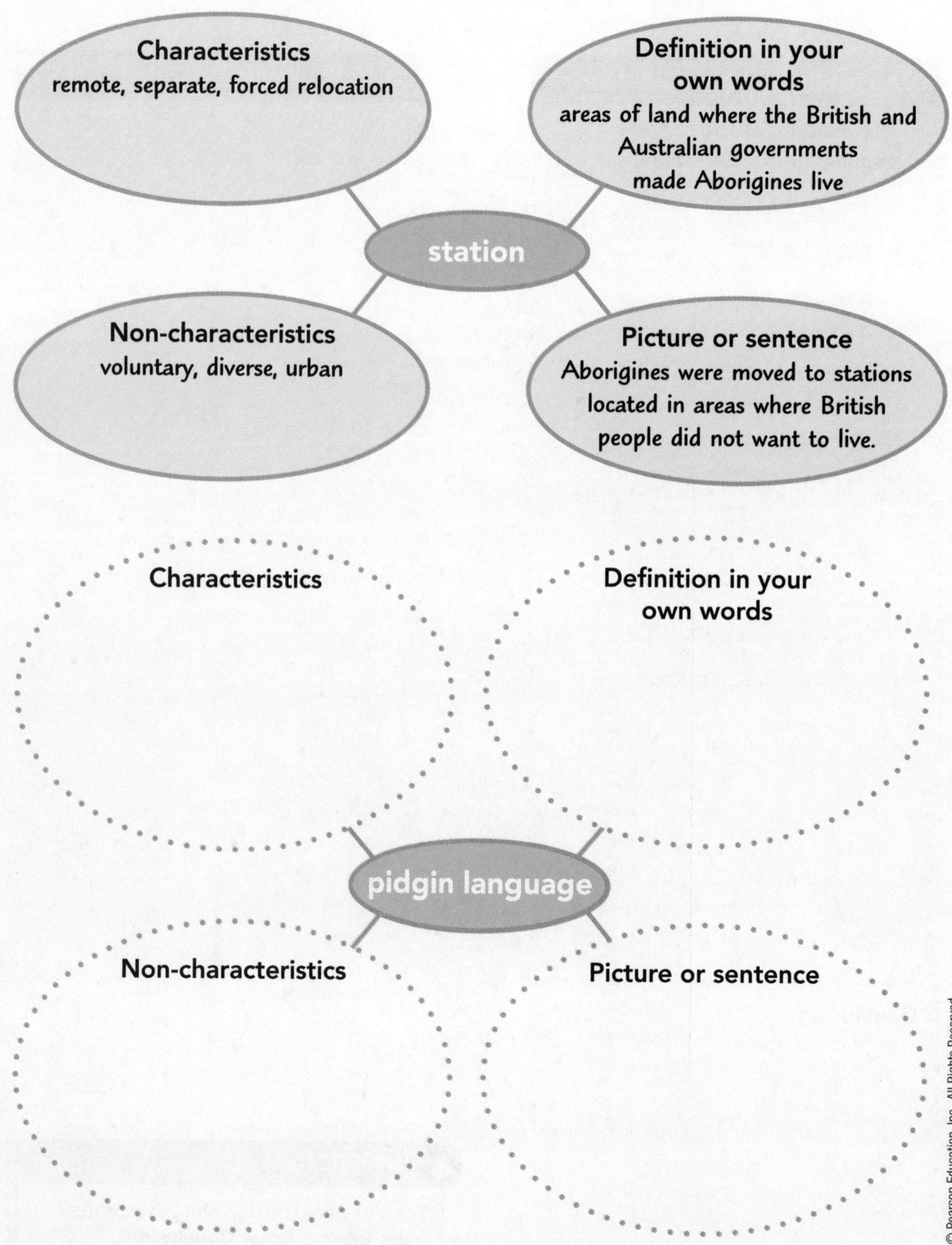

Quick Activity Modeling Distance in the Pacific

The table below shows the distance between several pairs of locations in the region.

Model these distances in your classroom. First, measure the longest side of the classroom. This will help you determine the scale of your model. The greatest distance from east to west in the region is approximately 5,900 miles from Australia to Pitcairn Island. Divide 5,900 by the length of the longest side of your classroom to determine the scale. For instance, if your room is 30 feet wide, 5,900 divided by 30 produces a scale of 196 to 1. Write the scale in the box. Then, calculate the other model distances by dividing each distance by the scale. Record the results.

Scale	

Countries	Approximate Distance (miles)	Number of Feet in the Room
Australia to Pitcairn Island	5,900	
Australia to New Zealand	2,600	
Australia to New Guinea	1,500	
Australia to Northern Marianas	2,500	
Australia to Wake Island	3,800	
New Zealand to Wake Island	4,200	

Team Challenge! Make a model of the region in your classroom. Each student will be assigned a country or dependency in the Pacific, including those listed in the table. Make a sign naming the place you represent. As a class, determine which sides of the room will represent the four cardinal directions—north, south, east, and west. Begin by having the students who represent Australia, New Zealand, New Guinea, the Northern Marianas, Wake Island, and Pitcairn Island stand in the position that matches the position of each location. If you are representing a location not in the table, estimate the distance from one of these locations to your place by using the Regional Atlas map. As a class, discuss the relative distances between parts of the region. What impact would that have on trade or on working together on common issues?

Take Notes

Literacy Skills: Compare and Contrast Use what you have read to complete the chart. In the first chart, write details about the forms of government in the region. In the second chart, list the important aspects of the economies of the region. How are they alike? How are they different? The first detail has been filled in for you.

Government

Australia and New Zealand	Pacific Islands
• Both are parliamentary democracies that are constitutional monarchies, modeled after the British.	

Economies

INTERACTIVE

For extra help, review the 21st Century Skills Tutorial: **Compare and Contrast**.

Practice Vocabulary

Words in Context **For each question below, write an answer that shows your understanding of the boldfaced key term.**

1. What role does the **governor general** play in the governments of Australia and New Zealand?

2. Why are **remittances** important in the Pacific islands?

Take Notes

Literacy Skills: Identify Main Ideas Use what you have read to complete the table. In each row write a main idea and at least two supporting details. The first item has been completed for you.

Environmental Challenges Facing Australia and the Pacific	
Main Idea	**Supporting Details**
Rising sea levels caused by climate change are threatening Australia, New Zealand, and the Pacific islands.	• Climate warming causes ocean waters to warm and expand and causes ice to melt, raising sea levels. • The rising sea level will make parts of the coastal areas unlivable, or make atoll islands disappear completely.

INTERACTIVE

For extra help, review the 21st Century Skills Tutorial: **Identify Main Ideas and Details**.

Practice Vocabulary

Sentence Builder Finish the sentences below with a key term from this section. You may have to change the form of the terms to complete the sentences.

Word Bank

atoll
coral bleaching
coral reef

1. Exposure to pollution, the sun, or warm ocean waters can result in

2. Low sandy islands that form around extinct volcanoes that have sunk into the sea are

3. A living formation of rock-like material made out of the skeletons of tiny sea creatures is

Take Notes

Literacy Skills: Use Evidence Use what you have read to complete the table. In each space write details about Antarctica. The first detail has been added for you. Then use the evidence you have gathered to draw a conclusion about what makes Antarctica unique.

Physical Geography	History and Political Status	Scientific Research
• Ice sheet covering 98% of land area		

Conclusion

INTERACTIVE

For extra help, review the 21st Century Skills Tutorial: **Identify Evidence**.

Practice Vocabulary

True or False? **Decide whether each statement below is true or false. Circle T or F, and then explain your answer. Be sure to include the underlined vocabulary term in your explanation. The first one is done for you.**

1. **T / F** Glaciers form at Antarctica's coast and flow slowly inland.
   False. Glaciers are slow-moving bodies of ice that form in Antarctica's valleys and flow toward the coast.

2. **T / F** The ozone layer filters out harmful ultraviolet radiation from the sun.

3. **T / F** The Antarctic Treaty specified where each signing nation was required to keep its military presence in Antarctica.

4. **T / F** Pack ice permanently covers the surface of the sea around Antarctica.

5. **T / F** The Antarctic ice sheet is a large mass of compressed ice.

6. **T / F** When pack ice detaches from the land, it breaks apart into icebergs.

Writing Workshop Argument

As you read, build a response to this question: How has geography affected people's lives in Australia and the Pacific? The prompts below will help walk you through the process.

Lessons 1 and 2 Writing Task: Gather Evidence As you read Lessons 1 and 2, take notes on how geography affected the lives of different groups of people over time.

Effects of Geography on Early Peoples	Effects of Geography on Modern Societies

Lesson 3 Writing Task: Introduce Claims Write one or more claims about the effect of geography on people's lives in Australia and the Pacific. You should be able to support your claims with the evidence you have gathered. If necessary, gather additional evidence to support your claims.

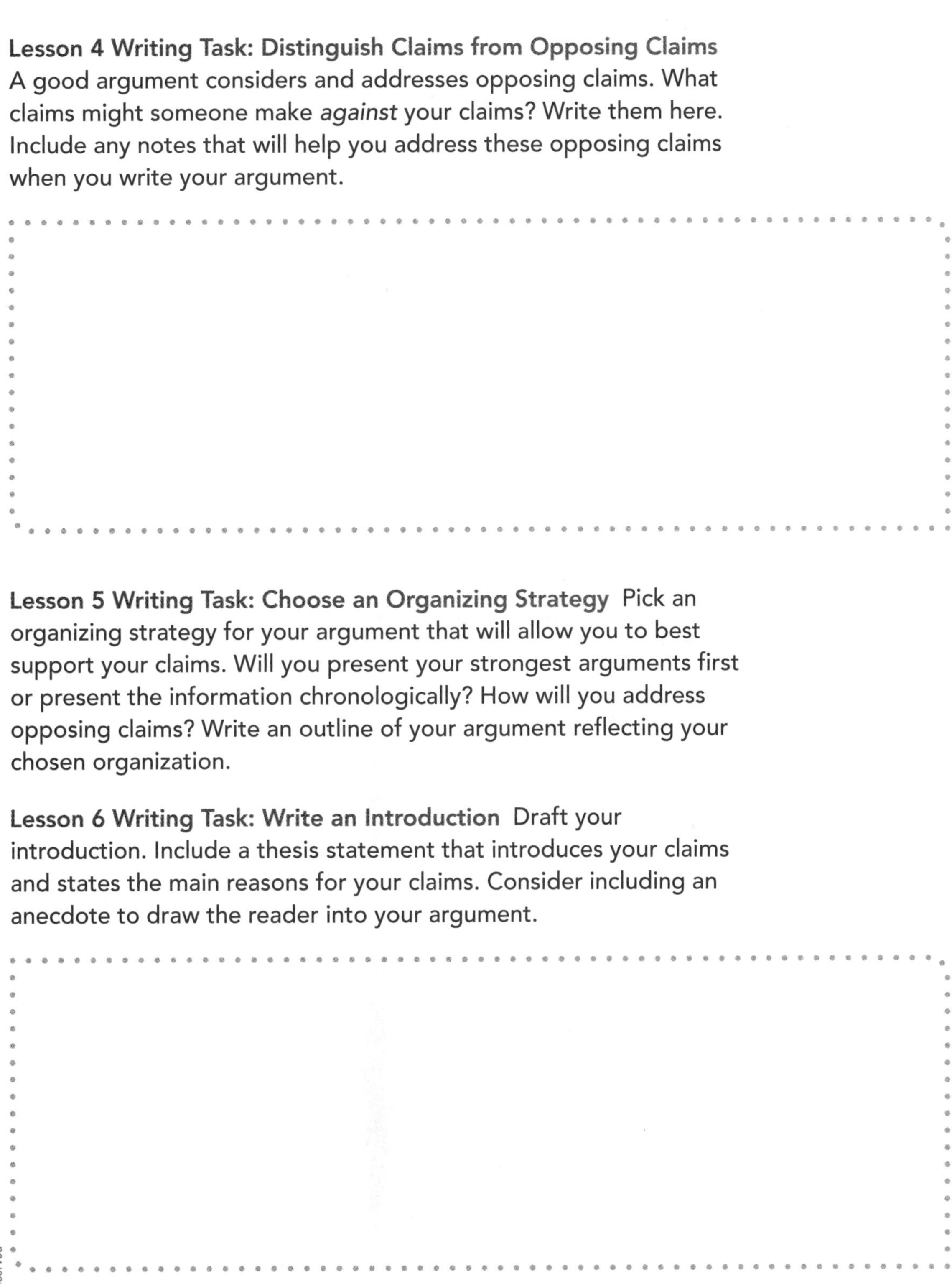

Lesson 4 Writing Task: Distinguish Claims from Opposing Claims
A good argument considers and addresses opposing claims. What claims might someone make *against* your claims? Write them here. Include any notes that will help you address these opposing claims when you write your argument.

Lesson 5 Writing Task: Choose an Organizing Strategy Pick an organizing strategy for your argument that will allow you to best support your claims. Will you present your strongest arguments first or present the information chronologically? How will you address opposing claims? Write an outline of your argument reflecting your chosen organization.

Lesson 6 Writing Task: Write an Introduction Draft your introduction. Include a thesis statement that introduces your claims and states the main reasons for your claims. Consider including an anecdote to draw the reader into your argument.

Writing Task Using the outline you created and the introduction you drafted, write an argument that answers the following question: How has geography affected people's lives in Australia and the Pacific? Clearly state your claims, reasons, and be sure to support your reasons with convincing evidence. Use words that strengthen your argument and sound authoritative.

Acknowledgments

Photography

004 Igor Mojzes/Alamy Stock Photo; **006** Rick Dalton–Ag/Alamy Stock Photo; **007** Kristoffer Tripplaar/Alamy Stock Photo; **009** Dmitry Kalinovsky/Shutterstock; **010** Michael Warren/iStock/Getty Images; **036** Michel Loiselle/Alamy Stock Photo; **038** Todd Taulman/Shutterstock; **039** Image BROKER/Alamy Stock Photo; **040** Orhan Cam/Shutterstock; **041** Art Babych/Shutterstock; **044** IanDagnall Computing/Alamy Stock Photo; **067** J Gerard Sidaner/Science Source/Getty Images; **068** EDU Vision/Alamy Stock Photo; **069** Jose Goitia/Gamma-Rapho/Getty Images; **071** Omar Torres/AFP/Getty Images; **096** Raul Arboleda/Stringer/AFP/Getty Images; **098** EPA european pressphoto agency b.v./Alamy Stock Photo; **100** Deco/Alamy Stock Photo; **101** Pulsar Images/Alamy Stock Photo; **103** Frilet Patrick/Hemis/Alamy Stock Photo; **104** Yohei Osada/Nippon News/Aflo Sport/Alamy; **124** Derrick E. Witty/National Trust Photo Library/Art Resource, NY; **126** Marek Druszcz/AFB/Getty Images; **127** Lebrecht Music and Arts Photo Library/Alamy Stock Photo; **128** Lambros Kazan/Shutterstock; **129** World History Archive/Alamy Stock Photo; **142T** Zev Radovan/BibleLandPictures.com/Alamy Stock Photo; **142C** Lambros Kazan/Shutterstock; **142BL** Hercules Milas/Alamy Stock Photo; **142BR** Evannovostro/Shutterstock; **154** Eye35/Alamy Stock Photo; **156** VLIET/iStock Unreleased/Getty Images; **157** Ian G Dagnall/Alamy Stock Photo; **158** Eduardo Gonzalez Diaz/Alamy Stock Photo; **159** Alex Segre/Alamy Stock Photo; **162** Michael Brooks/Alamy Stock Photo; **178** SVF2/Universal Images Group/Getty Images; **180** Everett Collection Historical/Alamy Stock Photo; **181** ITAR-TASS Photo Agency/Alamy Stock Photo; **184** Shamil Zhumatov/Reuters/Alamy Stock Photo; **200** Bartosz Hadyniak/E+/Getty Images; **202** Marion Kaplan/Alamy Stock Photo; **203** Pius Utomi Ekpei/AFP/Getty Images; **204** Greenshoots Communications/Alamy Stock Photo; **207** Peter Treanor/Alamy Stock Photo; **228** Universal Images Group North America LLC/DeAgostini/Alamy Stock Photo; **230** Interfoto/Personalities/Alamy Stock Photo; **231** Mirrorpix/Newscom; **232** Image Asset Management/World History Archive/Age Fotostock; **233** Bettmann/Getty Images; **235** Grenville Collins Postcard Collection/Chronicle/Alamy Stock Photo; **236** Adam Eastland Art + Architecture/Alamy Stock Photo; **256** Ahmed Jadallah/REUTERS/Alamy Stock Photo; **258** Ammar Awad/Reuters/Alamy Stock Photo; **259** Said Khatib/Afp/Getty Images; **260** Schmitz, Walter/TravelCollection/Alamy Stock Photo; **261** Thitivong/IStock/Getty Images; **263** Richard I'Anson/Lonely Planet Images/Getty Images; **278** Dani Friedman/Vario Images RM/Age Fotostock; **280** David Weyand/ImageBROKER/Alamy Stock Photo; **281** John Bennet/Alamy Stock Photo; **282** Eromaze/E+/Getty Images; **283** David Pearson/Alamy Stock Photo; **285** Michael Runkel/Robertharding/Alamy Stock Photo; **286** Jayanta Shaw/Reuters/Alamy Stock Photo; **308** Issei Kato/Reuters/Alamy Stock Photo; **309** Raga/Photolibrary/Getty Images; **310** PhotoNN/Shutterstock; **311** Top Photo Corporation/Alamy Stock Photo; **312** Hiroshi Higuchi/Age Fotostock/Alamy Stock Photo; **334** ESB Professional/Shutterstock; **335** Prasit Rodphan/Alamy Stock Photo; **336** Luis Barreto Photos/RooM the Agency/Alamy Stock Photo; **337** Afriadi Hikmal/ZUMA Wire/Zuma Press, Inc./Alamy Stock Photo; **339** Ivan Vdovin/Alamy Stock Photo; **340** Liushengfilm/Shutterstock; **341** Toby Williams/Alamy Stock Photo; **351** Ian Buswell/Zuma Press/Newscom; **358** Steffen Binke/Alamy Stock Photo; **359** Andrew McInnes/Alamy Stock Photo; **360** Peter Hendrie/Lonely Planet Images/Getty Images; **361** Axily/Getty Images; **363** Justin Mcmanus/The AGE/Fairfax Media/Getty Images; **368** David Kirkland/Axiom/Design Pics Inc/Alamy Stock Photo